Can Prisons Work?

The Prisoner as
Object and Subject
in Modern Corrections

STEPHEN DUGUID

UNIVERSITY OF TORONTO PRESS
Toronto Buffalo London

© University of Toronto Press Incorporated 2000
Toronto Buffalo London
Printed in Canada

ISBN 0-8020-4811-0 (cloth)
ISBN 0-8020-8350-1 (paper)

Canadian Cataloguing in Publication Data

Duguid, Stephen
    Can prisons work? : the prisoner as object and subject in modern corrections

    Includes bibliographical references and index.
    ISBN 0-8020-4811-0 (bound)
    ISBN 0-8020-8350-1 (pbk.)

    1. Criminals – Rehabilitation . 2. Prisoners – Education. 3. Corrections –
    Philosophy. I. Title.

    HV9275.D83 2000   364.6'01   C00-930659-5

This book has been published with the help of a grant from the Humanities
and Social Sciences Federation of Canada, using funds provided by the Social
Sciences and Humanities Research Council of Canada.

The University of Toronto Press acknowledges the financial assistance to its
publishing program of the Canada Council for the Arts and the Ontario
Arts Council.

University of Toronto Press acknowledges the financial support for its
publishing activities of the Government of Canada through the Book
Publishing Industry Development Program (BPIDP).

Contents

Preface

I often wondered how I would approach writing about my twenty-year experience with prisons, prisoners, and prison education, what theme or issue I would focus on, and the form it might take. After a lengthy immersion in the research industry that surrounds these areas of endeavour, including psychology, criminology, sociology, and even biology I have retreated to the humanities realm I know the best and chosen Thomas Jefferson as my guide. I was an amateur in 1973 when I first entered the maximum security British Columbia Penitentiary, a recently minted historian hired to teach European history to prisoners enrolled in an experimental university-level prison education program. Twenty-five years and much pondering later I have concluded that my efforts and those of my fellow teachers at that penitentiary were successful (and thanks to research we now can show just how successful) precisely because we were outsiders, interacting with our prisoner-students in the context of reciprocal teaching and learning, not as counsellors, keepers, or fixers. Jefferson was right in his insight that 'experts' are not really essential for people to sort out right from wrong, but he also knew that sometimes people had difficulty seeing their way through to right action and that they might therefore require some help. This was the situation I confronted in the prison, and to help me out Jefferson offered some further advice: 'I know of no safe depository of the ultimate powers of society but the people themselves. And if we think them not enlightened enough to exercise their control with a wholesome discretion, the remedy is not to take it from them, but to inform their discretion.' (Thomas Jefferson, *Letter to William Jarvis*, 29 September 1820). In dealing with crime, society had obviously not taken Jefferson's advice but that did not prevent others from attempting to follow it even within the limitations imposed by the carceral world. In reflecting on this experience and this advice, and in examining the ways in which others have done so in similar ways I have concluded that imprisoned criminals can be persuaded to reassess principles of right and wrong, and they can become informed of alternative ways to exercise their power as citizens with a 'wholesome discretion.'

But do prisons work? Can individuals be reformed or rehabilitated in prisons, or are these institutions modern versions of the medieval dungeon? A growing body of data indicates that rehabilitation and/or reformation through incarceration is illusory. Exceptions, according to this research, result by accident rather than from design. Rejecting an earlier optimistic belief in the transformative power of incarceration, writers in the 1970s such as Norval Morris, Robert Martinson, and Michel Foucault insisted that the primary function of the prisons is a combination of punishment, retribution, and revenge. Although these assertions have deeply influenced academic and some popular views, they have had little impact on policy making within the 'corrections community' which is charged with managing incarceration. For these practitioners the incarceration of criminals is a 'fact,' and the task of prisons to isolate, punish, and perhaps reform the criminal remains unquestioned. In this context the task of the modern criminal justice system remains to develop 'scientific' management principles to apply to interventions in prisons that can best serve to control or eradicate criminal behaviour. Ironically, both the critics and defenders of incarceration have made prisoners the object rather than the subject of their discourses, the one seeing them as victims of a monstrous institution and the other as incorrigibles persuaded only by coercion or manipulation. The issue is sharpened by the dramatic extensions of 'deviance' in contemporary times, with the criminal justice system thereby extending its reach and its mandate to deter, correct, and rehabilitate.

In *Can Prisons Work?* I contend that the debate between critics and the corrections community is not mutually exclusive. Imprisoned individuals can indeed be persuaded to change their attitudes, values, and behaviours. However, this process occurs most effectively when directed by 'outsiders' focusing on education rather than therapy or coercion. Taking an interdisciplinary approach, which draws on a combination of literary sources, prison interviews, statistical data, and my own experience of teaching in prisons, I re-examine the history of treatment and education programs in prisons in the United States, Canada, and the United Kingdom in the modern era. The central issue of 'what works in prison' is addressed by examining the meaning of the word 'works' in the context of the modern criminal justice system and in the culture as a whole. Revisiting the record of successful rehabilitation efforts, I argue that through education programs prisons can provide for a more 'natural,' 'organic,' or 'authentic' process of self-transformation through empowerment, communication of values, and the formation of new interests. Since neither this nor any other approach will work for every prisoner, it is essential to understand how it works for some and why it fails for others. Once we do this, we may be able to move beyond the stale arguments that reflect issues of another decade and generate instead a dialogue that allows us to view prisoners as subjects rather than objects of an ancient debate.

Acknowledgments

This work is the result of assistance from and collaboration with a number of associations and individuals. Much of the research data stems from a generous three-year grant from the Social Sciences and Humanities Research Council of Canada (1993–6). The success of that research was greatly enhanced by intellectual and methodological contributions from Ray Pawson, Wayne Knights, and others from IFEPS, the International Forum for the Study of Education in Penal Systems. Crucial to this research was the access to data provided by the Correctional Service of Canada through the good offices of Mr Chuck MacInnes in British Columbia and the archival staff at National Headquarters in Ottawa. I began the book, however, long before this research when I left full-time prison teaching in 1980 and moved to Simon Fraser University. For the opportunities I have had at Simon Fraser to pursue this and other projects I especially acknowledge the efforts of Jack Blaney, who gave me the chance, and Bob Brown, who gave me the time. In thinking through the issues addressed in *Can Prisons Work?* I profited from working with a vibrant group of interdisciplinary colleagues and students in the humanities at Simon Fraser University. The final text owes much to extensive discussions with Karlene Faith at Simon Fraser, Norman Jepson at Leeds University, Williain Forster at Leicester University, and especially to the critical and generous responses to a first draft by John Dennison at the University of British Columbia, Ray Pawson at Leeds University, Howard Kushner at San Diego State University, and Jery Zaslove and Margaret Jackson at Simon Fraser. And finally, for her collaboration, confidence, and endurance I acknowledge the contribution of my wife Colleen Hawkey, who gave me the will to finish the job.

CAN PRISONS WORK?

CHAPTER ONE

Introduction

Crime is a nasty business for the victim, the criminal, for those charged with doing something about it, and also for the moralists among us who would wish it away. Crime is also an occupation, at least for most criminals and for all of those charged with responding to it. Crime in almost all cases involves an action, 'thought crime' being something we reserve for history and science fiction, but those actions have deep roots in the inner structure of the self and in the visible structure of society and it is these roots that most interest us – the motives, the causes, the excuses, and the explanations. And it is our ambition to understand these roots that leads us to hope for change or renewal in the criminal or resigns us to retribution when understanding proves elusive. But unlike other queries we might have about unsettling human behaviours, the sheer nastiness of crime always draws our attention back to the action – the theft, the swindle, the brutality, the death. It is appropriate, then, to start this exploration of crime, criminals, and corrections with a look at some specifics and ask ourselves whether the action does speak for itself. For a start, portrayed here in Table 1.1 in stark black and white are the criminal careers of four young men, typical of those who frequent our prisons.

The four 'John Does' whose criminal records are so starkly set out could easily be interpreted as typical criminal 'careers,' social and economic options chosen by some individuals as a means of acquiring goods or status or simply as a means of 'getting on' in a world in which they see themselves as disadvantaged. These criminal careers begin with minor economic crimes and then escalate steadily, interrupted only by terms in prison until they erupt in full violent bloom in the form of robbery, assault, and rape: One need only turn to any daily

Table 1.1. Four typical young men in Canadian prisons

John Doe 1	John Doe 2	John Doe 3	John Doe 4
1955 Auto theft	1966 Theft	1969 Auto theft	1974 Poss stolen prop
1957 Assault CBH	1970 Theft under $50	1970 Assault CBH	1974 Poss narcotic
1958 B&E	1971 Cause disturbance	1975 Armed robbery	1974 Robbery
1960 Assault CBH	1972 Theft under $200	1976 Escape	1975 Theft under $200
1961 B&E/theft (5)	1973 Theft under $200	1977 Robbery	1975 Poss narcotic
1962 Escape	1974 Poss stolen prop	1978 Escape	1975 B&E/theft
1963 B&E/theft	1974 Forgery	1984 Armed robbery	1976 Poss traff
1965 B&E/theft	1976 Traff in narcotic		1976 B&E/theft
1971 Poss narc traff	1979 Poss stolen prop		1978 Assault CBH
1976 Robbery	1980 Armed robbery		1978 B&E/theft
	1984 Robbery/firearm		1980 Obstruct police
	1985 Robbery		1981 Attempted rape

B&E, breaking and entering; CBH, causing bodily harm; Poss Narc Traff, possession of narcotics for the purposes of trafficking; Poss Stolen Prop, possession of stolen property newspaper to give these careers some substance, as the following examples attest, and to begin the process of filling in the details that might lead us to some understandings.

Violent Teen, Pal, Accused of Killing Parents, Brother
(Vancouver *Sun*, 15 August 1995)

McCleary, Washington (AP) A teenager whose increasingly violent behaviour had his mother so frightened she slept with a baseball bat was held Monday on charges he helped shoot his parents to death and drown his five-year-old brother.

'He was always mad at them, but I don't know why,' a former girl-friend said of Brian Bassett, accused of killing his family with the help of a friend, Nicholaus McDonald.

Wendy and Michael Bassett died of multiple gunshot wounds and their younger son, Austin, was drowned in the bathtub at the family home, about 175 kilometres southwest of Seattle, coroner John Bebich said.

Bassett, 16, and McDonald, 17, were charged Monday with three counts each of aggravated first degree murder.

Friends and relatives said Bassett had been quiet and shy, an average student, until about a year ago, when he started 'hanging out with the wrong crowd' – including McDonald, said Wendy Bassett's brother-in-law, Ed Olsen.

Pat Bodine, a Bassett family friend, called McDonald 'a strange kid with a bad reputation in town.' Olsen said Bassett had become so violent lately that Wendy Bassett began sleeping with a baseball bat next to her bed.

The Bassetts recently told their son to move out.

Teen Sisters Admit Killing Mom; One Recounts Slaying in Poem
(Miami *Herald*, 9 July 1992)

Gulfport, Mississippi (AP) One of two teenage sisters who admitted kill-ing their mother wrote a poem for a school literary magazine in which the narrator describes giving her mother 'a taste of your own medicine,' authorities said Wednesday.

Shannon Garrison, 17; her sister Melissa, 15; and Melissa's boyfriend, Allen Robert Goul, 15, were charged as adults in the slaying Tuesday of Betty Garrison, 45.

In the poem published in this year's issue of *Perspectives*, a Gulfport High School arts magazine, Shannon wrote:

'My eyes were two burning embers of hatred

'My face cold and uncaring
'I laughed into your dead (silent) face ...
'I am your creation gone awry
'It looks like You got A Taste
'Of your own medicine Mommy.'

Police said that after the boyfriend implicated them, the sisters told investigators that they had held their mother down and choked her while Goul stabbed her. Garrison fought back, scratching Goul on the neck and trying to crawl under the bed to get away, police said.

The sisters were angry because their mother punished them for sneaking out at night and threatened to send them to a girls' camp if they did not behave.

Contrasted with the horribly malevolent, deadly, and mysterious outburst of Brian and Nicholaus, our four 'John Does' seem almost transparent. For sixteen-year-old Brian Bassett was it the sociological explanation of the 'bad crowd' that we should explore to make sense of the act, or was it the case of the influence of a biological 'bad seed'? Or do we look instead to the pressures on the modern family as a means of putting this case to rest? Or did something go awry in the way that Brian and his friend came to 'see' and 'understand' the world around them, their family, and their selves? Likewise for the Garrison sisters and Allen Goul – are these simply demon-children or has some catastrophe, gradual or sudden, occurred in this family that has driven them to murder most foul? And even if there was such a catastrophe in that family, surely there were other possible responses: Why were they not pursued by these young people?

Man with Tragic Past Dangerous, Crown Argues

(Vancouver *Sun*, 20 November 1995)

Marvin Tom remembers nothing of his mother, except her funeral. He was age five when she died of an overdose in Oakalla Prison. Because she drank heavily during pregnancy, Tom, at age 30, is intellectually impaired. He's also a chronic alcoholic.

Tom does have memories of his father – all of them horrific. His father was a drunken brute who regularly kicked, burned and beat his young son. Mercifully, the child was taken into care by social services and spent his formative years in a series of foster homes ...

Former teacher Norma Smith, who taught Tom when he was a teenager ... said he functioned at about the Grade 3 level. He was placed among special needs children. By age 15, he was an alcoholic. His brushes with the law included car theft and being unlawfully in a building ... Tom was placed on probation but he was uncooperative with probation officers and social workers ... During the next few years, as his alcohol problem increased, Tom fathered three children by three different women. In 1989, he unaccountably attacked one of the women with a knife.

Sentenced to four years, he was twice released on parole, but each time returned to jail for violations involving the use of alcohol ... In 1993, having completed his four-year sentence, Tom was released from prison. Within days of his release, Tom committed the brutal sex-slaying of L, 24. The next day he attacked two other women. Although tried for first degree murder ... a jury decided the evidence of Tom's drunkenness at the time reduced the offence to manslaughter.

During the hearing (to have Tom declared a dangerous offender and given an indeterminate sentence) Crown counsel told the court she intends to prove Tom has established a pattern of persistent aggressiveness [and that] his low intellectual capacity, coupled with his chronic alcoholism, suggest he won't respond to treatment.

Poor Marvin Tom, a victim of alcoholism and, no doubt, racism as well as a life of poverty and mental disadvantage – how do we consider his deviance? Escaping from our world via alcohol, his subsequent actions in that world were horrific, both to himself and others, and were matched in spirit if not in substance by actions done to him by family and society. Is prison the appropriate home for the untreatable but dangerous victim? Is it the best we can do? And if we suppose that the offender's actions are deeply rooted in culture and psychology, what are the deeper origins of society's bureaucratic response to those actions, and to what extent are they revealed in modern correctional practice?

Inmate Profiles, M Prison, 1977: JD

He is doing 8 years, having served 6 months. Conviction charge: trafficking in narcotics and theft. Prognosis: measured. Liabilities: He has been part of the criminal culture for a number of years and has been quite successful. His contact with the regular community is criminal. Assets: He is willing to upgrade and look at career options.

Educationally he finished Grade 12 (GED) within the academic program without any apparent difficulties. His present plans are to upgrade and develop career options from that perspective.

Occupationally, he considers himself the business type, as he speaks of sales experience. Manual labour is not how he perceives employment. He enjoys relating to people, specifically in the persuasive level (business). At the same time, the prestige element ranks very high in him. Jobs in the business world must provide visible esteem otherwise he will not function at his best. If esteem is present or in sight, he will be a very aggressive worker. He is an entrepreneur.

Incident Report, K Prison, 1987

On September 10 at approximately 12:20 p.m. I was confronted by Mr G in the prison courtyard. He came up to me and threatened to gouge my eyes out and kill me upon his release from prison. He stated that he would find me and carry out the action. This is not the first time that he has acted in a threatening manner. Previous threats were made in June and July inside the school. Those threats came in response to me trying to solve some behaviour problems that Mr G displayed.

My response to Mr G's threat was to walk away. I do, however, take his threats seriously and I feel very cautious when approached by him.

As far as I can ascertain, his threats stem from his previous involvement in the school program. Due to his aggressive behaviour and disruptions while a student, I found it necessary to ban and suspend him from the school and the program. He appears to be very unpredictable and acts in a very aggressive manner whenever he approaches myself and other instructors.

The immediate solution appears to be simply to avoid Mr G, though that is not always possible within the confines of this institution. We are concerned about his potential violence while he is in prison and also upon his release. We don't relish the idea of being targets for his anger.

Psychologist Report (excerpts): Inmate A

On examination, Mr A presented as an attractive and extremely articulate man ... He most definitely does not present as the stereotype of the prison inmate ... Previous psychological testing indicated that he functions in the very superior range of intellectual ability.

Both of the previous assessments concluded that Mr A met the criteria for a diagnosis of antisocial personality disorder, that condition previously known as psychopathy ... Mr A maintains that he has changed from the man described in the earlier assessments. The credibility of this claim is in my judgment central to an assessment of the risk this man represents to the public ...

Such is not always the case, as in instances where crimes are motivated by economic necessity. Here, however, the likelihood of recidivism depends on the degree to which one believes that the previously diagnosed psychopathic personality has changed. While there is some evidence to suggest something of an improvement in recent years ... there is unfortunately evidence that key elements of the psychopathic personality structure remain. In particular, there is a lack of affective tone when discussing the plight of others ... This lack of empathy is in my judgment a significant indicator that whatever progress Mr A has made in accepting responsibility for his actions, his fundamental personality remains psychopathic, and as such he continues to pose a risk to society. If released, I think that he might do well as long as things continued to go his way, as well they might given his extraordinary intellectual prowess. In the face of frustrating obstacles, however, it is my opinion that Mr A would continue to be ruthlessly self-serving, and I can not therefore reassure the Parole Board as to his safety in the community.

Once in prison, is the kind of objectification that JD experiences an example of our 'making sense' of the criminal and prescribing a cure? And Mr G, who in the face of disappointment threatens to gouge out the eyes of his perceived persecutor – is this Brian Bassett grown up, with violent assertion no longer uncontrollably explosive, but measured and owned as a social tactic? And finally, Mr A, whose criminal path is not escapist, not a response to poverty, discrimination, or low self-esteem, and not an alternative means of employment, but rather is an informed choice – what to do with him in our need to understand? Mr A emerges as the 'purest deviant,' the errant self driven not by demons or devils as in an earlier age but by deep, internal mental structures that seem to amount to much the same thing in their quality of mystification.

What can one make of all this? In a culture built on assumptions of enlightenment one is more often than not persuaded that it is possible and important to 'make sense' of phenomena, especially when they may in some way be either beneficial or harmful to ourselves, other humans, or existence per se. Thus, our ancestors sought to understand seasons, tides, and social deviance, and we seek to understand earthquakes, sunspots and social deviance. How can we, then, make sense of a range of deviant human behaviours such as those outlined above? Indeed, is 'deviance' the right lens through which to see and understand them? How do we draw a distinction between JD's entrepreneurial drive and need for status and the same qualities in the 'respectable,' achieving citizen? Are there really correct or 'true' ways of being a citizen of a community that are qualitatively superior? Or must we accept the postmodern frame that questions the question and the possibility of any 'true' answer – of any one answer being necessarily, absolutely, better than another? Or, avoiding such a duality, can we through social consensus agree at least on a ranking of human behaviours that would include doubts as well as proscriptions?

All these individuals, actions, and aberrations are collapsed in modern parlance under the term 'deviance' – a classically modern notion, a product of beliefs that were born in the seventeenth-century age of rationalism and science and that came to political fruition in the eighteenth-century Enlightenment, the application of the new science to human problems and thus the true 'dawn of the modern era.' In Woody Allen's film *Love and Death* (1975), a premodern Russian village can be the site of a 'town fool's convention' and nothing is awry – in modern Soviet Russia as in all modern systems, the town fools were sent away for cures – sometimes forever. Criminology, like psychiatry, is an archetypal Enlightenment product, an attempt to apply science (it is, after all, a social *science*) to understanding a phenomenon in order to intervene and thereby control or eradicate it – much the same as modern medicine has its origins in struggles against diseases such as smallpox. And just as the medical establishment has used its claims of beneficence to expand its field of operation, so has criminology managed to extend dramatically the field of behaviours designated as deviant and subject to cure. Michel Foucault argued that criminology in its modernist hubris has pushed the envelope of exploration beyond the act of the crime itself, to the 'shadows behind the act.'[1] Thus, aggressivity is punished along with acts of aggression – rape is punished but also perversions – murders are punished but also drives and desires. The central issue here is not the punishing, but rather the core belief that the aggression, perversion, or desire can be located within the human soul/personality/mind – depending of the theology or theory of the approach – and subsequently repaired or excised. More sceptical moderns insist that such quests yield only shadows and never the prey.

The behaviours we now characterize as 'deviant' are hardly new – theft, murder, drug use and sexual aberration being constants in human affairs. For much of Western history, however, they were considered almost mundane in nature, controlled or deterred through random if brutal punishments, banishment, or execution. Given a sensual world doomed to imperfection, these behaviours were inevitable; indeed they were welcome proof of that very imperfection. The idea of a 'cure,' or even the need to 'understand' was reserved for heresy, a crime of the spirit or the mind. With the coming of a modern and increasingly secular world-view by the eighteenth-century these two sets of behaviours change places, and the mundane becomes criminal or deviant and in need of correcting, while deviance in the realm of the spirit or mind is either allowed free rein or reclassified from crime to illness.

Deviance is far too complex and morally ambiguous, however, to allow for any singular modern understanding. While any number of philosophic traditions in Western culture can be illustrative of these modern understandings of deviance, a particularly useful entry point may be the positions of three French eighteenth-century writers, creatures of the Enlightenment all, who give us a choice of modern lenses through which to view human deviance.

Voltaire (1694–1778), the senior of the three, embodied the more conservative, almost pre-modern view, suggesting that we should view the phenomena as a whole, deviance and crime being simply reflective of 'human nature' – these are the kinds of things that humans do, and while it would be foolish to assume (as does Candide's companion Dr Pangloss) that these behaviours are perverse proof that ours is a 'best of all possible worlds,' it would be equally foolish to undertake attempts at systemic or spiritual reform. That said, Voltaire, in the classic tradition of the modern liberal crusader for the rights of the individual, spent his life struggling to support individual victims of injustice, punish specific offenders, and right specific wrongs. Modern Voltaireans acknowledge that the world is an unjust place and that injustice, which bears hardest on the poor, will lead inevitably to crime and deviance which must be punished if overall order is to be maintained. Here, even in the face of evil of holocaust proportions, deviance remains merely 'banal' and can only be mediated by individual actions. The task, therefore, is to focus on justice, on the righting of wrongs, on moderating punishment, and pursuing those who by their actions add to the intrinsic pains of existence. At the end of Voltaire's *Candide* the characters who have endured countless privations, brutalities, and injustices are counselled that the best response is to 'tend to their own garden' rather than launch a crusade. This brings to mind Hannah Arendt's book *Eichmann in Jerusalem*, an account of the greatest deviance of the twentieth century, where the most heroic figure is

Sgt Anton Schmidt, a German soldier who for five months of the war quietly and for no reward assisted Jewish refugees – and was just as quietly executed as a result.[2]

Jean-Jacques Rousseau (1712–1778), in a sense responding to Voltaire, assumed the opposite position, insisting that deviance is abhorrent and contrary to an essentially 'good' human nature and that reform of selves is possible via a combination of personal reflection and reform of society and its institutions. By agreements freely entered into – social contracts – the injustices and pains of existence can be, if not eliminated, certainly made tolerable and deliberate deviance outlawed. This 'social' side of the Rousseauist position was complemented by the psychological perspective that education coupled with introspection can lead to self-understanding and thereby to the desire to live equitably and humanely with humans and nature. This tripartite plan for humane existence – contract + education + introspection – was designed by Rousseau for operation in small, egalitarian, and agrarian communities, but modern 'Rousseaueans' have left that caveat behind and seized upon the optimistic (some would say utopian) message that deviance can be eliminated by (a) education, (b) agreement, (c) reflection, or if all else fails, (d) exile or execution. This tolerance for the idea that it might be necessary to sometimes 'force one to be free' enables us to locate Rousseauean roots in both liberal and authoritarian attempts to 'bring forth a better world.'

Finally the last of our trio, the Marquis de Sade (1740–1814), who took a position that may enjoy more current popularity, namely, that deviance is inherent in all, embedded in human nature, and that this should be 'appreciated' rather than denied or abhorred. If Voltaire was the practical 'realist' and Rousseau the naive utopian, then de Sade represents the celebratory 'dualist': Love and Hate, Good and Bad, Beast and Man are inextricably unitary, and we can only know the one through the other. To deny or repress deviance or the 'other' is simply to invite illness or pathology. Individuals and societies must acknowledge deviance, 'validate' it to use the modern jargon, and by doing so keep it within the bounds of the tolerable. Modern scepticism about the potential of the criminological or penal solutions to deviance and accompanying calls to 'legalize' or 'decriminalize' many behaviours find a home in the tradition of de Sade, as do many so-called perverse celebrations of what others perceive as deviance.

Since each of these perspectives, these lenses through which we see and understand what is before us, is part of the modern repertoire one can reasonably approach the issue of crime and punishment through any or all of them. Viewing crime and punishment through the Voltairean lens would see us focusing on issues of justice and injustice, the folly of attempts at universal reformation, the futility of mandating behaviours, the insidious corruption that lies at the heart of all bureaucratic systems – political, economic, or social – the inevitability of individuals falling victim to such systems, and the corresponding necessity of struggling for justice on behalf of those individuals. The field of crime, criminal justice, and prisons is particularly ripe for Voltairean pickings.

The Rousseauean lens would see us examining the various attempts to bring about change in individuals and justice in societies. At the political level, great societies, just societies, new deals and fair deals are all Rousseauean in spirit if not in substance. In our prisons, education programs, therapy and counselling, token economies, and just communities are Rousseauean in their social sentiment. The Rousseauean lens retains much of the social perspective stemming from a Voltairean view, but is at the same time microscopic in its search for the origin of both illness and cure within the self. Until the era of postmodern doubt, this was the most prominent lens through which one conceptualized crime and punishment – indeed most professionals in corrections remain stubborn adherents to the Rousseauean view (though few would identify it as such).

Finally, the Sadean lens prefers to train its eye on the extravagant and bizarre, preferring Hannibal Lector to the petty thief, the 'Butcher of Buchenwald' to Adolf Eichmann, Ted Bundy to the neighbourhood flasher. In an age of increasing cynicism, alienation, and relativism, this is currently the most popular lens through which crime and punishment are viewed – indeed the popular media is awash in a sea of Sadean images and the postmodernists in our universities celebrate 'difference' in order to denigrate the universal, the homogeneous, the banal.

This book takes up the methodology if not the ideology of the Rousseauean position, examining the 'modern reformational project' within the prison. In doing so the focus is not on the most bizarre crimes or the most unjust penalties, but on persons whose acts have been labelled deviant but who are nonetheless familiar to us, people we can recognize most clearly, perhaps even empathize with. The claim here is that the 'critical distance' needed to achieve some measure of disinterested understanding can be attained without restricting the phenomena to be studied to its extreme manifestations. As a form of human behaviour, criminal activity per se is distant enough from the everyday lives of most citizens for such a perspective to be attainable. Hence, like Hannah Arendt's decision to focus on Adolf Eichmann in her effort to 'understand' fascism, attention is paid here to the 'uncomfortably familiar' rather than the bizarre in an effort to comprehend both the criminal and the efforts of the state to effect a transformation of selves and souls from outlaw to citizen.

This examination of the 'reformational project' has a dual quality. On the one hand, I mean to explore and – more aggressively – to interrogate the modern corrections enterprise using certain critical perspectives and tools of humanistic inquiry. On the other hand, I seek to use the corrections enterprise as a means of coming to some conclusions about some central aspects of contemporary culture.[3] To do this, I will aspire to the status of what sociologists call the 'insider/outsider' or the 'stranger,' in my case a status earned after a decade as a teacher in several prisons, another decade of prison research, accompanied by a parallel 'normal' academic career. Thus, I am insider enough to have come to know many prisoners quite well and to call some of them friends, but outsider enough to detest crime as an unreasonable intrusion on civil life and, inevitably in these times, on my life – an insider in the sense of having visited prisons and immersed myself through research in the lives of individual criminals, but outsider in the sense of sustaining a deep antipathy for prisons and fences. While laying no claim to objectivity, I hope to approach the issues at hand with a combination of 'distance and nearness, indifference and involvement.'[4] Like Tocqueville in his wanderings through early nineteenth-century America, this position of 'stranger' should make it possible to see in from the outside as well as out from the inside and thereby provide a perspective different from those of criminologists or the advocates of either keeper or the kept.

This sense of 'medium cool' that the outsider entails with its hint of essential indifference cannot, in fact, be sustained throughout an exploration of such an emotion-ridden subject as the fate of the imprisoned selves in our midst and our complicity in the perpetuation of their condition. There is as well an advocacy agenda implicit throughout this book, an assertion that we are on the wrong path and that alternatives are readily available and accessible. Here the outsider becomes iconoclast, a 'breaker of icons' in the name of opening up the prison, deprofessionalizing 'corrections,' and in the process addressing prisoners as people rather than offenders.

There are three steps necessary in addressing the dual objectives of examining this modern project and assessing what it tells us about contemporary culture and about modern selves. First, we need to discover the basis for our modern belief in 'deviance' and in 'transformation' – to examine by what process we come to believe that violators of either a social contract or a moral imperative must and can be 'reformulated,' 'rehabilitated,' and thereby 'transformed' into citizens through either authoritarian or therapeutic interventions by the state. This will require a recurring look at the Enlightenment and its reverberations through the twentieth century. Second, we need to identify the human and humane implications of such a belief, determining how its mechanisms are formulated – how a perspective or idea system is transformed into action through ideology, structures, and institutions. As well we need to assess the degree to which these rehabilitative efforts are successful. Since the record is patently not good, we need to question whether selves can, in fact, be purposefully transformed against their will or in opposition to their perceived interests – are 'will' and 'interest' malleable qualities? Third, we will need to discover whether there are alternatives, whether even in prisons there can be a more 'natural,' 'organic,' or 'authentic' process of transformation or maturation that works through empowerment of the will, communication of values, and the formation of new interests. And, if there is, how does it work, for whom does it work, and under what conditions can it work?

There is no point in attempting to explore this reformational project in the abstract. It is carried out within specific contexts – historical and institutional – and can only be taken and understood within those contexts. Rousseau's classic study of maturation and reformation, *Emile*, unfolds in the gilded prison created by the boy's tutor, a prison young Emile does not perceive but which in essence was just as authoritarian and behaviourist as the modern penitentiary. The initial focus must, therefore, be on the prison-as-context, the prison as mirror and staring eye, the prison as arbiter of the means and limits of possible change. This will necessitate several detours into the field of sight of a fourth French lens, that provided by Michel Foucault and through him into the realms of language, bureaucracy, and authority.

Our collection of modern Emiles must as well be followed out of the prison and into the community in order to assess the resilience of their reformational experience. Unlike Rousseau's thought experiment, in this study we can utilize the careers of real people, in this case about 700 former prisoners from several Canadian prisons who were released into society in the 1970s and 1980s. A cross-section of the population of Canadian federal prisons, these men are 'serious offenders' who have in common participation in a particular prison education program and who, as well, took advantage of and/or were subjected to a variety of other programs designed to change, improve, repair, or in some way alter their personalities, behaviours, aspirations, or needs. It is the lives of these men – as criminals, prisoners, and parolees – that provide the visceral substance of the book. The focus throughout will combine an analysis of the larger cultural and political patterns that dictate the shape and direction of the modern correctional project with perspectives gained from the lives of specific individuals caught up within the systems spawned by that project, lives recorded in sometimes excruciating detail by the various functionaries of the correctional system.

This book addresses this central issue of 'what works in prison' and just what this word 'works' means in the context of the modern criminal justice system and the culture as a whole. Some might say, with Voltaire, that it works simply by being there, by protecting society from the further depredations of specific criminals, either through community supervision, incarceration, or execution, or that it works by acting as a deterrent to countless would-be criminals, who instead choose an honest path from fear of arrest and incarceration. Still others, and these are the central figures of this study, are not content with this passive role and insist that it can only be said to work if it persuades apprehended criminals to change their ways after release from incarceration. The issue of recidivism, or the lack thereof, was used by Robert Martinson as his measure of success in his (in)famous 1974 research that asserted that in prison 'nothing works,' and it persists as the most common measure of 'success': The (vulgar) Rousseaueans among us insist that the civil society we deserve, need, and can have depends on our ability to create a voluntary conformity – by coercion if necessary.

This study of interventions in the lives of prisoners should serve to illuminate the larger issue of the state's ability, or lack thereof, to affect its citizens' fundamental beliefs, attitudes, and needs. There is a conviction at the heart of the Enlightenment or the modern 'project' that crime and deviance are 'in the mind', that it is indeed 'the thought that counts.' Rousseau has won out over Voltaire, despite a strong tradition within modernity that persists in seeing the criminal as victim and the deviant as desperate defender of threatened needs. The penal enterprise becomes a field not of punishment but of internal reformation, a field of struggle brilliantly explored by George Orwell in his book *1984.*

In this sense the prison becomes a laboratory, a 'refined' realm in which the state seemingly has all the advantages, the imprisoned having as resources only resistance, manipulation, will, or blind faith. Far from being a mere 'warehouse' for the apprehended and sentenced offender, the correctional archipelago (of which the penitentiary or prison is the major part) has defined its mission as being a persuader, reformer, and educator, and its products are meant to be compliant, productive, and obedient citizens. It is here that the bureaucratic recording of these imprisoned lives is most revealing for it provides us with a systematic and necessary, given the seriousness of the task, look at how we think we *work* as humans. In virtually all cases the correctional system rejects the medieval (and postmodern?) Sadean view of 'bad people' and opts for the Enlightenment's more generous and optimistic perspective of people 'gone bad' who are in most cases 'correctable.' The 'how' of this correcting is the stuff of meaning for criminologists, psychologists, and other specialists, but it is the correctable part per se that is of generic interest because it tells us how we have come to understand ourselves. The prisoner is the captured, dull, remorseless, dysfunctional, dis-engaged, ill-employed, and pleasure-seeking deviant – the opposite of which is the 'citizen,' the participant in the body politic, the contributor to the general welfare, and the self concerned for the well-being of fellow citizens. From the terror, boredom, and ecstasy of the criminal life, the state prescribes, indeed demands, a transition to the 'silent heroism of daily living'.[5]

It is a commonplace to refer at the close of the twentieth century to a 'crisis' in corrections, to crime being 'out of control,' and recidivism rampant. There is an increasing popular consensus that the correctional reformational project has been a failure – despite the persistent efforts of professionals in the field to find the right combination of treatments that will work the cure. Any discussion of crime and deviance in these times of renewed popular interest in chain gangs, three-strike laws, boot camps, the prison 'industry,' and capital punishment must, therefore, acknowledge that there are deeper contextual structures and forces that impinge upon our understandings, always tending to move us – often unwittingly and always with dismal consequences – from the complex to the simple. The overly optimistic social forecasts of the 'new' medical and social sciences of the twentieth century, the disillusionment with the fruits of 'victory' in the Cold

War, and the perhaps inherent vacuity of a culture grounded in materialism and consumption have produced a potent combination of popular frustration and despair which has manifested itself in, among other things, a low tolerance for criminal deviance. Coupled with this low tolerance is a rejection of complex 'contextual' explanations in favour of easy to comprehend and generally monocausal explanations and panaceas. If even these panaceas – for example, literacy, job training, transcendental meditation, therapy, harsh prison terms, or incapacitation – fail, there is always despair and its inevitable companions, frustration and anger. While the claim made in the mid-1970s that 'nothing works' in terms of 'correcting' criminal behaviour is now generally perceived to have been based on flawed research, it nonetheless touched a chord of latent bitterness and scepticism in the popular imagination, and its effect has long outlived its cause.

There is, however, another way of approaching the whole issue of deviance, reformation, and citizenship. The failure, by and large, of this reformation to take effect, the consistently poor record of the corrections system at 'correcting,' has been grist for the argument of Foucault and others that the fault lies at the core, with the 'Enlightenment project' itself and its rationalizing, bulldozing, universalizing *raison d'être* – its rigid belief that reason is the key to human behaviour and that understanding alone will deliver enlightenment. This accounts for the radical 'postmodern' insistence that the Enlightenment tradition must be abandoned, which in the field of criminal justice could leave us a choice between Voltairean fatalism, dungeons, or de Sade.

Here I argue that there is another, counter-tradition within the Enlightenment, a tradition less obsessed by reason and the rational, but instead grounded in a more agreeable blending of the rational and the romantic, reason and passion. Grounded in a more romantic version of Rousseau, this approach retains the modern universalist ideal that citizenship is possible even with most troubled of our peers if we appreciate their complexity, treat them with respect, and demand reciprocity – treat them, in other words, as subjects rather than objects. It was in my own experience with an education program in prison that I sensed the power of this alternative tradition, the power of the traditional subject matter of the liberal arts to, in Jefferson's words, 'inform their discretion,' discretion in this sense involving more than mere reason and certainly more than simply emotion, but rather a dynamic combination of the two. It was this conviction that something more than just education was going on in those seminars and endless discussions with the prisoner-students that persuaded me to make their post-prison lives my research project. These lives, taken collectively in statistical form or individually as case studies, become evidence for the transformative potential of this more romantic and authentic tradition within the modern.

In seeking explanations for the more successful attempts within correctional systems to facilitate the transition from outlaw to citizen we can turn to this alternative modern vision. Just as 'deep ecologists' warn us that we will continue to despoil the earth as long as we insist on perceiving the natural world as consisting of objects rather than subjects, so I argue that only by abandoning a relationship to the prisoner-as-object in favour of a reciprocal subjectness – what Martin Buber called the 'I/Thou' relationship – can an authentic process of rehabilitation, reformation, and even transformation occur. The central question posed in this book is whether educational approaches to human change and development can be especially conducive to generating a subject to subject relationship in the face of an authoritarian context that seems to demand a relationship of subject to object.

CHAPTER TWO

The Origins of Curing Crime and
Similar Popular Delusions

I believe the day has come when we can combine sensory deprivation with drugs, hyp-
nosis, and astute manipulation of reward and punishment to gain almost absolute con-
trol over an individual's behaviour ... We'd assume that a felony was clear evidence
that the criminal had somehow acquired full-blown social neurosis and needed to be
cured, not punished. We'd send him to a rehabilitation center where he'd undergo posi-
tive brainwashing ... We'd probably have to restructure his entire personality.[1]

James McConnell, *Understanding Human Behavior,* 1974

Given only a little advancement in our knowledge of the brain and our electronic
instrumentation, it will be feasible to have implanted electrodes appropriately placed in
the brain of a chronic recidivist that will reveal the fact that he is approaching a poten-
tially dangerous state of rage readiness, or sexual arousal, or anxiety nearing panic, or
other states which in his case are a major factor in producing episodes of antisocial con-
duct. This cerebral 'danger signal' could either be monitored by a central receiving sta-
tion or the patient trained to respond to his own electro-therapist by pushing the right
button on his equipment to 'turn off the undesirable state.'[2]

P.E. Meehl, 'Psychology and the Criminal Law,' 1970

Where did these utopian/dystopian ideas come from? Albeit perhaps
not the majority view, they were not atypical of the prognostications
that prevailed at the height of what was known in corrections during
the period 1945–75 as the 'medical model.' But that is getting ahead of
the story of how we moved from dungeons to 'correctional' institutions, from convicts to inmates, from keepers to curers.

The movement starts from a very fundamental conversation that has
been going on in Western culture – indeed in almost all human cultures

– for centuries, a conversation about the nature of being human. Put in its most Manichean form, are we 'by nature' fundamentally 'bad' in the sense of being aggressive, acquisitive, selfish, and – for some – evil? Or are we 'by nature' fundamentally 'good,' even if often misguided, led astray, or just off-track in practice? The questions are fundamental to our politics, moral systems, and social arrangements and are guaranteed conversation starters at any social gathering.

The Dualism of Bad and Good

The human-as-bad perspective has a deep tradition in Western culture, rooted as it is in the Christian tradition of the 'Fall.' From St Paul to St Augustine to Rousseau to Bill Clinton, we are plagued by moralists who seem destined to 'know the good, feel the good, but do evil.' In St Paul's Epistle to the Romans we can read: 'For I know that in me (that is, in my flesh) dwelleth no good thing: for to will is present with me; but how to perform that which is good I find not. For the good that I would do, I do not; but the evil which I would not do, that I do.'[3] From the *Confessions* of St Augustine we learn that he tortured himself with guilt over his youthful pleasures in theft and carnality, admitting that 'the evil in me was foul, but I loved it.'[4] There was purpose to this, of course, the need to make the strongest case possible for divine intervention, for transcending the sensual in favour of the spiritual. Crime became an important piece of theological evidence, visible proof of the hopelessness of the secular world.

Closer to our time this dark view of human nature was given its modernist seal by the seventeenth-century English political philosopher Thomas Hobbes who, in seeking to explain the crucial importance of state power, warned us of the violent alternative that had its origins within each of us: 'During the time when men live without a common power to keep them all in awe, they are in that condition which is called war; and such a war, as is of every man, against every man ... In such condition, there is no place for industry, because the fruit thereof is uncertain; and consequently no culture of the earth; no navigation, nor use of the commodities that they be imported by sea; no commodious building; no instruments of moving ... no knowledge of the face of the earth; no account of time; no arts; no letters; no society; and which is worst of all, continual fear, and danger of violent death; and the life of man, solitary, poor, nasty, brutish, and short.'[5] This must be one of the most powerful modern pillars of support for the punitive power of the state to prevent this 'condition which is called war' by whatever means possible, including if necessary the forcible incarceration of a significant percentage of its citizens and even the execution of the incorrigibles. Hobbes also sets the scene for deterrence being a major factor in the state's penal policy, fueling popular fears of facing a 'war of all against all.' While certainly compatible with the earlier religious explanations of human nature as rent with 'evil,' Hobbes nonetheless moves the case onto a more secular – and hence modern – plane by grounding his state of war in a primitive, natural aggression and ignorance rather than in some innate moral failing or 'fall.'

By the early twentieth-century this view of human nature as fundamentally, instinctually aggressive, non-cooperative, and violent was given scientific pretensions in the work of Sigmund Freud, particularly in his book *Civilization and Its Discontents*, written in 1930. Focusing on the neurosis-producing conflict between the competing demand of human instinct and civilization, Freud pulled no punches in describing the base nature of the human animal: 'Men are not gentle creatures who want to be loved ... they are, on the contrary, creatures among whose instinctual endowments is to be reckoned a powerful share of aggressiveness ... In circumstances that are favorable to it, when the mental counter-forces which ordinarily inhibit it are out of action, it [aggressiveness] also manifests itself spontaneously and reveals man as a savage beast to whom consideration towards his own kind is something alien ... The existence of this inclination to aggression ... is the factor which disturbs our relations with our neighbor and which forces civilization into such a high expenditure of energy.'[6] Among those expenditures of energy which society must make to contain or repress this innate aggression are, of course, prisons and the entire range of institutions associated with the criminal justice system. Thus, we see that for some prisons are instruments of revenge or examples for deterrence, but for others, for those who accept this dark vision of humankind, prisons are simply necessary containers provided by the state for individuals who allow their innate tendencies towards aggression and 'war' on society to overstep the agreed-upon bounds.

The absolutist version of this perspective – 'people are wicked' – still persists in our time in both religious and secular communities, though the weaker version – 'wicked people exist' – is more current, especially among politicians, psychologists, and criminologists. As we will see, the latter version leads to fascinating and sometimes desperate attempts to identify through analysis and prediction just who among us might be (curably or incurably) wicked. The element of this perspective on human nature that tends to permeate popular and professional thinking about crime, criminals, and prisons is the argument that humans are not, by nature, social, but that there is a 'primitive' quality to the human that is both exotic and dangerous, that it takes great efforts at socialization to bring this to heel, and that a subsequent imposition of social controls is necessary to keep it repressed or channelled onto acceptable paths. Often couched in rhetoric that can take disturbingly racist turns, this 'story' of human nature can be used to rationalize the singling out of individuals, groups, and entire sectors of society for special treatment within a correctional system.

In a slightly different sense the popularity of this 'take' on humans and deviance is expressive of a general turn towards Aristotelean philosophical perspectives in the past few decades. It is a commonplace in philosophy texts that Plato and Aristotle sum up in their various works two distinct ways of considering most ethical and political issues. In the case of humans and evil, Aristotle presumed a pleasure-seeking decision maker as the norm for the human, and therefore if someone performed evil or non-virtuous acts these stemmed from intention rather than ignorance or accident. For Aristotle the issue was one of individual character which needed to be trained or predisposed towards virtuous acts. For instance, in an important and very contemporary-sounding passage in his *Ethics*, Aristotle argues for doubling any penalties for offences committed in a drunken state 'because the source of the action lay in the agent himself: he was capable of not getting drunk, and his drunkenness was the cause of his ignorance.'[7] One can sense in this lesson the current appeal of Aristotle for those who wish greater stress be placed on personal responsibility instead of appeals to circumstances, victimization, or prejudice.

At the opposite side of the philosophical-anthropological spectrum are those who consider humans to be, by nature, 'good.' Two great founding philosophers, Confucius and Socrates, ground their set of understandings in the idea that humans are social, reflective creatures who under the right conditions will always opt to do good rather than evil. For Socrates this predilection for good or, put another way, 'social' action in the world stemmed from two qualities innate in the human: reflection or the ability to reason and conscience or the ability to feel. Plato, Socrates' student, carried on this line of thought by insisting that the observed, bad behaviour of humans was the result of either 'some flaw in his physical make-up [or] failure in his education, neither of which he likes or chooses,' not solely to some innate quality or predisposition.[8] In his rendition of the debate between Socrates and Protagoras, Plato has Socrates proving that when people are taught properly, when their reflective and moral capacities are sufficiently developed along with knowledge of the good, then they will always choose the correct or virtuous path.[9] Clearly, this was Jefferson's point when he urged that the task was to 'inform the discretion' of those who had erred.

Not wholly compatible with the Christian perspective that was dominant throughout the long medieval era in European history, this more optimistic approach to human nature was revived in the seventeenth and eighteenth centuries as political thinkers tried to develop more secular rationales for human behaviour. In contrast to the Hobbesian vision of mankind being on perpetual verge of a brutal state of war of all upon all, Enlightenment philosophers like Francis Hutcheson, David Hume, and Adam Smith in Scotland, along with John Locke in England, Jean-Jacques Rousseau in France, Immanuel Kant in Germany, and Thomas Jefferson in America all argued the position that humans were basically social, rational, and empathetic creatures.[10] One of the pillars of Enlightenment thought, therefore, was that through using reason and experience alone humans were capable of achieving perfection in this world rather than having to await such a possibility in a spiritual world to come. What stood in the way of achieving such perfection was not human nature but rather 'circumstances' in the forms of tyranny, ignorance, discrimination, and – for some – inequality.

This Enlightenment optimism that humans could construct social systems that operated for the good of all was based on a core belief in an 'instinctive benevolence,' 'fellow feeling,' or 'sympathy' that is innate, anterior to reason or reflection, and without which 'a man would enter an assembly of men as he enters a den of lions' – precisely Freud's point a hundred years later.[11] This innate benevolence manifested itself in sets of self-regulated behaviours that were unconsciously social as individuals adjusted their actions to the prevailing norms of propriety in order, as Smith argued, that one might 'stand well in the eyes of our fellows.'[12] This self-regulation, in the view of these Enlightenment thinkers, was both a subconscious order-seeking behaviour and as well an expression of the conscious belief in the utility and justice of such a restraint on behaviour.

It is this moral sense that enables, indeed impels, humans to share in the emotions of others, to sense both pleasure and pain in others, and to act appropriately in response to those feelings. While Locke and Hume held that this sense of compassion was or at least could be improved and enhanced as society developed, their more primitivist fellow thinkers Rousseau and Jefferson saw increasing social complexity as inevitably masking this innate sense of compassion or pity, a 'feeling that is obscure but strong in savage man, and developed but weak in civilized man.'[13] But what about the evidence, one might reasonably ask? Surely there was evil in the world despite this innate benevolence? Jefferson conceded that this 'moral instinct' was not present in every man and counselled advice offered earlier by Socrates – education – and by David Hume – appeals to utility.[14] Hume had argued throughout his *Enquiry Concerning the Principles of Morals* that there was a utilitarian pay-off to benevolence, an early version of the modern tit-for-tat component of evolutionary theory or a late version of 'do unto others,' and Jefferson was convinced that such a reasoned appeal to self-interest would sort out most wrongdoers. In his *Social Contract*, Rousseau also tackled this issue, advancing the more Draconian argument that the criminal was in fact a traitor who, by violating the laws of his country 'ceases to belong to it, and is even making war on it.'[15] Echoing his Platonic roots, the response Rousseau counsels is educational and correctional, in his own words, 'forcing the criminal to be free' by forcing him to learn to live in community.

These ideas retained their force throughout the nineteenth and much of the twentieth centuries, providing the basis for socialist and utopian political schemes and for a wave of liberalizing reform within criminal justice systems. Thus, the great trial lawyer Clarence Darrow could claim in 1902 that people commit crimes 'simply because they cannot avoid it on account of circumstances which are entirely beyond their control and for which they are in no way responsible.'[16] These circumstances are social in nature, to do with property, wealth, and discrimination, not with 'bad genes' or 'flawed character.' After suffering virtual demise following the mid-century horrors of fascism and Soviet totalitarianism, which seemed to make any claim to innate human goodness ludicrous, the position has made a tentative comeback thanks in part to the emergence of a neo-Darwinian paradigm which sees sympathy or the 'sense of suffering or experiencing with' as a 'biologically normal response of humans and perhaps other organisms.'[17] While philosophers of the Enlightenment believed in this benevolence, they could not explain its presence short of invoking the hand of God.

Now, in the late twentieth century the philosopher-scientists of the proposed new Darwinian enlightenment can confirm a 'firm genetic basis' for altruism, empathy, love, conscience, and a sense of justice.[18] As we are not simply 'driven by our genes,' this discovery is not contradicted by observational evidence of selfishness, egoism, hate, evil, and deliberate injustice, but as we shall see simply replaces the 'ghost in the machine' with 'matter in the machine' and provides encouragement to those who believe in improvement and even perfection.

The Deviant

Both of these essentially philosophical arguments are, of course, confronted by a vast array of criminal or 'deviant' human behaviours in the 'real world.' For our first set of philosophers this is hardly problematic, indeed it is to be expected. As the late behaviourist Hans Eysenck maintained, the problem is not the existence of evil, but rather the existence of good – people behave in ways that are selfish, aggressive, and immoral because such behaviours are self-reinforcing, giving the person acting in such a manner immediate satisfaction.[19] Former governor of California Jerry Brown conceded as much when he noted that 'for many people in this society, crime in fact pays.'[20]

For those who see humans as at core beneficent, sympathetic, and just, however, the moral carnage of the observed world presents both a challenge and an opportunity. Their response is to single out the 'deviant,' the individual – and sometimes groups of individuals – who for specific, identifiable reasons, has departed from behaviours that comprise the norm. The academic interpretations or schools of thought concerning deviance go by many names including positivist, realist, and Marxist, but essentially they fall into three categories or 'meta-interpretations': the reasons for deviance can be external to the person (the sociological view), internal to the person (the psychological view), or innate to the being (the biological view).

A deviation from the norm as understood by sociologists has traditionally involved an action – voluntary or involuntary – or a choice rather than a physical or mental condition completely independent of an actor's volition. In the 'sociology of deviance' language that surrounds this issue, a 'deviant' is one who steps or is pushed by circumstances outside the established moral or legal norms of a given society. That move might be seen as intentional as in the case of a political or criminal action freely entered into, it might be seen as reactive as in a response to discrimination or economic deprivation, or it might be seen as an action driven at least in part by chemical or biological factors internal to the actor. Even in the latter case, where the voluntary nature of the act is often unclear, unless mental incapacity can be proven there is still the assumption of some element of choice, a breaking of a social contract. The deviant in this set of understandings remains a free subject and responsible for his or her actions, a clear inheritance from the eighteenth-century Enlightenment. Only the mad or deranged became 'objects' consigned to involuntary treatment. Given its roots in the revolutionary era of the eighteenth century, when breaking a social contract deemed oppressive was an act which history has often come to celebrate, there is a reluctance to attach firm value judgments to such acts of deliberate deviance, since today's criminal could possibly become tomorrow's rebel and eventual hero.

This perspective of the deviant as active decision maker has its roots deep in the history of sociology, starting with Emile Durkheim's insistence that crime must be seen as normal, indeed healthy for any society. In Durkheim's view the criminal is not necessarily unsociable or parasitic but merely an indicator of dynamic and healthy social differences. Merton, following on from Durkheim, interprets deviance as a natural result of differential pressures being exerted on individuals within a given society, with crime rates rising from the pressures of aspirations of individuals rising faster than their means to fulfil them. From these insights sociology moved on the one hand towards a focus on lower classes or deprived communities as the locus of deviance and on the other hand towards an accusation that deviance was really just an issue of power, the power to label or designate certain behaviours as 'deviant' as opposed to 'normal' – drug use and prostitution easily come to mind. Nevertheless, despite the potential 'blamelessness' that such theories might prescribe for the deviant or criminal, the actions did result in crime and in the creation of violence-prone and contract-breaking individuals who needed to be dealt with. While this approach tended to deflect causative blame from the individual deviant to the social system, the deviant remained a subject for rehabilitation, for returning to a pre-deviant state.

Whatever the specific interpretation or analysis, what characterized the sociological approach to the deviant was its focus on context, on the conditions – whether economic, political, or ideological – that created the behaviours in certain individuals and groups that were perceived by others to be deviant. In policy terms this meant a focus on creating employment opportunities, providing skills and training both in prison and in targeted communities, and initiating social assistance programs for families, communities, and individuals deemed 'at risk.' And at the same time, in the tradition of social activists like Voltaire, working towards increasing social tolerance and assurances of justice free from unreasonable discrimination.

The approach of psychology has been quite different and with very different implications for the individual criminal. Instead of rehabilitation – returning the criminal to his or her pre-criminal state – the psychological approach centred the source of deviance within the individual rather than the context. The need was for treatment or transformation, not rehabilitation, and there was little interest in the contextual or social issues that so consumed sociologists and social workers. Prisons were seen as being full of individuals with existing job skills, social networks, and opportunities. While more education and training were always desirable, they were not the answer to crime but might, in fact, just create more literate and skilled criminal welders or computer programmers.

From their first forays into the world of deviance, psychologists and psychiatrists have tended to see the criminal deviant more in terms of someone who really cannot help himself, 'an object, a fit subject for treatment not conversation, inferior to the doctor or psychiatrist who is going to change him in desirable ways.'[21] Garland makes the point that this movement from subject to object has had a long and varied history of labelling, categorizing, and stigmatizing the criminal offender, including categories such as the degenerate, the feeble-minded, the inebriate, the moral imbecile, the habitual offender, and more recently, the psychopath.[22] All of these labels presume the powerful effect of a 'norm' from which individuals deviate, a norm in this case built on factors such as stable employment, stable marriages, deferred gratification, and planning.[23] Once internalized, this perspective enables experts to speak with ease about a 'delinquent mind' which conceives of the world quite differently than the presumably normal mind.[24] These labels are all designed to allow us to somehow make sense of the 'other,' the small minority of marginal and troublesome souls that we find in our midst.

Starting then from the position that something is wrong with the individual deviant, this wrongness quickly evolves within the psychological approach into the idea of deviance as illness, which moves it directly into a medical and 'helping' realm. From this perspective, psychology may lay claim to being a powerful force in the general reform and improvement of corrections systems. The sociological approach, prone to seeing the deviant as much victim as perpetrator, put little faith in the corrections enterprise and consigned prisons to the role of, at best, a benign container. The psychological approach, on the other hand, offers a hope for renewal of these deviant selves given a more enlightened, interventionist, and humane corrections system.

Both these approaches may, however, be about to be superseded by a third, a resurgent, biological explanation of the deviant that grew up in close conjunction with various psychological approaches, but with recent advances in genetic research, neurophysiology, and evolutionary psychology is poised to chart its own independent and dramatic course. At its heart is a shift in targeting from the 'delinquent mind' to the delinquent brain.[25] This may seem a minor point, but the genetic and brain chemistry research that is driving this new wave of speculations concerning the nature of the deviant is a long way from the theories of the developmental, Freudian, and behaviourist psychologists discussed above.

The biological approach is 'resurgent' because it, in fact, has a long tradition, much of which its current advocates might reasonably prefer to see forgotten. Nassi and Abramovitz list an impressive array of what they call 'scientific curiosa' in this field, starting in the mid-nineteenth century:

- Phrenology (1840–70)
- Criminal atavism – Lombroso – atavistic reversal to the primitive revealed physiologically
- Constitutional psychiatry – behaviour a function of body structure – 1930s
- Physique and delinquency – 1950s – mesomorphs and delinquency
- Heredity and crime – Jukes and Kallikaks – 1910 – bad gene theory
- Twin studies – 1940s
- Crime and mental deficiency – IQ – 1920s
- Hormonal imbalance – 1930s
- XYY genes – 1960s – extra Y and aggression
- Neurological disorders – EEGs – 1950s
- Epilepsy and violence – 1960s
- Brain dysfunction – episodic dyscontrol syndrome – 1960s[26]
- Testosterone – 1970s

While Nassi and Abramowitz see little empirical justification for these kinds of research initiatives, following the popular press provides ample evidence for the continued vibrancy of the search for a 'technical' solution to crime and the optimism of the searchers. The longing for a 'magic bullet' solution to crime has deep roots:

- 'Junk Food Diet Linked to Crime' (Vancouver *Sun*, 7 April 1981): 'The increase in the juvenile crime rate in the last 35 years is proportionate to the increase in America's processed and refined foods.'
- 'Language of Crimes Is One of Deficiency' (Vancouver *Province*, 7 January 1982): 'Canadian prisons may be packed with criminals who have never developed average language skills ... [and] a lack of development in language also leads to a lack of the ability to think analytically ... It would explain the habitual offender ... because people with such problems often don't learn from experience.'
- 'Delinquency: Do the Eyes Have It?' (Vancouver *Sun*, 24 October 1983): 'An eye research group has released a report linking vision problems to poor school performance and juvenile delinquency ... delinquents showed they were four times more likely than other children to have vision problems that make learning difficult.'
- 'Metals, Violence Linked' (Vancouver *Sun*, 1 August 1983): 'The findings of a research team ... suggest that a strong link exists between violent behaviour and the metallic elements that show up in hair. In fact ... chemical imbalances may have more to do with violent crime than psychological or environmental factors'.
- 'Hearing Loss and Crime' (*Chronicle of Higher Education*, 21 October 1987): 'Early hearing loss that goes untreated can cause serious learning problems ... Those problems can lead students to drop out, literally or psychologically, and then to become prime candidates for turning to crime.'
- 'Half of Violent Crimes Linked to Disorders that Could Be Treated' (Toronto *Globe and Mail*, 3 June 1987): 'Half of all violent crimes are committed by people who may have brain defects that are treatable with medication. A study of six repeat offenders who committed irrational violent acts found two of them had brain defects similar to those found in epileptics.'
- 'Scientists Link Defective Gene to Aggression' (Toronto *Globe and Mail*, 26 June 1993): 'Scientists have discovered an inherited gene defect [that] appears to cause a build-up of natural chemical messengers in the brain of male carriers which leads them to overreact in an aggressive manner.'[27]

- 'Researchers Discover Copper-Zinc Imbalance in Violent Children' (Vancouver *Sun*, 19 November 1994): 'Illinois researchers have announced the discovery of a mineral imbalance that seems to be shared among violent and aggressive children.'[28]
- 'Aggressiveness, Temper Lie in the Genes, Study Finds' (Vancouver *Sun*, 28 May 1994): 'Genes may account for 27% to 40% of a person's tendency toward irritability and several kinds of aggressiveness ... they may act by reducing the brain's supply of serotonin.'
- 'Looking to Biology for the Causes of Crime' (New York *Times*, 29 January 1994): '... A growing number of researchers are seeking to train the might of molecular science on the greatest sickness of all – violent crime. [One researcher] estimated that the heritability of impulsive-aggressive behaviour is between 25 and 40% [with] the neurotransmitter serotonin [being] a major player in aggressive and impulsive behaviours ... [and] that violent offenders had abnormally high levels of testosterone'.
- 'Violence Linked to Woes in Early Life' (Vancouver *Province*, 14 December 1994): 'Boys who experienced difficult births and rejection from their mothers were almost three times as likely to commit violent crimes as children who did not have those problems.'
- 'Clues to Human Behaviour Sought in Mice that Roar' (Vancouver *Sun*, 23 November 1995): 'Male mice lacking a single gene are oversexed and vicious ... The mice, which are a strain created in a laboratory, lacked a working copy of a gene that is needed to make a chemical messenger called nitric oxide in their brains. Their behaviour suggests that nitric oxide normally acts as a brake on behaviour ... but nobody knows yet whether lack of nitric oxide has anything to do with aggression in people.'
- 'Fragile X Syndrome – the Delinquency Gene' (London *Sunday Times*, 9 June 1996): 'Despite there being no treatment available for this syndrome, the Dept. of Health is funding a study to determine the efficacy of a mass screening program, in part with an eye to giving pregnant women an opportunity to abort children with the syndrome.'

The central advantage proffered by this approach compared with other more ameliorative approaches is the promise of prediction, a general issue explored in more detail in later chapters. Hopes for biology providing the key to solving the crime problem received a boost during the 1980s when studies by the RAND Corporation and other groups indicated that perhaps over 50 per cent of reported crimes were being committed by a small sub-group of mostly male criminals – estimated as low as 5 per cent of the total number of convicted felons. This led to the notion of a small group of 'super-deviants' who were in fact the 'real' problem and were perhaps 'driven by individual (biological) factors not shared by most men.'[29] One can sense the immediate appeal of such a proposition, both in terms of efficiency and blame. Much of the tension that existed between the generally accepted Enlightenment belief in human autonomy, free will, and the determinism of the biological perspective could perhaps be muted if only a few humans were denied that autonomy by a defect in their biology.

This image of most crime as essentially a 'molecular event' does, of course, have a political dimension which its critics are quick to identify. It takes tremendous pressure off the social system concerned since much criminal activity that might have been attributed to poverty, racism, family breakdowns, or general anomie resulting from bureaucratized capitalism or socialism is now seen purely in individual terms, extracted from context. 'The belief in genetic destiny implies that flaws and failings are inscribed in an unchangeable text – the DNA – that will persist in creating criminals even under the most ideal circumstances. The moral? There is no possible ideal social system or nurturing plan that can prevent the violent acts that seem to threaten the social fabric of American life.'[30]

Finally, all these speculations, theories, and phantasms about the nature of the deviants in our midst takes place against the backdrop of a looming generation of 'superpredators,' a new 'criminal class' of children aged six to seventeen who by the year 2010 are predicted to account for a quarter of a million violent crimes in the United States alone. These young people, according to theorists like DiLulio, have no adults in their lives (the result of the collapse of the family in certain sectors of society) and 'no apparent capacity for remorse.'[31] It is posited by some that these people are 'broken' and in some cases cannot be repaired – they are seen as being in essence 'moral flatliners.' In the face of this alarmist Sadean nightmare, the autonomous and educable moral selves posed by the Enlightenment ideology of Hume, Smith, Jefferson, and others appears to be woefully inadequate and the pretensions of psychological treatment a forlorn hope.

These catastrophic visions aside, what these theories concerning the deviants amidst us do accomplish is the preservation of at least the spirit of the Enlightenment dream of the essentially 'good' self, the reflective, potentially autonomous decision maker who is able to balance reasonable self-interest with consideration of justice and community. For the several reasons just outlined (and many more variations), it is accepted that not all humans are able to sustain or in some cases even envisage this balance. As Thomas Jefferson said as early as 1776, it would be a 'fantastical idea' to think that virtue and notions of the public good would be sufficient security against the depradations of criminals and traitors.[32] At the very birth of modernity Jefferson, Rousseau, Hume, Kant, and the other great philosophes and philosophers of the era acknowledged the flaw in their system, these errant characters who resisted or were denied access to virtue. Their counsel has guided us ever since – it is our duty to attempt to bring the criminal back into the fold and only as a last resort exile or execute him. Thus began modernity's great adventure with correction and treatment.

The Treatment Issue

North Americans cling stubbornly to the 'correctional' nomenclature attached to their carceral world. Prisons are 'correctional institutions,' prison guards are 'correctional officers,' teachers are 'correctional educators,' and the profession is called 'corrections.' The label conveys a powerful faith in what is clearly a mission and may as well be an illusion. Despite the dismal record of recidivism, violence, and programmatic failures, government and much of the public manage to sustain a belief that criminals can be 'corrected,' that crime can be 'cured,' that the social world can be made 'safe.' As we have seen this must be so, for at the base of the modern project is a determination to place an almost unlimited value on the individual, to see each as an end not a means, to paraphrase Kant. This explains our reluctance to banish, execute, or merely imprison and our endless search for the means of correcting, a search that invariably turns, as it does in other areas, to reason and science for direction.

From Socrates to the moderns we have been taught that reason is not a divine gift but rather a tool that we can use to further our survival in the best, happiest, and most virtuous means possible. We have therefore 'used' reason in the form of science to defeat or wrestle to a standstill many of the hostile elements that we confront in the natural world, such as diseases, floods, drought, and famine, and we as well yearn to apply reason to our more intractable moral and social problems. Indeed, in the modern, post-Enlightenment culture that we share with much of the globe there is a faith that with enough effort of application, rationality can address and solve our social problems. Or can it? John McKnight offers the counter view that the rational, medically derived approaches we utilize – what he calls the 'allopathic approach' – have had little impact on problems such as public health compared with more community-based and collective efforts like water purification, waste management, and milk pasteurization. McKnight sees the practice of prisoner rehabilitation as also essentially allopathic: 'What is most significant about the allopathic approach is the radical nature of its basic premise. For along the continuum of world healing practices, allopathic medicine stands at one pole – an extremist premise. Its radical position grows from the unique belief that the malady is *in* the person and the cure is achieved by professional intrusion *into* that person. In that understanding the allopathic faith stands isolated in therapeutic history as it ignores both the world around the person and the person as healers. Instead, it emphasizes the malady within and the expert assault upon that pathogen.'[33] Again we can see some fundamental divisions at work here. McKnight sides with a more sociological approach in emphasizing the 'social' nature of both the problem of crime and its solution, but he also presumes to critique in a very Rousseauean or romantic way the pretension of reason – whatever branch of the social sciences it operates in – to be the correct means through which the problem may be addressed.

Nietzsche, as a pre-postmodernist opponent of these same pretensions, points to Socrates as the originator of this modern project with his idea that knowledge and virtue are one and that the path to the latter can only be via the former. Socratism, Nietzsche claims, rejected instinct and intuition in favour of insight: '*Only instinctively*: the phrase touches the very heart and core of the Socratic intention. Socratism used it to depreciate all known art and ethics: wherever its piercing gaze alighted it found only a lack of insight and the power of delusion.'[34] The reason to be employed in carrying out this project, Nietzsche claimed, was of a very special kind, a 'discursive' reason that relied on observation, analysis, and speculation, but minimized the role of intuition. Refined further by Descartes and other modern rationalists, this reason came to see virtue in fragmentation, in taking things apart in order to describe the whole and provide meaning, indeed to identify truth.

Thus, Nietzsche claims, is born the central illusion of modernity, 'the unshakable belief that rational thought, guided by causality, can penetrate to the depths of being, and that it is capable not only of knowing but even of *correcting* being.'[35] Nowhere is this more evident than in the attempts by the state via the prison to change the behaviour of criminals. This change in behaviour is to come about by a change in thinking, a change to be brought about by a combination of introspection, interaction, and response to external pressure.

The idea of 'correcting' goes back at least as far as the eighteenth-century Walnut Street Jail in Philadelphia with its stress on being 'penitent,' introspective, self-analytical and remorseful as the path towards citizenship. But it is really with the latter half of the twentieth century that the treatment prison emerged in full flower, with the medical model as its rationale and provider of rational, scientific tools. We have seen already some of the rhetorical flourishes that accompanied this model, but a refresher will not hurt:

> Imprisonment and punishment do not present themselves as the proper methods of dealing with criminals. We have to treat them physically as sick people, which in every respect they are. It is no more reasonable to punish these individuals for behaviour over which they have no control than it is to punish an individual for breathing through his mouth because of enlarged adenoids ... It is the hope of the more progressive elements in psychopathology and criminology that the guard and jailer will be replaced by the nurse and the judge by the psychiatrist, whose sole attempt will be to treat and cure the individual instead of merely to punish him.[36]

In these times this may sound incredibly naïve and, indeed, foolish, but these were, after all, enlightened reformers, who saw their mission in terms of liberating the prisoner from the medieval darkness of mere confinement and the mundane belief in employment as the solution to crime. Taking over from more traditional education, training, and religious programs which maintained a rather more universalist approach to the issue of rehabilitation – taking on all comers as it were – the medical model opted for getting to know the prisoner, getting 'inside,' so to speak, in order to offer individualized treatment. Ideally, the new phalanx of specialized prison workers – the psychiatrists, psychologists, and social workers – would diagnose the inmate's needs, prescribe the necessary treatment, and ensure that it was effectively carried out. At the centre of this ambition is a subtle de-centring from the 'act' of deviance – the crime – and onto the individual deviant, the

Picture of B.C. Penitentiary is from Prison Journal #8 (1989), published by the Institute for the Humanities, Simon Fraser University.

concern being 'less to avenge the crime than to transform the criminal who stands behind it.'[37]

To illustrate the significance of this shift in belief we can examine two quite similar documents, each 'introducing' a recently arrived inmate to the staff who will be responsible for finding the appropriate placement for him in the prison regime. The document concerning 'Convict #5116 Jones' is from the chief keeper at the British Columbia Penitentiary and is dated November 1939 (Figure 2.1).

The second document, summarized here to ensure anonymity, is titled a 'Progress Summary – Appraisal and Recommendation' and is dated October 1984:

Mr P is a 36-year-old offender who is doing an aggregate 24-year sentence for armed robbery, use of firearm, escape, and unlawfully at large.

P was only six years old when he was deprived of parental affection and supervision due to his parent's separation. His mother took his older brother and sister in her custody and left P and his younger brother to live in foster homes through social workers. P found himself in foster homes, training schools, and police lock-ups in an age when he should have been

LQ/JA
File #5116

BRITISH COLUMBIA PENITENTIARY.
CHIEF KEEPER'S DEPARTMENT

Nov. 7/39

THE WARDEN:

Sir,

Re Convict #5116 JONES. (Indian)
Re Report for the Classification Board.

REMARKS Age approximately 35 years.   States he was born in
Owen Sound, Ontario. He is single, but lived with
a friend Clara Phillips, Chehalis Indian Reserve,B.C.
His parents are both dead, he states. Description:-
Complexion Dark (Indian), Eyes Brown, Hair Black,
Weight 163# Height 5'6". Religion Roman Catholic.
Is a repeater to this Institution.

CRIME He was sentenced at Ashcroft, B.C. on August 19/39,
by H.E.A.Robertson, CCJ, to serve Four years for the
crime of Steal in a dwelling house. He was received
into the Penitentiary on October 18/39 and his term
is due to expire on Nov. 25th. 1942.

PREVIOUS
CONVICTIONS. 1920 Parry Sound, Ont. Housbkg & Theft 3 yrs. Kingston,
                                                          Penity.

1922 Released on Tkt. of Lve.

1925 Fort William, Ont. Br.Rly.Act 30 days,Ft.William
                                                 Ind.Farm.

1925 Kerrobert,Sask. Assault & Vag. 30 days, Pr.Albert
                                                    Jail

1929 Grande Prairie,Alta. Att.Rape 3 yrs. & 10 L
                                               Sask.Penity.

1932 High River, Alta. Carry Revolver 3 mo.

1933 Wetaskiwin,Alta. Theft 5 chgs 5 years Sask.Penity.
1937 Victoria,B.C. Ret.Stln.Goods 2 yrs. B.C.Pen.#4830

He is apparently in good physical health. Mind seems
to be slightly deranged. He states he does not drink.
Uses tobacco but has never used drugs.

He was born of Indian parentage in the Georgian Bay
District but his parents are both dead. He has lived
with a common-law-wife on the Chehalis Indian Reserve,
B.C. by the name of Clara Phillips.

SUMMARY This convict has never attended school therefore can
read and write very little. He seems somewhat mentally
deranged and his statements cannot be relied upon.
He is untrustworthy and would have a violent temper
and should be kept under close observation. He is not
a fit type to put to work outside the walls. I would
recommend he work on Construction work.

Respectfully submitted,

....
Chief Keeper.

Illustration from B.C. Penitentiary Chief Keeper's Department was purchased
at a flea market in New Westminster, B.C., in 1998 from Bernard Spring, owner
of Antiquarius, #609 – 207 W. Hastings St., Vancouver, B.C., V6B 1H7

in mother's lap. The circumstances made him rebel against society to take revenge for deprivation of his childhood love and affection. He was in conflict with the law at an early age. He had been in police lock-ups and provincial prisons until he got his first federal term in 1968 for armed robbery. To draw a clear picture of his criminal history, the record from 1977 is as follows:

1977   10 years armed robbery
1977   Escape – apprehended
1978   1 year consecutive for escape
1980   Escape – apprehended
1982   Unlawfully at large
1984   1 year consecutive
1984   10 years concurrent armed robbery
1984   18 months consecutive – use of firearm

The foregoing criminal history shows his criminal activities progressed from car theft to armed robbery. He felt he had no home to go to, or no trustworthy friend or relative to return to. After every short release he found himself returning to lock-ups and prisons; places he referred to as 'homes.' It is evident that P had no meaning or purpose in his life. He was deeply institutionalized and was scared to get out. Subconsciously, he deliberately committed crime to return to jail. He was in different kinds and levels of jails, and all he picked up from those places were criminal activities. He considered himself a non-entity on the street but inside prison he was a leader. He survived in a brutal environment through crisis-like riots and disturbances in prison. But he could not feel and felt no confidence to cope with normal situations outside the prison. He was immature, insensitive, and careless of the consequences.

It is during his present incarceration that P has upgraded his education and has taken concrete steps towards personal development.

While the language of the 1939 document seems woefully amateurish and judgmental, and one senses that Jones is indeed less a subject than the object Convict #5116, can we be any more at ease with the progress made by 1984? One senses here the obfuscations of the amateur therapist and social worker, blithely identifying the primal, subconscious needs of P, including a mother, a home, meaning, purpose, and self-worth. This summative narrative of the life of P is constructed from a thick file of facts and interpretations produced by psychologists and social workers, resulting in an 'explanation' involving both social factors ('circumstances' drove him to crime) and deep-seated psychological problems stemming from deprivation of love. While the 'mental derangement' of Convict #5116 Jones was simply a *fait accompli* to be accommodated, P's 'immaturity' and insecurity were problems looking for solutions.

The difficulty faced by the advocates of the medical model centred on the prison itself (about which more will be said in a following chapter). The prison was simply too difficult, too intractable an institution to be easily transformed into a hospital or therapeutic community. Thomas Szasz[38] could warn us as early as 1963 about the dangers of what he called the therapeutic state with its ambition to 'manage' all aspects of social life, and this ambition was certainly present within the new world of 'corrections,' still it was less easily accomplished there than in the wider society. Prisons paid lip service to rehabilitation, but the treatment specialists always insisted that they did not go far enough, and that released prisoners remained criminals, despite the best efforts to provide treatment. The problem seemed to centre on the 'feelings and attitudes which underlie their antisocial behaviour ... many are little different in their hearts.' The answer of course was to push the model further, to truly transform the prison into a hospital, a 'total treatment agency where there can be harmony of purpose among the various kinds of employees who comprise the staff.'[39] One can easily imagine the tensions between the new treatment-oriented and professional do-gooders whose ambition was to medicalize the issue of crime and the career prison officers and prison administrators who wished only to remain proud and efficient keepers. Indeed, our two documents embody this conflict and many 'chief keepers' were still in positions of influence in the 1980s.

This need to penetrate, to get inside the mind and soul of the imprisoned criminal, had its roots in the Enlightenment insistence that there was a crucial distinction between 'intention' and 'action.' Nowhere is this clearer than in the complex rationalizations of Rousseau as he sought to assert the goodness of the self despite the questionable antics of the body in space and time. Rousseau was insistent that one could and must distinguish between intention and action in the sense that the decision to act is always dictated by something outside the person, something 'social' rather than 'personal' or 'internal.' Throughout his confessional writings, decisions Rousseau makes about mundane and decisive matters are made 'in spite of himself.' He writes his *Confessions* because he is forced to speak 'in spite of himself.' He insists throughout his writings that there are 'moments of a kind of delirium, in which men cannot be judged by what they do.'[40] From these insights spring Perry Mason and the obsession of our justice system with motive and intentionality, the means by which an act of killing can become transformed into various 'degrees' of 'murder' or 'manslaughter.'

For Rousseau and his many followers into modernity, the essence of the self is preserved in the depths of the heart; our being is essentially present in our feelings, not our actions.[41] Implicitly, the criminal could retain a crooked-timbered soul (or set of attitudes, or feelings, depending on the theory being applied), while in his or her actions seeming to cooperate with and learn from the correctional treatment. If we were all Rousseaus and veiled our feelings behind false actions, and if the root of the impulse to criminality lies deep within, then to be effective the treatment would have to penetrate to the soul in a manner disturbingly medieval, potentially assuming the form of a modern Inquisition.

In the Socratic tradition that permeates the modern bureaucratic world that includes the prison we gain access to this inner world by cognitive operations – we reflect, we think, we ponder, we review, we reassess, and analyse. Sometimes this is done in isolation, more often in group sessions, or with a counsellor. Within this world of correctional treatment there is a massive intolerance for ambiguity. The treatment staff and the parole board want to be sure that the person has changed, not just because the consequences of error are so pronounced and visible, but also because the cultural world in wihich the prison exists rejects ambiguity, complexity, and paradox. A prison should be or wants to be a Manichean world, a place for pure dichotomy, a setting in which Cartesian dualism can function without qualifications. There is insight or lack of insight, remorse or no remorse, sincerity or insincerity, truth and lies, good and evil. Drawn into this Manichean world in a cruel embrace, many prisoners come to accept its terms and seek themselves the transformation from black to white, while others find in such dualisms only the justification or validation of their chosen course.

The 'being' of the prisoner / criminal is in many ways a mystery to the observer responsible for correcting. Like with most phenomena, however, there are degrees of mystery. The thief is more comprehensible than the addict and the latter more comprehensible than the pedophile – though one might argue that these distinctions are self-imposed delusions or illusions, designed to mask or repress the observer's own inherent or culturally attuned drives towards violence, addiction, and sensual extremes. The thief commits the act we all commit, but does so clumsily or beyond the bounds of acceptable appropriation. For him, the correction needed is a question of tactics more than morals, of bringing within acceptable boundaries the socially generated disposition to acquire.

The violent persons we subdivide in terms of understanding: violence in the act of theft, violence with a certain utility, as it were, is again a matter for reason to work its magic. Control through improved insight, through a tactical understanding is the issue. There are better ways to steal, better ways to acquire, or, indeed, ways to sublimate the need to acquire. For the seemingly unmotivated violence, or violence that in degree moves past its utility – the violence of the people in our earlier examples – reason seems on less sure ground. Here the language of correcting moves beyond the bedrock of self-interest, utility, and common sense and into the mystical-rationalism of psychology, beginning the effort to probe the depths of being to find the proper insertion point for insight. The violence has no logical meaning, or at least seems not to have so in the light of a reconstruction of the act. Unlike the act of theft which contains no mystery, here the act itself is probed incessantly in search of a reason, a motivation, a cause that can then be addressed. Indeed, the search is insatiable, limited only by the availability of the subject.

The addict presages the true crisis for the modern Socratic project. Reason employs all its tools in the effort to explain this phenomenon, to find its cause, and effect its cure, all seemingly in vain. It is the will of the addict to feed the addiction and the will of the addict to starve it that is at the centre of the phenomenon, and reason finds itself a blunt object when it tries to confront the will. For the drug-addicted the appeal to reason over emotion is a non-starter. The addict lives in both worlds, revelling in a non-Cartesian universe completely absent of clarity. No one has captured the futility of reason in relation to the addict better than Irvine Welsh in *Trainspotting*. His addicts 'know' the evil they do to themselves, but the knowing carries no weight:

Ah'm just lettin it wash all over me, or wash through me ... clean me ott fae the inside.

This internal sea. The problem is that this beautiful ocean carries with it loads ay poisonous flotsam and jetsam ... that poison is diluted by the sea, but once the ocean rolls out, it leaves the shite behind, inside ma body. It takes as well as gives, it washes away ma endorphins, ma pain resistance

centres; they take a long time to come back .... and ma reflexes are not getting any better ... but it's all here, all within my sweaty grasp. Syringe,
needle, spoon, candle, lighter, packey ay powder. It's all okay, it's all
beautiful; but ah fear that this internal sea is gaunnae subside soon, leaving this poisonous shite all washed up, stranded up in ma body.

Ah start to cook up another shot. As ah shakily haud the spoon over the
candle, waitin for the junk tae dissolve, ah think; more short-term sea,
more long-term poison. This *thought* though, is naewhere near sufficient
tae stop us fae doing what ah huv tae dae.'[42]

The contest goes on, however, because the Socratic project has a pros-
thetic weapon beyond reasoning in the form of science and its many
creations. Chemical and other material interventions into the body of
the addict are a second wave of attack following the defeat of reason's
attack.

The sexual deviant is the most recent object of reason's intervention.
Here, finally, the state has decided to strip away the last frontier of private life and enter into the imaginations of its subjects. Not content to
merely punish violators of the ever-shifting sexual mores of a culture,
the Socratic must know why in order that they may correct. Unlike
theft or even violence, sensual predilections lie deep in the being, buried or made invisible by fear and loathing, covered over by carefully
and cleverly devised rationalizations, or made too quickly transparent
by practised and guilt-driven confessions.

In the classic version of the medical model, as operationalized in the
period circa 1949–77, these variations of deviance were minimized, all
offenders being seen as potential addicts, sex offenders, thieves, and
killers. Sentences issued by the courts varied based on the perceived
seriousness of the offence, but these distinctions faded as soon as the
verdict of guilty was decreed by a judge and the deviant criminal was
passed over to the penal wing of the criminal justice system. Now the
criminal, the offender, became in Foucault's terminology the 'delinquent.' Suddenly the action that precipitated the conviction and the
sentencing receded (at least temporarily) and the person of the delinquent became the subject of study. This transition generally began after
conviction and before sentencing as the judge requested a 'pre-sentence
report' outlining some specifics of the offender's life history that might
be relevant to the sentence. The prison thus accepts at its gate a convicted person but what it will subsequently act upon throughout the
duration of the sentence is a different 'object' than the 'subject' it
receives, an object:

Defined by variables which at the outset at least were not taken into account in the sentence, for they were relevant only for a corrective technology ... The delinquent is to be distinguished from the offender by the fact that it is not so much his act as his life that is relevant in characterizing him. The penitentiary operation, if it is to be a genuine re-education, must become the sum total existence of the delinquent, making the prison a sort of artificial and coercive theatre in which his life will be examined from top to bottom. The legal punishment bears upon the act; the punitive technique on a life; it falls to this punitive technique, therefore, to reconstitute all the sordid detail of a life in the form of knowledge, to fill in the gaps of that knowledge and to act upon it by a practice of compulsion.[43]

Behind the offender stands the delinquent, whose slow formation is shown via the creation of a biography – the criminal thus exists before the crime and even outside it. As Foucault says, he not only commits his crime, he 'has an affinity with it.' For the treatment practitioners it was an elective affinity, a set of links between self and act that were not necessarily freely or consciously chosen, could be identified, diagnosed, prescribed for, and treated.

Before moving on to examine the operation of the medical model in some detail, we need to establish more clearly what it looked like in practice. We can do this by examining a portion of the carceral history of one of the men included in the British Columbia research study. We will call the man Bill and fictionalize his case sufficiently to preserve his anonymity but not enough to blur the reality of his experience.

Bill was born in 1946 and was raised in what must have been a confusing and unhappy household. His alcoholic father died when he was an infant, his mother worked full-time, leaving him in the care of various female relatives. He suffered physical and mental abuse at the hands of a stepfather, frequently running away from home and being apprehended by the authorities. He had first started drinking alcohol at age seven and by twelve years old was a steady drinker, often mixing alcohol and barbiturates. He was made a ward of the Superintendent of Child Welfare and after numerous foster placements was sent to a juvenile delinquent institution but 'by the age of 14, punishment had no effect. *I do what I like* was his attitude and unfortunately this was allowed by the groups working with him since they had given up, describing him as incorrigible.' Reports from this period describe him as 'an extremely aggressive youngster, [with] little feeling of guilt and a high degree of self-love. Generally he

feels rejected by all adults and requires a good deal of kindness, understanding and patience from a substitute parent figure. Punishment for
misdemeanors has no affect.' As a last resort at the age of fifteen he was
sent to an adult institution where he had his first homosexual experiences. Upon release he committed a series of robberies and was sent to the
penitentiary.

In the 1963 induction process, Bill was described as having 'no deep
feeling regarding his behaviour. He has never learned to accept guidance
or limits nor has he respect for himself or society. Therefore his behaviour
is not wrong but something that is necessary. He resents authority and
presents a verbally hostile picture which possibly reflects general aggressive tendencies. He has few interests and feels school is useless for his
occupational goals.' Within the month Bill was transferred to a psychiatric
institution for treatment where he was described as being in a 'delusional
state, hearing people call him dirty names and considered suicidal, potentially homicidal if aroused.' To this point in his criminal career, Bill's only
actual crime had been the theft of cigarettes and groceries from two break-
ins. In the prison and the psychiatric centre he refused most food and
medication, felt that the staff 'had it in for him,' and had a particular fear
of homosexual attack. The provisional diagnosis was that Bill was 'a person who basically suffers from Sociopathic Personality Disturbance, Anti-
Social Reaction.' The prescription was ECT or electric shock therapy and
an intensive course of chlorpromazine. After four months of this 'treatment,' he was transferred back to prison where he was reported to have a
'somewhat withdrawn, suspicious attitude about life and people.'

Bill was released a year later and by 1968 had become addicted to heroin, returning to prison in 1973 for trafficking in that substance. The
medical model had mellowed with age by this time, the diagnosis now
being that: 'He is particularly vulnerable. He needs gentle confrontation and pushing with much ego support.' Bill ended up in the prison
high school and then college program and his counsellor concluded by
1974 that Bill 'appears to have re-examined his previous life-style and
discarded it for a new one.' This seems a somewhat extraordinary
notion, but in the mid-1970s it may have seemed more possible to shop
for lifestyles. By this time, as we will see in subsequent chapters, the
medical model was fading in the prisons and Bill's travels through it
were largely over. He remained, of course, a heroin addict and was in
and out of prison until the early 1980s, but during those years he experienced a quite different correctional regime.

CHAPTER THREE

Insight Wars:
The Struggle for the
Prisoner's Mind and Soul

Some paradox in our nature leads us, once we have made our fellow men the objects of our enlightened interest, to go on to make them the objects of our pity, then of our wisdom, ultimately of our coercion.[1]

Lionel Trilling, 'Manners, Morals, and the Novel,' 1947

This search for understanding explicit in the medical model had, as a corresponding demand, the insistence that the prisoner must gain insight (understanding) into himself. The instruments designed to reveal these understandings were embedded in a variety of bureaucratic processes, all subsumed under the general heading of the 'criminal justice system.' Unfortunately, diamonds become zircons when immersed in this system, as they do in virtually all bureaucratic systems. Language is debased as words such as 'insight,' 'communication,' and 'remorse' become mere code words for ritualized understandings stripped of precise or even actual meanings. The talents, motives, and ideals of the corrections staff are debased as they struggle with competing mandates, impossible expectations, and hopelessly inadequate resources. A sometimes vast gulf opens between the intentions of treatment and the results, in part because of the means through which the intentions are administered. The prisoners-patients either struggle to resist debasement by refusing to participate, actively resisting or going 'underground,' or become 'institutionalized,' voluntary partners in what becomes the game of corrections.

From Reformation to Transformation

This understanding sought by the new technicians of correction was radical in the sense that it demanded not merely the rehabilitation or reformation of the prisoner, but a transformation. Reformation implies a kind of partnership, an acknowledgment that a previous way of being was faulty and in need of reform and that the subject concerned will to some degree be a participant in the reformation project. This was certainly the sense that Martin Luther carried with him as he urged a reformation of Christianity in the sixteen century. The result was indeed a *re-formation*, a re-thinking of Catholicism, a re-formulation of its doctrines and core beliefs, and an invitation for all to participate. A transformation seems an altogether different thing, often imparted from outside the subject. It is as well more ambitious than a mere re-formation, being instead a new formation. For examples, the 'transformer' toys so popular for a while bear no resemblance to their pre-transformed shapes. While Lutheranism and Anglicanism can be clearly seen as re-formulations of Catholicism, Methodism and strict Presbyterianism are much more on the order of Christian transformations. Finally, as we saw in the case of Bill at the conclusion of the previous chapter, the transformations envisaged by proponents of the medical model involved the abandoning of one 'lifestyle' and the adoption of a 'new' one, in effect the creation of a new, improved self.

In this war for the soul, the attacker-transformer accepts the Socratic injunction that the central task in achieving authenticity and thereby sociability as opposed to criminality, is to 'know thyself,' but presumes that the criminal cannot accomplish this without a massive intervention by experts, the very antithesis of the Jeffersonian strictures cited in the Preface and a far cry from merely 'informing their discretion.' Adopting the metaphor of revolutionaries, the advocates of these interventions argue that the self the deviant could come to know is either a corrupted self – the crooked timber from which no respectable house can be built – or the processes they might use to come to that knowing are corrupted. There is a need for intervention to (a) change the self or (b) change the means by which one comes to know oneself. This must be a profound transformation, rather than a superficial training; a change of *morality*, rather than of *attitude*.[2]

This radical intervention into the soul of the criminal and prisoner during the administration of punishment is rationalized through the Enlightenment notion of the social contract. No matter the severity or seriousness of the criminal act per se, the criminal is perceived to have broken the social contract and is therefore the enemy of not just the victim of the act or the state that enforces the law, but of society as a whole. Foucault argues the point as follows, borrowing directly from Rousseau's formulation in The Social Contract: 'The offence opposes an individual to the entire social body; in order to punish him, society has the right to oppose him in its entirety ... thus a formidable right to punish is established, since the offender becomes the common enemy. Indeed, he is worse than an enemy, for it is from within society that he delivers his blows – he is nothing less than a traitor ... a wild fragment of nature, villain, a monster, a madman, perhaps, a sick and, before long, abnormal individual.'[3] In this modern formulation of punishment and treatment the offender has been saved from the premodern 'vengeance of the sovereign' – which could be horrible and arbitrary – but in turn is exposed to a penalty that 'seems to know no bounds.' There is implicit in all this the conversion of the 'self' of the imprisoned criminal from a subject to an object, an 'other' with needs that 'it' is unaware of but which informed, enlightened society is both aware of and can provide.

It is at this point that the analysis of Michel Foucault proves so powerful and persuasive. He argues that to carry out this 'education,' this transformative function, the prison must have more than mere administrative powers. In fact the legal authorities, those who passed the sentence, must withdraw from the scene and can have 'no immediate control over all these procedures that rectify the penalty as it proceeds.' Here, then, is the source of that stark distinction between the consideration of the crime and the criminal by a judge while sentencing and the consideration of the same by corrections staff. Once outside the courtroom another and sometimes quite distinct arm of the criminal justice system takes over. 'Those who administer detention must therefore have an indispensable autonomy, when it comes to the question of individualizing and varying the application of the penalty: supervisors, a prison governor, a chaplain, or an instructor are more capable of exercising this corrective function than those who hold the penal power. It is their judgment (understood as observation, diagnosis, characterization, information, differential classification) and not a verdict in the form of an attribution of guilt, that must serve as support for this internal modulation of the penalty – for its mitigation or even its interruption.'[4] In recent years this process has become more complex as discretion over sentencing has been systematically taken away from judge and judiciary and given to legislatures which base their decisions on crude assessments of public opinion.

Insight: The Get-Out-of-Jail-Free Card

Corrections professionals, occupying the space between the judiciary's judgment of guilt and the public's increasing demands for 'just desserts,' must assert their right to determine the substance of the actual sentence – that is, the time needed to reform, correct, and rehabilitate as well as the time needed to exact appropriate retribution and remorse. To make this assertion convincing, they must employ a 'technology,' a set of tools designed to diagnose and cure. Central to this task is the idea of 'insight.'

In reading through the correctional service files of prisoners one is quickly struck by the repetition of the word 'insight' (as in lack thereof) and by its apparent multiple meanings as it is deployed by psychologists, psychiatrists, case management officers, parole officers, counsellors, parole board members, and prisoners themselves. It is a slippery notion throughout, with prisoners lacking it, gaining it, losing it, pretending to have it, or not having the vaguest idea what it is. In the case of Prisoner A, he is seen to have 'some mature self-insight and some genuine motivation' in a 1975 interview, in 1981 he has gained sufficient insight to be a 'healthy emotional being,' and in 1990 prison staff conclude that despite all this, 'his lack of insight is complete.' Likewise, Prisoner B is described on two occasions in 1982 as having 'demonstrated good insight,' but in 1984 it is deemed he is 'unlikely to gain any insight,' though two months later he claims 'to have gained much insight' from a drug and alcohol program. Prisoner C progressed from lacking any 'useable insight' in February 1980, to apparently gaining 'insight and awareness' in July, to definitely having undergone 'genuine insight and change' in September. Following an almost immediate re-offence the system was more guarded regarding prisoner C, as late as 1988 describing him as 'an articulate man who verbalizes insight' and thus remains a risk to re-offend.

For drug addicts, predictably, the concept of insight was particularly troublesome. Prisoner D, a long-time heroin addict, is described as having 'apparent insight' in 1977, only possible insight in 1982, a 'lack of insight' in 1985, but as being 'not without insight' by 1991 – though by 1993 he is described as once again needing to 'develop insight into his self-defeating behaviour.' This is a not uncommon pattern, Prisoner E being described as having 'no insight' in May 1979, 'some insight' in June, 'not much insight' in July, a 'lack of personal insight' in 1980 and again in 1982 and 1984, but with 'good insights' in 1985, followed by a lack of insight in 1987. Often claims by line staff or parole staff are undercut by the more specialized and professional understandings of the psychologists who characterize what is often described by staff as insight as in fact 'mere intellectualizing,' while on other occasions the apparently professional discovery of insight by the psychologist is rejected by the corrections staff as a 'con job.'

Just what is it they are all looking for? We can start with the standard definitions from the *Oxford English Dictionary* (*OED*):

> Insight: The original notion appears to have been 'internal sight', i.e. with the eyes of the mind or understanding. But subsequently there arose a tendency to analyse the word as sight or seeing *into* a thing or subject, although even so there remained the notion of penetrating into things or seeing beneath their surface with the eyes of the understanding.
>
> 1 Internal sight, mental vision or perception, discernment; in early use sometimes, Understanding, intelligence, wisdom.
> 2 The fact of penetrating with the eyes of the understanding into the inner character or hidden nature of things; a glimpse or view beneath the surface; the faculty or power of thus seeing. In studies of behaviour and learning, the sudden perception of the solution to a problem or difficulty.[5]

Words such as 'insight' and 'remorse' could be described as 'diamond words,' words with many facets and multiple meanings. Their meanings change over time and the definitions utilized at an operational level of a bureaucratic system may lag behind more contemporary meanings used by 'experts' or professionals. 'Insight,' for instance, has its roots in the psychoanalytic tradition where it has a quite specific, even 'scientific' meaning. Here insight is a central aspect of the therapeutic process, contributing to adaptation, empowerment, forgiveness, guilt reduction, enhanced problem solving, reduction of tension, the release of psychic energy, increased self-knowledge, symptom relief, better understanding, and strengthened will.[6] For any of this to occur within the psychiatric framework the following qualities are said to be required:

1   Capacity for self-observation
2   Sound ego functioning
3   Sufficient cognitive abilities
4   A relationship between therapist and client based on a compliant and cooperative client
5   Viewing the therapist as competent, warm, helpful, and safe

This latter condition seems to take the psychiatric notion of insight some distance from at least the day-to-day world of the prison, though it may indeed prevail in the private relationship of the individual prisoner and the psychiatrist.

In recent decades, with the erosion of the psychoanalytic tradition within the correctional field, the word 'insight' was being used by staff in a more 'common sense' form or even in a form with religious or moral overtones rather than in a strict diagnostic or prescriptive sense. Overlaid with this 'lay' use of the term is its increasing centrality in cognitive psychology, with 'insight' assuming once again a quite specific meaning, in this case the ability of the prisoner to acknowledge and comprehend psychological or emotional difficulties. Thus, it is argued that 'some individuals are readily able to report why they committed a violent act and this realization may inhibit further offending. Others will put forward "the language of change" without necessarily having altered their outlook or intentions.'[7] Still other uses of the term occur in counselling psychology where in group situations it is hoped that the prisoner will gain 'insight' into his or her personal problems. As well, in developmental psychology, which tends to see much criminal activity as a factor of immaturity or underdeveloped cognitive and moral abilities, 'insight' is seen as one of the abilities that is to be developed. At the operational level, however, with the line staff correctional officers, case managers, and parole officers who write the bulk of the reports that to a large degree determine the short- and long-term fate of the imprisoned, the use of the word may still be grounded only in common sense or moral meanings. It is in this sense that the object of interventions, the prisoner, can be victimized by the language of corrections, never being sure which facet or face of the word is being employed.

In generalizing about the personality qualities of the imprisoned, the specific examples offered of lack of insight are legion, but in keeping with Foucault's analysis of the proper functioning of the modern prison and with the *OED* definition of 'insight,' all these qualities share a location 'beneath the surface' of the visible self. One of the earliest paradigms employed in attempting to characterize this area beneath the surface was the authoritarian personality, the set of traits first identified by Theodor Adorno and his colleagues in fascists and racists but quickly transferred to criminals as well. Rigidity, intolerance of ambiguity, compartmentalization of thought, cynicism, obsession with power relationships, and an adherence to conventional values are all hallmarks of authoritarianism and all have their parallels in the world of the criminal, especially as it is lived out in the world of the prison.[8] Other views add to this by stressing egocentrism, a lack of analytical skills, a tendency to view the world in an episodic manner, not always linking cause and effect or the past with the future, and a general impulsiveness.

These essentially internal components of the personality, formed in part by biology and part by culture, can under the right conditions manifest themselves in behaviours that are decidedly deviant and often criminal. For the authoritarian the average, honest, 'straight' citizen is held in contempt, regarded as weak, to be pitied, and, among the more hardened, stepped on or over. Goodness, justice, humility, honesty, and similar qualities are seen as hypocrisy or the attributes of a fool. When transformed into praxis, these qualities lead to an anaesthetized sensibility towards violence, a defence of violence as simply a tool of the trade, and the criminal's all too frequent stance towards the victim as someone who simply got in the way. If personality components like egocentrism, impulsivity, presentism, and the 'delusion of exceptionalistic exemption from the laws of cause and effect'[9] come to dominate the world-view of an individual, they wreak havoc with the idea of deterrence that is so central to our means of maintaining social order, since taken together they inhibit one's ability to assess risks adequately. Robert Ross calls such individuals 'sublimely optimistic,' believing – again, because of supposed lack of insight – that they will not be caught; if caught, not convicted; if convicted, not sentenced; if sentenced, not imprisoned; if imprisoned, quickly released.[10]

Examples from my own experience of teaching in prison spring easily to mind, making it easier for me to accept such a generalized view of the criminal. A bank robber who is angry at the customer who 'got in the way' during a robbery, thereby forcing him to shoot, stands out as an early introduction to the skewed perspective of the prisoner. In this case the result of the shooting was a much longer sentence, for which the errant customer was to blame. There is also the endless search for technicalities that might lead to overturning a conviction or gaining early release without the slightest interest in the issue of guilt or just desserts. One could easily generate a sense of having passed through the looking glass in this upside-down moral universe, especially during attempts to apply reason and ethics in discussions of prisoners' actions. Indeed, one might even suspect that prisoners deliberately seek such a separation of 'them' from 'us,' a wilful assertion and celebration of a cognitive and moral 'difference' to accompany their social stigmatization. (Thoughts of Samoans exaggerating the liberality of their sexual mores in order to put one over on the visiting anthropologist Margaret Mead come to mind.)

Nonetheless, these mental deficits, skewed patterns, or immaturely developed abilities were the raw material that the psychologically driven medical model was designed to correct in order that the prisoner could acquire sufficient insight into his or her actions to be trusted once again in society. In most cases this correcting came to be operationalized in terms of problem solving. Successful citizenship became equated with possessing and knowing how and when to use a range of problem-solving skills: 'To fully appreciate the efficiency with which the person navigates through the problem to a satisfactory solution, it is necessary to understand how well he thinks about and works through the interpersonal situation. It is this process, manifest in a set of cognitive skills, that defines his social problem-solving capacity. It is the manner in which he proceeds that largely determines the quality of the outcome. It is *how* he thinks it through, rather than what he might think at any given instant, that becomes the important issue in understanding the likelihood of long-range success or failure.'[11]

The medical model in this formation clearly focused on the 'form' as crucial in determining the 'content,' as well as focusing on the process of acquiring and utilizing insight rather than on the specific conclusions drawn. There was a kind of Enlightenment hubris operating here, a conviction on the part of the treatment experts that if the mechanics were right, if the processes were in place, if the analytical skills and perspective-taking and empathy-generating qualities were internalized, then the subsequent actions in the world would logically be law-abiding. Behind this hubris, of course, was the equally firm conviction that all of these processes could, in fact, be imparted to the imprisoned criminal.

The 'reasoning' and 'thinking' being advocated here is almost completely operational or procedural, a means of re-integrating the offender with the social contract community so central to Enlightenment ideology. The key words were 'development,' 'skills,' and 'decision making.' Each had powerful links with the general field of education and training, thus preparing the way for a shift in focus in corrections away from 'fixing' and towards 'developing.' This was not a shift towards the sociological analysis of deviance, the politics involved here being completely one-way – the offender was to learn how to conform. Thus, Paul Wagner, a criminologist at the University of Missouri and early proponent of this approach, has argued that 'an individual who is rehabilitated is one who takes care to ensure that his actions comply with those rules and regulations of society which are designed to insure that each person is treated justly.'[12] Of course, arguing that the offender could become a rational decision maker opens the door to that person rationally concluding that crime is justified or that crime does pay (that is, is rational). Wagner acknowledges this dilemma and concedes that, given a potentially unjust social contract, reasoning skills will have to be balanced by fear of punishment and practical assistance with employment.

This was surely the Achilles' heel of the reliance on critical thinking and problem solving. In many cases the criminal's perception that society was unjust, unequal, and discriminatory was correct. The argument that many laws were unjust or unnecessary often had merit, and the evidence of the impact of race, wealth, and social position on judgment and sentencing was too obvious to refute easily. In discussing these issues some twenty-five years ago with a well-practised thief, I was struck at his attack on the core of this approach to treatment via the following aphorism: 'Men who reason that theft is not a moral question, but only one of risk and consequence, will always take the risk.' Here was a problem and one that led to yet another dimension of insight. Was it sufficient to be analytically sophisticated enough to know the odds were poor (or good, as many would claim)? Returning to the ideas of Smith, Hume, and Rousseau, was it not central to citizenship to 'know,' to have the insight, that crime was wrong because it harmed others with whom you had a sympathetic link? Here was the moral or common-sense dimension to insight that most of the treatment experts were reluctant to engage with because it seemed to violate the moral relativism already pervasive in a culture heading full speed towards postmodern scepticism. Remorse, the demand of the first wave of enlightened prison reformers of the nineteenth century, had an oddly unscientific ring to it and was a difficult quality to assess, test for, and evaluate. It was, in fact, more in the realm of the notoriously subjective psychiatric experts and, of course, was much in the minds of lay members of parole boards and the citizenry in general.

As we will see, remorse has made a comeback in the 1990s, both in response to public pressure and because of a general disillusionment with the results from the more process-driven correctional policies that emanated from the medical model in the 1960s and 1970s. But first we need to explore in more detail just how that model worked in practice.

The Treatment Regime: Observation and Examination

Whether cognitive structures or remorse, the search for insight requires getting beneath the skin of the insight-less, insight-poor, or insight-wrong to reveal the source of the action that brought them to the prison, the deviance behind the deviant act. It means denying the 'insight' of Hannah Arendt in arguing that the quest is ultimately futile: 'To be sure, every deed has its motives as it has its goal and its principle; but the act itself, though it proclaims its goal and makes manifest its principle, does not reveal the innermost motivation of the agent. His motives remain dark, they do not shine but are hidden not only from others but, most of the time from himself, from his self-inspection as well.'[13] One has the sense here of veils upon veils, of answers that only delude the questioner and the respondent, of a deep unfathomable and circular mind that will never yield itself up to insight. Or cannot! It is worth recalling that Arendt would have been influenced here by the vacuous inability of Adolf Eichmann to show either insight or remorse as much as by Robespierre's even more frightening deliberate blindness in consigning both enemies and friends to the guillotine in the name of a higher purpose. But could the psychiatric ambition hold out for a middle ground of understanding, a functional way station for insight that does not require full disclosure of the entire set of assumptions and predispositions that an actor utilizes in taking action or assigning meaning? This, surely, is the hope of the medicalized correctional treatment regime.

This approach to corrections has as its primary mandate the need to understand the prisoner and his or her relation to the act that resulted in the prison sentence. The mandate to protect society through incarceration is subsumed under this larger, more complex mission since the examination of the soul, the 'being' of the prisoner, follows on into the parole period when protection of society is, in fact, more pretense than reality. It is only by understanding the person and his or her act that the state can reform the criminal or at least come to reasonable predictions about future behaviours. The act itself, however, is history and cannot be recreated in the world that is the prison, a world that bears no practical resemblance to society outside the prison. What is left of the act is the file, a sparse, scattered, and frequently contradictory collection of documents ranging from police notes from the 'scene of the crime,' the trial transcript or parts thereof, the truncated narratives of victim and convict, and the speculations of various officials. And, of course, the inevitable imperfections of bureaucracies means that the file is always incomplete, sections having gone missing or having failed to keep up with the physical movement of the person through the system. The language of this bureaucratic discourse is chaotic and does not easily disclose meaning. Some of the discourse is blatantly self-serving, other parts are pompously moralistic, while yet others claim to assert only the 'facts.' The act, however – whether murder or a sale of drugs – remains the crucial entry point for the treatment regime's journey back to its origins in search of the primal cause(s).

Nowhere is this cacaphony of voices, assertions, and discourses more clearly portrayed than in Foucault's resurrection of the case of the French 1835 parricide Pierre Rivière, in the text *I, Pierre Rivière, having slaughtered my mother, my sister and my brother*.[14] In reprinting the documents from this case Foucault illustrates several of the more theoretical points he makes in *Discipline and Punish*. The documents display first the 'facts' in all their contradictory, irrelevant, and observed detail as recorded by neighbours, the press, and family members: there was a vicious 'slaughter,' and Rivière was obviously the perpetrator. Next, words of the experts of the second rank are recorded, the police investigators, prosecutors and trial witnesses, all trying to make sense of the crime, establish intention, and – in what Foucault certainly saw as a landmark case – come to a conclusion about Rivière's mental state, whether he was sane and hence 'responsible.' Next comes the voluble statement by Rivière himself, his *Memoir*, an extraordinarily sophisticated recounting of what drove him to kill his mother, sister, and brother. It is an explanation grounded deeply in the social history of the time, in property relations between husband and wife, in intrafamily disputes, quarrels over money, and the nature of marital sexual obligations. Immediately the reader's attention is shifted from Rivière to the context – from psychology to sociology, and back again. To sort this out experts of the first order are brought in – doctors and lawyers – to decide the disposition of Rivière based on his being sane or not The result was a victory for the doctors, imprisonment rather than execution for Rivière, followed rather quickly by his suicide. Then, in the final section, essays by Foucault and his students are included as a discourse upon the discourse.

Pierre Rivière was one of the first criminals subjected to the new, modern treatment version of the criminal justice system. He had expected a simple execution but instead was incarcerated in the hopes of a cure. The facts indicating that he committed the crime were insufficient for the state to dispose of the matter quickly – as would have been the case in earlier times – but rather only opened up the larger questions about why and what could be done. In a sense every criminal case since this has – at least theoretically – repeated the same exercise with degrees of complexity varying with the seriousness of the crime and the resources of the investigators. In Rivière's case the exploration really ceased with the disposition of the case, few prisons in the early nineteenth century actually being able to carry on the search for 'understanding.' This changed gradually until by the 1950s the correctional component of the criminal justice system had become just as obsessed with understanding motive, intention, and cause as the investigative branch.

This was a gradual process, but throughout the nineteenth and early twentieth centuries these new approaches to crime and the criminal began to find and refine their structures and systems. At what was clearly the trail-blazer in this work, the Walnut Street Jail in Philadelphia, in 1790, the Quaker-inspired jailers met the new prisoner with a request for information, the first step in their determination to develop knowledge of the individual. Like now, when the prisoner arrived at the jail he was accompanied by a file containing information concerning his crime, the circumstances in which it was committed, a summary of the examinations of the defendant, and notes on his behaviour before and after sentence. Throughout his sentence he would be observed and his conduct noted daily – a process requiring new technologies of observation. Just as the discovery of the 'true' soul of the cosmos required the telescope of Galileo as well as the mathematics of Copernicus, so the discovery of the 'criminal soul' of the prisoner required the logic of Socratism and the technology of the panopticon. The new architecture of the prison served the same function as Galileo's telescope; it rendered visible those who were inside it and as well operated to transform individuals, 'to act on those it shelters, to provide a hold on their conduct, to carry the effects of power right to them, to make it possible to know them, to alter them.'[15] In discussing the eventual model for this 'telescope', Foucault describes the panoptic prison as a 'museum of human nature' in which the 'codified power to punish turns into a disciplinary power to observe.'[16]

Within this human observatory the examination becomes the most public of all observations. In the modern penal system this process of examination takes place during the periodic interviews with 'case managers' or their equivalent functionary, interviews with parole or probation officers and, the potentially most intense observation site of all, the interview with the parole board. During each of these person-to-person examinations the subject/object being examined is subjected to multiple observations, focusing on words, body, and emotions as well as the intentions behind the words, the masking of the body, and the sincerity of the emotions. As Foucault rightly observes, the process 'manifests the subjection of those who are perceived as objects and the objectification of those who are subjected.'[17] This subject/object confusion that has been alluded to before is a crucial dimension of the treatment model. The imprisoned criminal (being incessantly examined, observed, and judged) clearly becomes an 'object' in the sense of being subjected to the gaze of authority in the form of the panoptic eye.[18] On the other hand, that authority is demanding that the imprisoned criminal reflect on the past, on present behaviour, and on future prospects – such reflection clearly requires the skills, qualities, and attributes of a subject, an authentic, reflective self. Hence the dilemma for both prisoner and keeper – given a number, a label, and severely restricted freedoms the prisoner as object is nonetheless required at specific times and under examination to make a temporary transition (back) to subjectness, an adroit feat managed by only a few.

Intention versus Result

The correctional system starts with a person/prisoner and an act/narrative. The prisoner is not the same person as the one who committed the act. In the first place time has passed, the situation or context of the act has passed, a history of arrest, confinement, and judgment has intervened, and the person has had to adjust and adapt to facing incarceration. Second, the person is now a prisoner, trapped like a 'rat,' caught up in a system which, though he or she may have been there before, will always be alien to his or her more 'natural' way of living. He or she must adopt a survival, freedom-seeking persona at all costs, and do it quickly, even as the gate shuts behind him or her. Everything the prisoner does or says, his or her appearance, even if possible his or her thoughts must be directed towards regaining freedom as soon as possible. But ideally this freedom must be gained without loss of self, with pride intact, with reputation in place. Hence compromise and conciliation with the system become a tactical issue – how to gain freedom with minimal loss of self. There may, of course, be aspects of one's self better left behind – such as addictions or skill deficits – and the person may very well be open to addressing these issues, but only carefully. So, when the classification officer or other member of the case management team (CMT) first sits down with Convict #4879 Smith in order to 'get to know him,' to 'assess his needs,' and 'prescribe treatment,' he is really talking only with #4879, not with Smith. For the criminal, the veils are in place as soon as the gate is shut behind him or her.

The process of examination is dominated by documentation, written words that seek to situate individuals in 'a network of writing; it engages them in a whole mass of documents that capture and fix them.'[19] These documents are meant to transform the individual into a case, but do they? Foucault seems overly optimistic here, captured perhaps by the idiosyncratic efficiency of the French penal bureaucrats who may indeed keep a respectable paper trail. In most jurisdictions the ideal is far from realized, and the intention of written observation not fulfilled. Michael Ignatieff, in calling into question some of the sweeping claims explicit in a Foucaultean analysis of the criminal justice system, warns us that 'the gulf between the reformers' rationalizing intentions and the institutionalized results of their work ought to make us rethink this equation of modernity and rationalization, or at least to give greater room for the idea that modernity is the site of a recurring battle between rationalizing intention and institutions, interests, and communities which resist, often with persistent success.'[20] This 'recurring battle' may be fought most visibly on the high plains of theory, policy, and politics but its gritty reality is at the chalk face, in the inherent resistance of large bureaucratic institutions – the proverbial mountains of mud into which cannonballs are ineffectually fired[21] – the weaknesses of staff and resources, and the passive and active resistance of the objects of rationalization.

Charged with initiating the process of treatment, the correctional officer, counsellor, or case manager will have in front of her or him, if lucky, a version of Foucault's notorious file, ideally containing the narrative of the act, the biography of the person, and the commentary of the pre-prison experts. It will be rare, in fact, if the file contains much of this. More than likely the forms in the file consist of compressions of the former information, presented often in staccato form – single lines summarizing paragraphs. The court-demanded luxury of the richly endowed 'pre-sentence report' with its information on family background, education, employment, and its analysis of the offence and previous record is most likely reduced to a few points deemed relevant by someone with much less time at his or her disposal than the author of the original report. A complex sexual assault charge that, like, in the film *Roshomon*, assumes radically different meanings depending on the teller, can here be reduced to 'what amounts to haggling over the price with a local prostitute.'[22]

Armed with the intuitive knowledge that Smith is not Smith, but just a number, and vividly aware that the resources are not there for a truly biographical or historicist approach to the person, the act, or the relationship between them, the correctional service must choose the behavioural path and start with the person-as-is and the act as an objective and isolated phenomenon. That is, while aspects of the subject's personal background may be acknowledged, its substance is too shadowy to be trusted. The criminal background of which the state is aware is credited, but in a very abstract way. No attempt is made to 'reconstruct' past crimes or convictions – instead the list of 'official' descriptors (such as 'indecent assault,' 'uttering,' and 'theft,') is tabulated to arrive at a rough idea of how 'serious' a criminal one is faced with, and behaviour in previous incarcerations is reviewed to assess the appropriate penitentiary placement. In most cases, the process of understanding begins afresh, with only minimal contamination from previous understandings.

Even with repeat offenders who circulate within a specific circle of prisons, the correctional paper trail is weak and the personnel constantly changing, thus inhibiting the creation of a historical file or treatment or response to the person. Two additional factors militate against any such continuity. First is the fact that the return of the person to prison symbolizes a failure on the part of the correctional system – an imperfect understanding, a failure of insight, so to speak. The person has failed, of course – or perhaps not if his or her intention always had been to continue in crime and even to return to prison. But the system itself bears the greatest burden (cross?) because in its Socratic hubris it took on the task of transformation through understanding. Better to start over with the person and his or her new act than to dwell on past diagnoses and prescriptions that were obviously flawed. Second, the bureaucracy that is corrections endures shifts in policy at about the same pace that many offenders recidivate. Each policy entails a dedication to a very different means of understanding – a 'better' means of understanding. Hence the understanding achieved at one point may be superseded following a new policy initiative that involves a whole new way of looking at the person and the act. Needless to say this is a useful palliative for those who might otherwise shoulder some guilt about 'failing' with a recidivist – in this world of revolving paradigms they did not fail, it was the means of understanding that was faulty.

At each station at which the imprisoned criminal is examined the same set of faults undermine the intention of the process. Sudden transfers to new institutions occur, most often the result of factors unrelated to the specifics of the treatment regime (for example, over-crowding, 'deals' between prisons concerning difficult inmates, access to families, cascading to lower security, or simply at the request of the prisoner). Staff changes take place on a regular basis, requiring incessant re-familiarization with cases, personality clashes as objects adjust to new subjects and vice versa, and subtle shifts in ideology and focus. Furthermore, there is the simple problem of excessive case loads for both prison and parole staff, a result of increasing levels of incarceration and decreasing levels of funding.

These weaknesses are particularly vivid in those jurisdictions that employ some form of parole or conditional release. Here, at the point where the most important decision for the prisoner, the correctional system, and society at large is to take place, the gap between intention and result seems most profound. Ideally, the Foucaultean gaze would be at its most intense at this moment, the paper file examined in detail, and the prisoner subjected to full scrutiny. The decision made here is to be the final piece of the trilogy – conviction, sentencing, release. In theory the parole decision should be a 'balanced scientific decision made by experts at a comparatively leisurely pace, upon ample and accurate information accumulated in the real-life, post-conviction milieu.'[23] In fact, in their review of over one hundred California parole hearings, Garber and Maslach conclude that they are merely 'short, unstructured interview sessions where the hearing officers typically ask psychologically oriented questions and the prisoners respond passively in a minimally informative, nonaffirmative manner.' The parole process is an exceedingly complex issue, and as we will examine later, those involved have gone to great lengths to improve upon decision making by utilizing various risk and recidivism prediction devices, increasing reliance on 'expert' testimony, and a new attention to the interests and rights of victims – but it remains annoyingly unscientific, increasingly politicized, and disliked by public and prisoner.

Treatment and the Self or, 'Rehabilitation Means the Surrender ay the Self'[24]

> Why is it that because ye use hard drugs every cunt feels that they have a right tae dissect and analyse ye?
>
> Once ye accept that they huv that right, ye'll join them in the search fir this holy grail, this thing that makes ye tick. Ye'll then defer tae them, allowin yersel tae be conned intae believin any biscuit-ersed theory ay behaviour they choose tae attach tae ye. Then yir theirs, no yir ain; the dependency shifts from the drug to them.
>
> Society invents a spurious convoluted logic tae absorb and change people whae's behaviour is outside its mainstream. Suppose that ah ken aw the pros and cons, know that ah'm gaunnae huv a short life, am ay sound mind, etcetera, but still want tae use smack? They won't let ye do it. They won't let ye dae it, because it's seen as a sign ay *thir failure*. The fact that ye jist simply choose tae reject whit they huv tae offer. Choose us. Choose life. Choose mortgage payments; choose washing machines; choose cars; choose sitting on a couch watching mind-numbing and spirit-crushing game shows, stuffing fuckin junk food intae yir mooth. Choose rotting away, pishing and shiteing yersewl in a home, a total fuckin embarassment tae the selfish, fucked-up brats ye've produced. Choose life.
>
> Well I choose no tae choose life. If the cunts cannae handle that, it's thair fuckin problem.

So says the defiant self in the film *Trainspotting*, addicted yes, but still on the street and subject merely to a benign observation and examination that only on occasion becomes intolerably intrusive. Resistance or surrender – in this view it is a dichotomous world in the treatment society – you are either your own self, or you are their self. According to Charles Taylor we ought to be placing the highest possible value on the idea of 'authenticity,' of an 'authentic self,' based on the notion that 'each one of us has an original way of being human.'[25] But is the addicted self possibly an authentic self? Can a life spent divided between thieving and prison be an authentic life? Is a murderer's 'original way of being human' one we should respect, or even allow? Can we really perform a kind of psychic lobotomy, removing the addiction, the urge to steal, and the drive to kill while leaving enough of a self from which authenticity can be reformulated? Or, following on from the utopian vision of many medical model adherents, must this self be transformed into a 'new' self and, if so, can that new self ever be authentic? These are the very real concerns faced by prisoners as they confront the treatment engine, and their responses are varied. Consider the following example:

Tom was the youngest of six siblings – his parents divorced when Tom was four years old, the children were divided between the two parents. Tom lived with his mother until he was twelve, when he went to live with his father. He refers to her as a 'slut' who was 'always running off with various men ... very cold, unloving and mean ... a woman who never wanted children and always belittled them ... the town whore.' The father is described as 'a very violent man who drank excessively,' but Tom refers to him as a hard-working man. All the siblings acknowledge difficulties with authority, perhaps stemming from both their father and from their experience in divorce court, with a judge deciding where they should live.

Tom completed grade 10 and was employed irregularly as a mechanic and auto body repairman. He started drinking when he was about fifteen and is a steady user of various soft drugs and cocaine. His criminal career began at age sixteen and continued steadily for the following fifteen years with offences ranging from theft to robbery to murder. In prison he is constantly in trouble, most of it of his own creation. As a young man of twenty-two, during his first serious period of incarceration, he informed his living unit officer that 'where I come from staff who screw around end up leaving in a pine box. I am physically and mentally stronger than all the staff here ... I'm doing ten years and I don't give a damn about anything.' The staff concluded at the time that 'Clearly, this is a young man who has no regard for rules and regulations of any sort and he is prepared to risk his personal well-being as well as that of correctional staff to maintain his tough-guy image ... his institutional conduct continues to show an alarming decline. Clearly, Tom is a very angry young man and his anger is currently being channeled in a very destructive pattern.' A year later, despite completing several university courses and the prison's life skills program, Tom was charged with threatening the life of his counsellor and family when he gets out of prison.

This pattern continued throughout his sentence with Tom completing various programs, showing some promise, and then descending to violent confrontations with staff and eventually to an escape after transfer to lesser security. When apprehended, true to form, Tom's 'institutional behaviour has deteriorated to the point that he has become a grievous security concern and the writer feels that staff safety with this individual is in jeopardy.' He has been involved in several physical confrontations with prison staff and had just barely avoided being sent to the system's 'special handling unit.' His teachers in the prison university program credited him with intelligence, tact, and a 'critical and inquiring habit of mind.'

The psychologist called upon to assess Tom's readiness for conditional release described a 'dramatic escalation in criminal behaviour ... motivated initially by the need for funds to pay off a gambling debt.' He paid back the debts from the proceeds of the robberies but then continued the behaviour, showing 'little in the way of remorse.' Tom claims his anti-authoritarian stance is 'my natural disposition.' He has little patience with correctional staff, does not like being told what to do, and is uncomfortable being cooped up with 'serious criminals.' He is described as antisocial and aggressive, impulsive with an 'inordinate need for stimulation and excitement', egocentric, shallow and often callous in his orientation to others. He is prone to act and react with insufficient thought, deliberation, and delay. He is cynical, sceptical, and untrusting. He almost constantly feels misunderstood, unappreciated, and demeaned and is resentful, obstinate, and touchy to an extreme as a result.

In the following months Tom was denied day parole, was a participant in a major prison disturbance, and was described once again as having 'a very serious anger control problem, a history of tantrums when he doesn't get what he wants ... which has not been addressed through programs or psychological counseling.' Then Tom received a series of institutional charges, including setting fire to his mattress, disobeying orders, causing a disturbance, and refusing to allow the door to his cell to be shut. Staff responded by trying to handcuff him to move him to segregation at which point Tom screamed: 'I'm not listening to you!' He resisted being handcuffed, fought with staff on the way to segregation, attempted to burn his mattress once again, threw his food on the floor, and stripped in front of female staff.

Finally, two years later and a month from his statutory release date the parole board conceded defeat, refusing to grant a full parole, though they acknowledge that Tom has 'admitted and accepted responsibility for your actions. You have expressed empathy for your victims for the fear and trauma they would have experienced as a result of your criminal actions. You admit you do not know why you react in such an unacceptable manner towards authority but expressed an interest in pursuing the manner upon release through professional assistance.'

One year later Tom was back in maximum security convicted of murder during the course of a robbery.

Tom's resistance was to scream out his defiance, to assert his right 'not to listen.' One might argue that while not a particularly admirable citizen prior to his last major period of incarceration, he had been employed, had done reasonably well in school and had seemed to be making some progress at overcoming the social and psychological handicaps of a difficult childhood. Was he a murderer just waiting to strike? Was the constant anger displayed in prison evidence of the violence that was to erupt during the final robbery? Or was Tom right in his constant refrain throughout his imprisonment that he was only responding to being 'treated like a dog' (that is, an object), to being stuck in a brutalizing environment of prisoners and keepers, to being shown no respect? Were his teachers and the few correctional staff who agreed, correct in their judgment that Tom was intelligent, capable, and had definite career options in the publishing or printing field if he continued his education after release? Assuming he was not already 'crooked timber out of which nothing straight could ever be made,' did his decision to resist by violent means predestine him to be unable to turn off the violence after prison? If so, then clearly this issue of retaining a sense of self in the face of the treatment regime can be a dangerous business.

Are there other ways than the open resistance that Tom chose? Rousseau can give us a clue, given that he felt he spent most of his adult life under the gaze of a panoptic society, personified in this case by his readers and critics. Feeling transformed into an 'object' and defeated in his attempt to 'confess' (via his *Confessions*, which had only opened the door to more 'interpretation' by his examiners-observers), Rousseau responded by composing two more texts towards the end of his life, the *Dialogues, or Rousseau, Judge of Jean-Jacques* and his *Reveries of a Solitary Walker*. In the *Dialogues* he trifurcates himself into Rousseau, Jean-Jacques, and a 'Frenchman' who wishes to get to 'know' Jean-Jacques – the self therefore carrying on a three-way conversation with itself and thereby exposing the errors that stem inevitably from attempts to judge, know, or understand from outside. In his *Reveries* Rousseau recalls his ultimate method for resisting panopticism, 'namely, his rare capacity to withdraw into himself and experience reverie ... his adversaries appropriate his discourses, they spy on him, they create new versions of him, but his psyche and intellect remain intact, resistant to their disciplinary regime.'[26]

Thomas Jefferson, another Rousseauean who felt constantly misunderstood, and who hated the public gaze and the private interrogation, retreated to his beloved Monticello and enjoyed his own reveries, inventing machines and surveying his land. The retreat into reverie, then, is another field of resistance. I recollect conversing with a prisoner while sitting on the grass inside the prison grounds, the barbed fence being only a few feet away. He assured me that when he looked out from the prison there was no fence, there were no towers – he simply elided them from his vision in a kind of reverie of freedom. The notorious Charles Manson maintains: 'There's no prison. Not to me. I'm just here. The people that are in prison are locked up in their mind.'[27] Victor Frankl, in talking about the survival of the self in the concentration camps, insisted that 'although held in the vicious grip of brutal circumstances, a human being still has one great residual power ... to choose one's attitude in any given set of circumstances, to choose one's own way.'[28] Thus, we return to Charles Taylor's idea of authenticity as one's unique way of being human.

There are other ways to resist treatment as well, ways that appear to be cooperative but are in fact duplicitous. Bruno Bettelheim survived in the concentration camps by trying to go along with the system as did many others, all the while preserving their selves by enjoying the charade and examining themselves and the system they were caught up in. A prisoner at the State Prison of Southern Michigan put his finger on this little bit of Foucaultean wisdom when he recounted: 'From my point of view, the entire counseling-treatment program is a game, the rules of which I must try to learn in order to placate the prison officials and manipulate the parole board at my parole hearing. I have to serve my time, but in addition, I must also prove that the counselor has been successful and that I am rehabilitated and ready for parole.'[29]

After my decade working in prisons, and further years working with people who work in prisons, the truth of this field of resistance rings uncomfortably true. Prisoners do not, by and large feel sick or deviant – lawbreakers perhaps, but not sick. Part of being a lawbreaker is a central dynamic of competition and disdain or hatred for lawkeepers, whether police or corrections. It is thus a direct attack on the pride of the prisoner – on her or his sense of self – to expect her or him to acknowledge being cured of an imagined illness by a doctor for whom she or he intrinsically has no respect. Hence the spread of this most cynical, and damaging form of resistance, more damaging even than Tom's violence.

Violence, reverie, and manipulation are all 'reasonable' responses to the determination of the state to alter the soul, but the most impressively 'reasonable' is the assertion by a few prisoners of a counterargument. Eldridge Cleaver's book *Soul on Ice* was a classic modern version of such an assertion as was the *Memoir* of Pierre Rivière. In reviewing the files of the Canadian prisoner-students, the following 'memoir' from the mid-1970s surfaced in one man's file: 'Treatment Plan: Philosophy of Don R. Prisoner #744:

> It was proposed to me by various people, on numerous occaisions [*sic*], that I prepare and submit a *'Treatment Plan.'* I find the quoted, capitalized, and italicized phrase and its implications unacceptable and have therefore chosen this alternative method for documenting certain facets of my personality and philosophy. In no way should this be interpreted as obligating me to act in total accord with any statement contained herein.
>
> At present my aims within the X Institution are directed at education in accredited university courses ... In regard to release plans; at this period in my incarceration I have formulated none. I have indulged in thoughts about what I could do after my discharge from captivity but these are of such a tenuous nature that I shall not embellish them with articulate sophistry.
>
> It is my most fervent conviction that I am an individual possessing abilities surpassing those of the 'herd' in general. More precisely, I refuse to allow myself to be submerged in the 'groupness' of the herd. The rational human animal has neither a need nor a desire for the emotional parasitism that characterizes congregations of Homo Sapiens. When an individual submits his will to the control of any group, no matter what the quantitative dimension, he immediately ceases to be an independent entity capable of directing his own existence. It is this condition which I shall strive to avoid, even at the cost of material comforts, or whatever. To illustrate my point I direct your attention to the Llamas of Tibet, who, until the Communist occupation of that country, lived their lives in virtual isolation from the world and its excruciating masses for protracted periods of time. This life of isolation seems to have aided in producing minds capable of feats of cerebral gymnastics so astounding as to boggle the imagination of Western man. Obviously, these Llamas did not acquire superlative intellectual powers by flocking together like sheep, indeed, to the contrary. They are individuals!
>
> In considering Kant's Categorical Imperative, I regard this to be a base upon which one may construct the sum of his personal philosophy. How-

ever, in the barbaric society in which I find myself striving for mundane creature comforts, Kant's suggestion becomes dysfunctional in terms of finding one's way to a satisfactory and materially rewarding conclusion. The Categorical Imperative is irreconcilable with the Protestant Ethic, which glorifies one of the most objectionable conditions of human endeavour: Work! Because of this difference, or rather conflict, of philosophies it has been necessary for me to choose a dogma that combines the two, or more aptly, is between them. This is where I am at present and where I shall remain until I choose to pursue either the aestheticism of Kant, or the vulgarity of Work!

Concluding. My position in any given situation is determined by my perception of that situation and I will react in accordance with that perception. I must avoid externalization of my 'self' as this will lead to submersion of my ego and loss of my identity as an autonomous individual. This does not mean that I am impervious to intelligent argument, only to the vacant, futile meddlings of bureaucrats and petty dictators inflated with their own misplaced self-importance and confused priorities.

One can only speculate on the reaction of the prison treatment staff when they received this document. Don was a difficult prisoner, student, person – a loner with a quick temper but prone to verbal rather than physical assaults. He was typical of the self-taught, isolated, stubborn, proud, and perversely elitist prisoner. Contemptuous of his fellow prisoners, he was alone against the state, and in concluding that he could preserve his identity only by refusing to cooperate he paid a heavy price. That falsely heroic and vulgar-Nietzschean identity, of course, contributed to his criminal career of primitive accumulation through armed robbery and to his decision, when cornered by the police following his release, to commit suicide rather than face a return to prison.

It would be nice if the medical model and its related schools of thought were correct in presuming that the problem was simply identifying what was 'wrong' with people like Don or Tom or Bill – a deficit or disorder, a missing piece, or an incorrectly programmed child, a wounded being needing care and attention, or the myriad of other explanations of why people do bad things. If that were the case, then we should be able to fix them, and undoubtedly with some offenders that is the case. But with the seasoned troops that occupy our adult prisons, the reality is quite different. The pathology, deficit, or disorder, whatever its origin, has long since been incorporated into an identity and into a world in which it can qualify as a fully developed subject: 'The Life,' it is often called.

There is an interesting analogy with the natural world here. In *Natural Alien*, Neil Evernden recounts the story of the wood tick, which bears exploration in some detail. The wood tick is literally blind to the world as we know it, with our list of preferences, insights, and observations being unknown and irrelevant to it. It knows no colours, hears nothing, smells almost nothing, and if you could somehow communicate to it that such a world of senses exists, it would consider you a liar. Instead, the wood tick relies on three elements of the planet:

- A general photosensivity of its skin leads the mature, fertilized female wood tick to the top of the bush, to which she clings awaiting a mammal and a meal of blood in order to complete a life cycle;
- A smell of butyric acid – sweat – heralds the arrival of the meal, and she executes her ambush by dropping from the bush;
- Assuming the target is hit and she lands on something warm she heads for open skin and drinks what for her is only a warm liquid, then drops to the ground, lays her eggs, and dies.

The world for the tick is a world of light, sweat, heat, and blood. Evernden insists that this is indeed a world 'every bit as valid and adequate as our own' and should not be dismissed as mere 'instinct' or 'reflex.' The tick occupies a world that is meaningful to it, only sensing information that is perceptually significant to it, what Evernden and others refer to as its *Umwelt*, the environment of an individual organism.

What is the connection between the tick and the prisoner? Within the human species we may have several forms of *Umwelt*. The conventional environment consists of the standard biological factors such as sight, sound, touch, but also values, preferences, customs, aspirations, beliefs, and cognitive patterns of cause and effect. And they work for us. Indeed, that is why we have them.

Criminals, of whom prisoners are a sub-set, may operate within a different environment that works for them. Jean Genet, for instance, makes a powerful case for the erotic appeal of theft. We know that for some individuals violence per se is pleasurable and socially significant. Irvine Welsh, in *Trainspotting*, describes the attraction of self-destruction through drug addiction. For many, this is the most troubling encounter in prison, the seemingly irrational appeal of persistent drug use when it leads almost inevitably back to prison. In attempting to explain the appeal, many addicts fall back on banalities: 'I'm just not myself unless I'm high.'

The tick's environment is functional for the tick – indeed it is the best of all possible tick worlds. The environment of the criminal is likewise functional for him or her. Even illiteracy, one might argue, can be functional in a community that relies little on the text. Addiction can be a badge of membership, a quick temper an admired attribute, and callousness or lack of empathy a valued quality in a friend and fellow thief. But this world is clearly dysfunctional for the rest of us. And, I would argue, it is only functional for the criminal because, for whatever reason, access to the more conventional world of human society has been denied or rejected.

Understanding that the criminal's environment in some way 'works' for him does not mean, of course, that we should therefore celebrate or even tolerate it. What it does mean, however, is that the criminal does have a world, a 'life,' in which he or she is a subject. In the prison, therefore, we are not offering a life of subjectness – the life of citizen – to a mere object – a criminal. Instead we are trying to persuade a subject disguised to our eyes as an object to, in fact, switch subjectivities – a much more complicated task.

The assault by the state on the offending subject is not, however, the primary concern in this book, but rather the inherent limitations of bureaucratic state power as it attempts to grapple with issues as complex as crime, criminal recidivism, and the transformation of individuals. The medical model in corrections was a product of the technological and scientific triumphs enjoyed by governments like those in the United States during the successful prosecution of the Second World War. After defeating fascism – itself perceived by many at the time to be a kind of illness – there were widespread hopes that other social ills could be dealt with in a similar manner, by mobilizing resources and bringing to bear the best that science had to offer. Crime was a logical target, especially as it shared many of the militaristic overtones of the earlier struggle. Just as the Marshall Plan offered balm to defeated and needy former enemies, the treatment proponents in criminal justice offered a path to the good life for defeated criminals. But the analogy did not hold, the science was flawed, and hence the optimism was misplaced. Despite being granted considerable influence within corrections – though never enough, of course – and money sufficient to carry out a myriad number and variety of interventions, the imprisoned continued to resist and after release continued in great numbers to return to crime.

Finally, in 1974, the whistle was blown with the publication of Robert Martinson's review of prison rehabilitation programs in the influential journal *Public Interest*. In the so-called nothing works essay, Martinson said the following about his review of current research:

> These data, involving over 200 studies and hundreds of thousands of individuals as they do, are the best available and give us very little reason to hope that we have in fact found a sure way of reducing recidivism through rehabilitation ... It may be simply that our programs aren't yet good enough ... It may be, on the other hand, that there is a more radical flaw in our present strategies – that education at its best, or that psychotherapy at its best, cannot overcome, or even appreciably reduce, the powerful tendency for offenders to continue in criminal behaviour. Our present treatment programs are based on a theory of crime as a *disease* – that is to say, as something foreign and abnormal in the individual which can presumably be cured. This theory may well be flawed, in that it overlooks – indeed denies – both the normality of crime in society and the personal normality of a very large proportion of offenders, criminals who are merely responding to the facts and conditions of our society.[30]

Here was the sociologist resurgent! The psychologists were wrong, crime was by and large a normal response to poverty, discrimination, inequality, and a society based on material accumulation. It should be dealt with through 'decarceration for low-risk offenders – and, presumably, keeping high-risk offenders in prisons which are nothing more (and aim to be nothing more) than custodial institutions.'[31] In the following chapter we will examine the dramatic alterations this attack on rehabilitation had on the corrections system.

CHAPTER FOUR

Let a Hundred Flowers Bloom, a Hundred Schools of Thought Contend[1]

Perhaps, leaving the prison he is not an honest man, but he has contracted honest habits. He was an idler, now he knows how to work ... Without loving virtue, he may detest the crime of which he has suffered the cruel consequences, and if he is not more virtuous he has become at best more judicious; his morality is not honor, but interest. His religious faith is perhaps neither lively nor deep; but even supposing that religion has not touched his heart, his mind has contracted habits of order, and he possesses rules for his conduct in life.[2]

Alexis de Tocqueville, cited, in Joel Stewards,
'The Penitentiary and Perfectibility in Tocqueville,' 1985

So argued Alexis de Tocqueville in 1832 after viewing the earliest version of prison-based treatment at the Walnut Street Jail during his North American visit. Imprisoning for the purpose of imparting 'virtue' – the nineteenth-century word for reformation or transformation – was a worthy religious objective for 'saving' individuals, but given the unlikelihood of high rates of success not a worthy or practical objective for the state. The state's objective, Tocqueville thought, should be focused on the attainable, namely, a bit of deterrence, some acquisition of skills related to employability, better work habits, and a dose of citizenship education. By the late 1970s, after having flirted once again with imparting virtue as a *raison d'être*, correctional jurisdictions in the United States, Canada, and Britain were once again ready to consider such a pragmatic approach to 'corrections.'

In part this was the result of research like that of Martinson, but the shift was also part of a more general cultural shift, a shift we have come to associate with the postmodern and which had at its core an increasingly pervasive questioning in the postwar era of science, progress, and the modern. Science had become militarized by the Cold War and thereby linked with growing fears of mass destruction. Progress, since the appearance of Rachel Carson's book *Silent Spring* in the early 1960s, seemed to portend only environmental collapse, material plenty as portrayed in the media and in art seemed to result in only greater alienation, and poverty, crime, and civil strife continued to expand despite promises of 'cures' just around the corner. This early version of what came to be seen by the 1990s as a postmodern turn was brought home to the world of corrections by the appearance of writings by, among others, Martinson (1974), Morris (1973), and Foucault (1977).

Martinson, Morris, and Nothing Works

Martinson, as we saw at the end of Chapter 2, based his conclusion that in corrections 'nothing works' on exhaustive research into the claims made by rehabilitation programs. He described a tremendous waste of money and resources throughout the corrections 'business' and concluded that even though some prison programs might be effective in reducing rates of recidivism, that was a 'pipsqueak of an issue' compared with the more important (and sociological) issue of reducing the rate of crime itself.[3] So once again the practical endeavour of dealing with crime, criminals, and recidivism was the subject of a paradigm war in the social sciences. The seminal 1973 book by Norval Morris from the University of Chicago, *The Future of Imprisonment*, when read in conjunction with Martinson, helped convince people in the criminal justice system that 'a prison can't set itself up as an agent for helping an individual (rehabilitation) when its reason for existing is to do violence (by robbing him of his freedom) ... Sentencing and parole policies should be changed so as not to make a prisoner's release contingent on participation in such programs.'[4] Morris attacked directly the scientific pretensions of the medical model, specifically its claims for predictive insight into the future behaviour of individuals and its faith that rehabilitation could occur in a coercive environment. At the same time, he attempted to make a case for the 'rehabilitation ideal' when, and only when, it was cleansed of its coercive dimension. Foucault, as we have seen, went even further in his critique of the medical model, condemning not just its impracticality or unjust features, but rather its role in the justice systems' actual 'creation' of the criminal.

There followed a growing crescendo of voices all tending to confirm the absolute failure of the medical model and, indeed, of virtually all prison-based rehabilitative activities. Alfred Blumstein and Jacqueline Cohen announced in 1974 that 'the various forms of treatment do little or nothing to improve the post-release behaviour of those treated,' Robert Ross and Bryan MacKay in 1978 reported the many behaviour modification programs found in prisons (such as token economies and programmed learning) were 'singularly unimpressive' as rehabilitative tools. And in their extensive review of the literature on prison programs in 1986, Louis Genevie and his colleagues found that not only were rehabilitation programs ineffective, they were in fact 'consistently associated with higher rates of recidivism'![5] In the case of evaluations of prison education programs, the special focus of this book, while it was clear that the efforts were well received by the prisoners and that they had a generally positive impact on the prison and measurable effects on the offenders as prisoners, no post-release effect could be verified in terms of lower rates of recidivism. In virtually all of these studies the prison itself was seen as the problem, successfully negating whatever hopes the intervention might have had in changing the lives of the inmates.[6]

Foucault's radical suggestions seemed in this case to have garnered some empirical support, especially as at the heart of these conclusions was the growing conviction that the problems associated with rehabilitation were as much the fault of the prison per se as the programs concerned. This was, after all, the mid-1970s and prisons were not immune from the cultural and political trends of the time. This was the era of Attica and a wave of other prison riots, a time when civil and individual rights rather than public order were at the forefront of political concern, and a time still in the midst of a general anti-establishment mood that had begun in the late 1960s. Following Foucault's lead in his book *Discipline and Punish*, and supported by the evidence of Martinson and others, it became an accepted truth that the very nature of the incarceration process was the cause of failure, that 'whatever is gained by the rehabilitative programs and treatment efforts is greatly overshadowed and diminished by the counterproductive forces operating within the prison community.'[7] We will look at this issue in more detail later in this chapter, but first we need to examine the policy responses to this apparent collapse of the medical model.

The Medical Model in Retreat

Government response to the news that expensive rehabilitation programs in prisons were ineffective and possibly harmful was quick in coming. In Canada the federally sponsored Law Reform Commission came out against any linkage between sentencing and rehabilitation, insisting that an offender should never be sent to prison for the purpose of receiving treatment. By 1976 the federal solicitor general admitted that rehabilitation efforts were a failure and proposed instead that 'in the future, instead of trying to prescribe appropriate treatment to rehabilitate offenders, the correction system will expect prisoners to make use of available opportunities to earn their way out ... the offender has the capacity to make choices.'[8] This was a dramatic reversal of policy and a blanket rejection of the idea that criminals had internal deficits or pathologies that effectively blocked their ability to make appropriate decisions. In the Correctional Service of Canada's *Orientation Manual* for staff the new 'opportunities model' was seen as the sponsor of 'offender development programs,' programs 'not premised on a belief that the offender is sick [but] on a belief that the better an offender's personal resources, relationships with others, educational and vocational strengths, and situations at completion of sentence, the lower the possibility of recidivism.'[9] Rather than 'transforming' inmates the corrections system retreated to the more pragmatic objectives identified by Alexis de Tocqueville 150 years earlier, providing an environment in which individual prisoners could make responsible choices among reasonable opportunities designed to assist them in preparing for an eventual return to the community.

In the United States the attorney general came to much the same conclusion as early as 1973, with a national Advisory Commission on Criminal Justice agreeing, concluding that prisons were 'obsolete, cannot be reformed, should not be perpetuated through the false hope of forced treatment, and should be repudiated as useless for any other purpose than locking away persons who are too dangerous to be allowed at large in a free society.'[10] These thoughts led directly to the 'just desserts' model of corrections advocated by criminologists like Marvin Wolfgang and Norval Morris, an approach that called for shorter, fewer, but more certain sentences and for increased attention to victim's rights and restitution. In a dramatic fulfilment of these suggestions, the State of California after years of being at the leading edge of treatment regimes, abolished the indeterminate sentence – the cornerstone of the medical model which had enabled courts to base sentencing on the personal characteristics and perceived needs of the offender. As in the Canadian Law Reform Commission's recommendations, the indeterminate or open-ended sentence was seen as leading to differential sentencing based on race and class and to longer time spent incarcerated, even to the point of 'fostering the illusion that inmates were locked up for their own good.'[11]

As in Canada, officials in the United States placed rehabilitation as simply one of the aims of corrections, on an even par with retribution, deterrence, and incapacitation. The ball was tossed into the prisoners' court, placing the onus on them to choose to make changes and in the process of course, conveniently absolving the corrections system of any responsibility for the fate of those prisoners who 'chose' not to attempt rehabilitation. Unlike many scholarly critics of the prison as institution (for example, Foucault, Martinson, and Morris), policy makers presumed the proverbial 'level playing field' or 'neutral ground' in the arena shared by prison and prisoner so that the choices made by the latter were in essence free and informed choices. This is an important distinction and marked a very real point of contrast between the dominant thinking among criminologists and the determination of correctional administrators to keep the door ajar for rehabilitation.

These North American policy shifts were similar to those in the United Kingdom, though with less prevarication about the potential for prisons playing a role as rehabilitative institutions. In a 1969 White Paper entitled *People in Prison* the Prison Service in the United Kingdom was firmly committed to the idea that treatment programs in prison could reform and rehabilitate offenders. By the time of the next official review of this question, the 1977 *Prisons and the Prisoner*, this faith was gone, the recommendation to the Prison Service being that it abandon concerns for crime causation and recidivism and focus instead on the 'management of prisons.'[12] Closely following from this, the decisive blow to the treatment model was delivered by the May Report (Committee of Inquiry into the U.K. Prison Services), in 1979, which proclaimed the end of the rehabilitation ideal in favour of 'positive custody,' echoing the North Americans in holding that 'if a man wants to reform himself, then it is up to us, within the resources available, to provide the means by which he can do so.'[13] Again, this was the best that advocates for rehabilitation could do in responding to repeated calls for incarceration being used only as a last resort and as 'humane containment.'

The approaches of the positive custody and opportunities models were devised during this era as much to benefit corrections staff as they were genuine efforts to make a case for rehabilitative programs. The director general of England's Prison Service put it quite bluntly in insisting that humane containment was not enough, 'people must have a purpose.'[14] The 'people' he refers to are, of course, the 'dedicated and caring people who serve within the Prison Service.' Thus, an uneasy peace was established between the two factions of experts. The academics, who insisted that since 'nothing comes from nothing' there could be no meaningful rehabilitation within prisons, were happy to see 'treatment' abandoned and hopeful that the focus of efforts would now be on crime prevention and community corrections. The corrections professionals, on the other hand, remained committed to the idea that a significant number of prisoners could be helped to lead better lives once the medical approach had been replaced by one based more on a partnership with the inmate. Missing in this negotiated settlement was, of course, the perspective of the imprisoned.

In effect the 'opportunities approach', which characterized corrections policy in all three jurisdictions post–Martinson/Morris did tend to open up, partially at least, a kind of public sphere within the formerly closed-off punitive and experimental world of the prison. But it was a tentative opening at best and one fraught with contradictions. Wayne Knights points out in his critique of the Canadian policy at the time that by insisting on the ability of most offenders to 'know and appreciate the nature and quality of their actions.'[15] the government was presuming a social contract reality in which all men are 'viewed as egoistic, autonomous, and rational individuals who come freely together to create civil society.'[16] Even Rousseau was more candid than this, insisting that a genuine social contract community had to be grounded in at least a reasonable level of equality from the start. In the case of the prison, the imprisoned are neither equal in circumstance nor genuinely able to 'come freely together,' being still subjected to a variety of punitive and reward-based measures that conditioned their choice of opportunities. Knights rightly points out that the prison tries to have it both ways with this approach, conceding the prisoner's right and ability to choose participation or non-participation, while keeping sufficient overall control to ensure that its functionalist, bureaucratic goals are met by retaining the right to transpose those choices into a language of 'success' and 'failure.' But nothing in a system as complex as the modern criminal justice system is ever airtight, and the argument being made here is that the opportunities approach, for all its duplicity and contradictions, did nevertheless create a space for activities that were both subversive and progressive.

It is the presence of this contested space within the prison – sometimes quite literally 'square footage' – that creates an environment conducive to the possibility that actual 'transformations' might occur. The tentative language is deliberate here since the prison remains authoritarian even with the door thus slightly ajar. Just as social movements (for example, feminism and environmentalism) in the larger society began to operate in the 1970s in what some theorists refer to as 'counterpublic spheres,' even the very limited public sphere within the carceral world itself spawns or allows entrance to various groups and social formations, which, in combination with prisoners who choose to attach themselves to these 'movements', demand a space or counterpublic sphere within which to operate. Trapped in its proclaimed openness to new initiatives, programs, and opportunities, the prison, for the moment, has often been forced to concede the space.

Three general types of prison programming emerged in this new potentially subversive space which, while referred to differently in various jurisdictions, can be categorized under the headings of life skills, vocational training, and education. They were easy program areas for the prison to look towards because they had been there all the time in the form of school programs, industrial and training shops, and various religious, recreation, and counselling services. Within the prison, however, these three areas often competed with each other for access to funds, staff positions, and in many cases inmates, despite the fact that the new, more sociologically driven research was clearly indicating that the post-release difficulties faced by ex-prisoners involved a combination of skills, education, and attitudes. Thus, literacy, high school graduation, and even some post-secondary education might be important in gaining access to employment opportunities, and in many cases evidence of training in specific skills might be necessary, but all this would go for naught if absenteeism was commonplace or workplace friction endemic. Most research into post-release employment showed that these attitudinal factors were in fact the primary difficulties faced by ex-offenders. In other words the problems ex-prisoners faced in the community had less to do with job-finding, but rather with job-keeping[17]: 'Training well spent would be in how to get along with or tolerate co-workers, how to hang on to an unexciting job long enough for promotions or better opportunities to present themselves, how to use informal peer networks for support or to air gripes, and how to get on the job or part-time training for better employment when motivation for it develops.[18] In very few instances, however, were prison systems ever able to integrate social development or living skills programs with education and training programs. Typically they each fell under different boxes in the staffing flow chart, and if prisoners did manage to participate in all three areas they did so in no particular sequence and with no attempt at integration. With the new 'opportunities' approach, the prison had to rely on the prisoner's willingness to participate in what would necessarily be a complex and demanding exercise. As a result most prisoners ended up with only one piece of the pie, if that. Further to the point, were Morris and his fellow critics correct in their supposition that affective, cooperation-dependent, and complex objectives such as attitude change, assumption of personal responsibility, enhanced critical thinking, and expanded moral reasoning simply could not be imparted within the context of the prison?

There were three possibilities in explaining the poor results of the medical model within the prison setting. On the one hand, the 'mechanisms' – the treatment programs themselves – could have been irretrievably flawed and thus fated to fail. This was the conclusion come to by corrections professionals which led them logically to a search for alternative mechanisms with education, training, and life skills being close at hand and therefore their initial choice. Or the fault could lie with the 'circumstances' – the prison context itself – which would undercut and sabotage whatever rehabilitative mechanism was tried. This was the argument of those who argued for options ranging from humane containment to prison abolition. The third possible explanation centres on the prisoners themselves, whether they through resistance, stubbornness, or some other means managed to make rehabilitative attempts dysfunctional. So far in this study a case has been made that the mechanisms associated with the medical model were clearly flawed, but what about the argument that the prison itself is the problem?

The Prison

In the earlier review of Foucault's work on the transition of the 'prison' into the 'correctional institution' beginning in the eighteenth century, the argument was advanced that this new institution actually played a direct role in the 'fabrication' of criminals by singling out a class of people not just as convicted offenders – the straightforward judgment of the court – but as people whose very character was linked to their criminality. This insight has led to a series of speculations as to the specific role of the prison-as-institution in forming the various attributes one can observe in any population of prisoners. One school of thought argues that criminals 'import' into the prison the mores of the subcultures to which they belong, while the other school of thought insists that the prison imposes a set of attitudes and a culture of its own (the 'prisonization' thesis). The truth, as in most dichotomies, probably lies in between, but the end result is much the same, namely,the creation of a unique world of the unfree, gendered, class bound, and ethnically unbalanced. Jean Harris of 'Scarsdale diet doctor murder' fame, describes it as follows: 'It is an alien world in here. One that is difficult to think about let alone describe. It is virtually impossible to be consistent about what one thinks. One doesn't expect friendship from these women. It is almost beyond the ken of many. They trust no one and value no one – least of all themselves. Their instincts are sometimes very kind, but they're unreliable. You don't know whether they will hug the wounded animal or kick it. They don't know either.'[20] It was, of course, 'alien' to this upper-middle-class woman who suddenly found herself locked in with the 'underclass' and, like the Samoans with Margaret Mead, Ms Harris's fellow prisoners were no doubt 'having her on' at times. Still, as a classic 'outsider' Harris has a valuable perspective. Innocent in her mind if not in deed, she shared the sense of outrage and injustice felt by many of the women in the prison who felt they were there because of race, poverty, injustice, or bad luck rather than as a result of anything they had actually done. Was it the prison that made them 'trust no one,' or did they import that into the prison from their lives of not so quiet desperation? Did the prison rules make them inconsistent in their opinions and habits, or did they bring that to the prison from fractured families, sexual exploitation, and welfare dependency? Did the prison rob them of self-love, or self-esteem as we call it now, or had it always been denied them by the vicissitudes of their lives? And was the amoral world of a brutal and corrupt prison the cause of their moral indecision, or was this a street-survival technique adapted to the dead-end streets in prison?

Trust, consistency, self-respect, and morality – these are difficult habits of mind to sort out as are the behaviours that must inevitably stem from them. Clearly, such components of our personalities are affected by the community in which we reside as well as having deeper roots in our individual biographies, and so the prison as community must have a role in shaping, if not in necessarily creating – or fabricating as Foucault insists – the particular forms in which they appear. What is there about the structure of the prison and the mandate it is given by the state that might be decisive in this shaping process? I can recall vividly a conversation with the head of security at a high-medium security prison in which he described – in a completely serious tone – his 'ideal' prison as one in which each prisoner upon arriving from sentencing was assigned a cell and remained in that cell until his release date. His greatest anxiety came when thinking about any form of 'inmate movement,' those times when prisoners could interact, congregate, plot, and undermine. This was his starting point for negotiating any concessions to people like myself who were interested in 'opening up' the prison to innovative programs, outside visitors, and new ideas.

Prison services have throughout the modern period made various claims to rehabilitative ideals, to teaching moral virtues and forming therapeutic communities, but at their base they are bureaucratic organizations whose primary concern is a management style that centers on the basic demands of order and discipline. Whatever reformative or humanistic deals may be communicated from above or from outside the prison itself are in most cases muted or undermined in the name of administrative convenience or security considerations.[20] John Irwin puts the management imperative front and centre, arguing that far from any interest in rehabilitation the priority (though unstated) goals of corrections are:

1   Increasing the ease of employee work routines
2   Reducing outside criticism
3   Maintaining the moral superiority of employees over prisoners
4   Maximizing the autonomy of the bureaucracy[21]

Let us review Irwin's claim. Like the post office, the U.S. Internal Revenue Service, or any other large bureaucracy with a near monopoly in its area of endeavour, the prison system of any given jurisdiction is first and foremost a system that looks in on itself before it nods in the direction of its clients, inmates, or assigned mission. In that inward gaze the prison sees itself first as an employer, as an institution with potential labour difficulties, a tight budget, and difficult working conditions. Labour peace, worker contentment, and job satisfaction are thus high priorities for prison wardens, directors, or governors – certainly more important than inmate happiness or even well-being! Irwin's second point seems likewise accurate, the prison's job being a 'nasty' one and often open to criticism from all sides of the political spectrum. Prisons can be seen as too harsh, too soft, too porous, or too walled off, and as public institutions they are constantly vulnerable to the impact of public opinion. The response of the prison system has been to isolate the prison itself, to place prisons in rural or deserted regions or regions of high unemployment where criticisms might mean local job loss. This geographical placement, of course, directly inhibits any mission the prison might adopt that involved reintegration of the offender into the community.

Irwin's third point may seem an odd one at first glance, but it has deep resonance within the literature on criminals and prisons. Often from similar backgrounds, prisoners and guards share a virtual lifetime of companionship within the prison and some have argued that they 'live the same life on both sides of the same bolted door.'[22] Jean Genet, perhaps the most eloquent writer on this point, describes the relationship between guards and prisoners as follows: 'They openly hated the inmates, but cherished them in secret ... one feels that the guards are on intimate terms with the hoodlums, not because there is intimacy between them in the usual sense of the word, but because there wells up from the hoodlums the horror in which the guards are caught, in which they melt. A family air merges them, as it merges masters and old servants, who are the seamy side of the masters, their opposite and, in a way, their unwholesome exhalations.'[23]

One hears the strong echo of Hegel's notion of the master-slave relationship, the dialectical trap in which both are caught. The prison service must, therefore, go to great lengths to create a moral distance between its employees and the imprisoned, the keepers and the kept. It does this in part by reinforcing, through uniforms, numbers in place of names, strict if often nonsensical rules, and even sometimes the sanctioning of brutality, the identity of the prisoner as 'other,' as object rather than subject. For instance, in the prison I taught in the staff went to lunch during the prisoners' 'feeding time.' All this adds immeasurably, as can be imagined, to the difficulties encountered by rehabilitation efforts that include prison staff.

Irwin's final point concerning maximizing bureaucratic autonomy is perhaps a given in any large system but especially important for the prison given the lengths it must sometimes go to in order to carry out the first three objectives.

These 'bureaucratic imperatives' create conditions, traditions, and practices within the prison that severely hamper the various policy initiatives associated with inmate programs. William Outerbridge, the long-time chairman of the Canadian National Parole Board, pointed out the contradictions implicit in a national policy directed towards prisoners choosing among several 'opportunities' when the prison regimes takes away 'every opportunity of choice he has' and yet expects that same individual to 'be able to make the right choices after he's been released.'[24] The socialist writer Victor Serge, reflecting on his own experience of French prisons in the 1930s, saw prison life as 'a kind of mechanized madness; everything in it seems to have been conceived in a spirit of mean calculation how best to enfeeble, stupefy and numb the prisoner.'[25] Peter Scharf, bemoaning the collapse of any pretense at rehabilitation in the 1970s, likewise observes that in the modern prison the inmate 'is simply to be (to exist) and to obey. There is nothing expected of him other than cooperation and good behaviour.'[26] The individuality of the prisoner thus becomes completely subservient to the larger needs of the prison as institution, thereby preventing any unnecessary 'eruptions of humanness' which could only serve to disrupt an efficient and changeless system.[27]

The Convict's Response to the Prison

As outlined earlier, there is no consensus among academic writers about the nature of the convict's response to the prison, there being two primary academic analyses of the prison inmate: one that the prisoner is fundamentally shaped by the prison (the prisonization thesis), and the other that the subculture from which the prisoner originates is the decisive force in shaping his or her behaviour while imprisoned (the criminalization thesis). One can imagine a wide range of responses depending on factors such as age, experience, commitment to a criminal 'vocation,' and family ties, and indeed most commentators not wedded to one or the other of these two models generally attest to both versions being present in the prison.

The contemporary debate over the nature of the prison's impact on the prisoner stems in large part from the theorizing about the 'total institution' undertaken by Erving Goffman in the early 1960s, part of the general suspicion of large institutions and state power that came to characterize the 1960s and 1970s. Goffman argued that prisons, hospitals, and mental institutions 'stripped' the patient/inmate of any meaningful manifestations of self and justified this through reasonable-sounding security or health objectives. This is a particularly important issue when it comes to considering whether the prison can ever provide a context or setting for individual growth or transformation. A statement by a prisoner in the State Prison of Southern Michigan captures this sense of the prison experience:

> To describe what it means to be a prisoner, how it feels to be confined, is impossible for one who has not experienced it. The psychological state of complete passivity and dependence on the decisions of guards and officers must be included among the pains of imprisonment, along with the restriction of physical liberty, the possession of goods and services, and heterosexual relations. The frustration of the prisoner's ability to make choices and the frequent refusals to provide an explanation for the regulation and commands descending from the bureaucratic staff involve a ... threat to the prisoner's self-image and reduce the prisoner to a weak, helpless, dependent status of childhood. The imprisoned criminal finds his picture of himself as a self-determining individual being destroyed by the regime of the custodian.[28]

There is another, more complex, more Kafkaesque critique of the world of the prison offered by Robby Wideman, thief, addict, murderer, and brother of the American novelist John Wideman. Here the focus of the prison is on unsettling the prisoner, keeping him off-balance and unsure of rules, identity, and environment:

> I wasn't prepared to step through the looking glass. Giving up one version of reality for another. That's what entering the prison was about. Not a dramatic flip-flop of values. That would be too easy. If black became white and good became bad and fast became slow, the players could learn the trick of reversing labels, and soon the upside-down world would seem natural. Prison is more perverse. Inside the walls nothing is certain, nothing can be taken for granted except the arbitrary exercise of absolute power. Rules engraved in stone one day will be superseded the next. What you don't know can always hurt you. And the prison rules are designed to keep you ignorant, keep you guessing, insure your vulnerability ... Prison rules and regulations, the day-to-day operation of the institution, confront the inmate with an image of himself that is grotesque, absurd. A prisoner who refuses to internalize this image, who insists upon seeing other versions of himself, is in constant danger.[29]

At its core, this critique could apply to many classic interfaces between citizens and a bureaucracy. One thinks of the citizen facing the tax official, or being hospitalized, and so forth. Petty rules subject to constant change and interpretation and enforced by brute authority rather than reasoned and reciprocal discourse (because of the assumption that they serve good a purpose), disempowerment through denial of information and context, and the restriction of choices are all tools used by those in positions of bureaucratic authority. For most citizens, however, these are occasional confrontations, momentary collapses of self-image quickly restored within a life context of one's choosing. For the prisoner this *is* the full life context, at least to the degree that the prison can penetrate inmate society. If the prison really has no other aim or purpose beyond pragmatic custody and control enforced by punishment, authority, and petty rules, then it will necessarily lack any of the elements of experience required for intellectual, social, or moral growth. Indeed, the prison becomes a hotbed of cynicism, hypocrisy, and illusion as the imprisoned cooperate with their keepers – including treatment staff – solely in order to avoid institutional punishments and to secure some kind of relief or release from the more punitive aspects of their confinement.[30] This is the prison we know most directly from films and the news media and via our osmotic incorporation of the 'nothing works' and 'total institution' messages of the previous decades. But there are other images of the prison that contradict or at least complicate this negative or static view. For instance, we know that for many – some young males in particular – prison is an attraction, a place where one establishes a reputation in the criminal world, proves one's toughness, and begins the construction of social networks useful 'on the street'. Jean Genet speaks of this eloquently in his memory of observing a young boy entering the prison with 'haughty elegance ... a tough among other toughs ... his longing to be a big shot ... great enough for him to sacrifice his youth and life to it.'[31] Recent trends aimed at eliminating incarceration for most juvenile offenders are motivated more by an acknowledgment of Genet's insight than any desire to show mercy or compassion for such young 'toughs.'

There is another, even more challenging image of the prison refuge, an attractive centre of calm in a world of turmoil. Martha Duncan cites Solzhenitsyn and many others who extol the nature of prison friendships and prison as a 'calm place in the midst of motion,' a place where 'serious things happen,' where things are more 'real' than in the outside world. Malcolm X, for instance, saw prison as a place of learning.[32] For Duncan prison is a place where deep friendships flourish, in part because all other (competing) types of relationships, such as work or family, are absent. These attractions are made all the more powerful because life lived outside the prison in the criminal fast lanes was so unpleasant in comparison. She then develops the idea of prison as 'mother,' as a place of refuge, protection, with the subsequent idea of being 'reborn' through prison, entering society again as a 'new person.' At a materialist or almost nutritional level Duncan is quite correct in seeing the prison as refuge, a place where drug addicts can 'bulk up' after months or years of dietary chaos and malnutrition stemming from heroin abuse. The thieving life is notoriously hard work at the journeyman level, and many of these men and women might very well look forward to a light prison term as a time to rest and recuperate. More challenging is the notion of prison as a source of friendship, an alternative social world. Robby Wideman, despite having to move through the looking glass, confirms much of Duncan's insight. His brother reports that at mid-sentence 'Robby had achieved an inner calm, a degree of self-sufficiency and self-reliance never apparent when he was running the streets.'[33]

So the prison is both authoritarian destroyer of selves and nurturing centre for the creation of new selves, the appropriate metaphor being the modern machine, a processing plant of sorts taking in individuals who have committed criminal acts and who in most cases are engaged – admittedly to varying degrees – with an entire criminal lifestyle. It is not unlike its university and hospital counterparts in this way, except these latter two seem on the whole to be more successful in terms of their stated mission. The university shapes the post-adolescent youth more or less successfully into producers and consumers, creators and critics, with only a small number of failures and deviant products. Likewise the hospital system claims high success rates in at least deterring the ravages of time, disease, and tension. But the prison can make no such claim. While in general successfully contained while under its care and supervision, one of every two of its products returns as failures after release: the 'treatment regime' seems less successful than the 'convict code' in reformulating identities while inside.

Before examining in more detail the role of the prison itself in generating these failures, however, we need more information about just who these prisoners are. Most descriptions of prisoner populations begin with the deficits along with background specifics that indicate a critical accumulation of negative factors. These include problematic home environments, previous incarcerations as adults and possibly juveniles, and frequent shifts in employment and living arrangements – a general lack of stability. The profiles are remarkably similar within the developed countries, with at least half of all prisoners attaining grade 10 or less in schooling, generally more than half being single, drug addiction rates of about 30 per cent with drug and alcohol abuse rates much higher, in many cases nearly 100 per cent. More than half of all prisoners come from families with histories of serious discord, what in the review of the files of our 800 Canadian prisoners we came to call 'toxic families.' Pre-incarceration unemployment rates for prisoners run as high as 40 per cent, and of those employed a majority report earning less than recognized poverty levels of income.[34] In the penitentiaries (as opposed to jails or community corrections facilities), well over half of the prisoners have three or more prior incarcerations with high levels of violence and crimes against the person. Increasingly, as mental institutions fall out of favour with government and the public, prison populations accumulate more and more inmates diagnosed as severely mentally disturbed. As well, prisons are notorious holding tanks for high percentages of any nation's ethnic minorities, particularly young, 20- to 30-year-old males. In the United States this is a particularly high profile issue with, for example, a third of African-American men in their twenties in California living behind bars – compared with 5.4 per cent of white males and 9.4 per cent of Latino males in the same age group.[35]

As we have seen in discussing the origins of the medical model, these commonalities in the 'look' of the prisoner population were seized upon as being indicative of a similar layer of internal, psychological commonalities. More recent research tends to focus on the 'differences' rather than the similarities in the psychological make-up of the prisoner population. After testing a cross-section of prisoners using five psychological measures, Patricia Van Voorhis described them as a 'heterogeneous population' and concluded that 'the belief that adult, male, inmate populations are made up primarily of psychopathic, character disordered, subcultural, or manipulative personalities cannot be supported by these data. Similarly, these data should cast doubts upon sweeping generalizations about the nature of the "criminal mind," or the criminal personality.'[36] The urge to such generalizations is, however, powerful. In one of my own early reflections on thinking about the prisoners I was teaching in my history classes at Matsqui Institution in British Columbia I described the progress of my own theorizing as follows:

My first impulse upon reflecting on my students was to see them almost exclusively as individuals. This was reinforced by my initial impression that while they may be criminals, they did not appear to be all that different from myself, an impression that was heightened by the opposite expectation upon first entering the institution. This individualist analysis lasted for some time. The first signs of disillusionment appeared with the first recidivist. The more I learned about my students' behaviour, the patterns that seemed to lead to a return to crime, the more I began to question my initial assumptions. By that time the empirical and impressionistic data of several years of constant exposure to and discussions with the prisoner/students began to have its effect. Intellectual struggles in the classroom that had seemed random or isolated at first became repetitive as each class seemed to pursue the same questions ... Starting from no *a priori* assumptions myself concerning criminals as a group, the common attitudes, thought patterns and assumptions of most of my students were leading to some sort of a general theory.[37]

In my case this 'general theory' became centred on the work of Jean Piaget and Lawrence Kohlberg in the fields of moral education and developmental psychology, and I mined this pit for several years in seeking an explanation for the behaviours and attitudes of my students both in prison and after release. And, of course, I found them; but as Thomas Jefferson warned his more avidly generalist colleagues, 'the moment a person forms a theory his imagination sees in every object only the traits which favor the theory.'[38] Seven years after my initial foray into theorizing about prisoners I had already begin to equivocate, fearing that the prisoners were 'too complex a group about which to generalize,' and the theory of cognitive development requiring 'too much leveling of prisoners to common stages and too little differentiation.'[39] I had been away from the prison for some years by that time, having left in part because of an increasing inability to see my prisoner-students as individuals as opposed to types or categories. With several years subsequent hindsight I can now appreciate both the validity or at least utility of the theory – in this case cognitive development theory – and its limitations. The point is not my own struggles with this issue but rather the universality of this tendency among people who work with prisoners and total(izing) institutions like prisons.

Nowhere is this dance of the theories more evident than in the aforementioned prisonization versus criminalization debate, the review of which will be mercifully brief. The prisonization approach is most closely related to the work of Sykes and Messinger in their work described in the 'Inmate Social System.'[40] They argued that the pains associated with imprisonment led to the development of an inmate code of behaviour, movement towards which eased the pains of imprisonment: 'A cohesive inmate society provides the prisoner with a meaningful social group with which he can identify himself and which will support him in his struggles against his condemners.'[41] The inmate code, a set of 'normative imperatives that are held forth as guides for the behaviour of the inmate in his relations with his fellow prisoners and custodians,'[42] consists of the following:

1   Don't interfere with inmate interests, that is, serving the least possible time and enjoying the greatest possible number of privileges while in prison.
2   Don't lose your head; ignore the irritants of daily life in prison.
3   Don't exploit inmates by breaking your word, stealing, etc.
4   Don't weaken; stand up to frustration or threatening situations without complaining or resorting to subservience
5   Don't be a sucker by working hard, submitting to authority, or thinking guards can be all right.

By following these precepts the theory is that the prisoner can maintain a measure of autonomy and self-respect in the face of the carceral regime that is determined in Foucaultean fashion to deny him of both. The prison is served as well, since the code allows for a considerable degree of inmate self-management while at the same time it is an essentially conservative, system-maintenance ideology, 'acting like a brake on the unfettered exercise of force and cunning in the interaction of men in prison.'[43] By embracing the inmate code, however, the prisoner becomes in effect a 'convict' and, upon release, an 'ex-con': 'Thus by struggling to avoid an institutional identity which was despised (the good inmate) prisoners often took on another one (the con) which the public had reason to fear and despise.'[44] By allowing the prisoner only two options (good inmate or con) instead of three (those two plus a self with pride and moral self-respect), the prison thus guarantees the perpetuation of the prisoner or the creation of the quiescent subject – but never the autonomous citizen.

The criminalization or 'importation' theory accepts that some prisoners, especially long-term prisoners, may adopt attitudes and behaviours as described by the inmate code, but that there also exists within the prison a thriving convict code that is linked to a criminal code that exists outside the prison. Irwin and Cressy, the authors most closely linked to this view, stress the importance within the prison of the 'thief subculture' which emphasized the importance of getting out of prison quickly, stressed that one was a 'man' not a 'prisoner' and that the proper response to the prison was to 'do your own time' and not interfere with others.[45] Prison was 'an annoying interval in one's career,'[46] and one remained committed to the criminal life, not the prison life.

Complexity, then, is more likely the order of the day in considering how individuals respond to imprisonment, while simplicity is more likely the explanation of how prisons respond to individuals. The latter are operating on the basis of institutional imperatives that tend to override well-meaning or even ill-meaning shifts in policy of waves of public opinion, imperatives that are as operative in minimum security work camps as they are in concentration camps, though prison or correctional staff must live with the conviction that this is not the case in order to sustain their professional integrity. Prisoners, on the other hand, come into the prison from such a variety of circumstances, ranging from embittered innocence to exhausted relief, that their responses are necessarily diverse. As well, they are themselves a diverse group in terms of biography, ability, and attitude, and this is reflected in the range of responses they devise.

Cats among the Pigeons

It was in this divided and hostile carceral universe that a wave of outsiders appeared in the 1970s in response to the programmatic vacuum created by the sudden collapse of the medical or treatment model. The existing educational and training programs in the prisons had for so long laboured in the shadows of the treatment programs that they were virtually moribund and were generally unable to fill the space. As well, the prison systems were reluctant to expand their in-house programs because that would require adding staff which, if these programs too proved ineffective, would be difficult to get rid of. Instead, the prison systems across North America in particular moved towards contracting out for programs and the personnel that accompanied them, thereby avoiding long-term commitments and expansions of base budgets.

Private contractors, school districts, charitable associations, community colleges, universities, and other community-based bodies now began to propose activities and programs designed to address prison and prisoner needs, whether for recreation, education, counselling, or therapy. Local chambers of commerce got involved, along with national bodies concerned with topics from literacy and learning disabilities to prison arts and Black Studies. In the absence of the singular approach to understanding crime and the prisoner that had characterized the earlier decades, the range of possible interventions was now limited only by the availability of interested parties, money, and the favoured approach of institution-based or regional corrections administrators.

These new faces in the prison came with minimal 'baggage' in terms of the patterns that had been established by prisoners, treatment staff, and corrections staff. Indeed, one of the defining characteristics of most of the people associated with these new initiatives was their fundamental unfamiliarity with prisons. They came from other institutions by and large, but institutions with quite different traditions, objectives, and expectations. The result was often chaos, sometimes innovation, and frequently frustration, both for the outsiders and for prison staff, but as we will see in the next chapter, this inexperience more often than not worked to the advantage of the prison rather than the outsider.

CHAPTER FIVE

Reeling About:
The Era of Opportunities

What I think about Humanities is that it widens your vocabulary and the way I think, tremendously I mean. Geoff's girlfriend was mucking about and calling me all sorts of insulting names, and so on, and I just told her to stop making superfluous remarks – and she didn't know where to put herself. A normal everyday sort of person just doesn't use words like that; they've got no answer if you say something like that to them, you know. And I found it the same way, well, in the street, or in arguments with teachers, you don't have to revert to violence, but more to vocabulary, and if you come out with a lot of linked up, very long words that mean very small things – but they've never heard them before – they get all upset and don't know what to say and sort of reel about, you know.[1]

Barry MacDonald, *The Experience of Innovation*, 1978

There are a wealth of insights packed into this stream of words by a young near-juvenile delinquent enrolled in a humanities program for school leavers in England. Instead of reverting immediately to a violent response when called names by Geoff's girlfriend, which was clearly in his repertoire of possible responses, the young man felled her with a word – 'superfluous.' This is a new weapon in the social war, a new way of winning that does not involve precipitous action. The more words one can string together, the more victories one can win, even against powerful entrenched enemies like teachers. Words, not deeds, can get the job done. But first you have to have the words, and that is where education comes in. Not training in job skills or conflict resolution, but good old-fashioned education that offers up a vocabulary and a set of critical insights about when and how to use it. Words are also linked closely to social class and affiliations. The 'normal everyday sort of person' in this young man's life is the sort that probably got him into trouble in the past, but with his new words he begins the process of moving towards other social networks in which people do not just 'reel about' when spoken to, but respond in kind.

This is not a particularly new idea in prison work, intensive and solitary Bible study being one of the first forms of rehabilitation envisaged by eighteenth-century prison reformers. The idea was to instil a moral 'brake' on precipitous or unwise actions, a set of rules imbibed through study that would give the criminal an alternative way of approaching personal problems, social relations, and excessive or inappropriate desires. Education as experienced by this young man was more instrumental in nature, giving him the tools without the explanation.

The issue is taken a step further in the following from John McVicar, a notorious English criminal who used his experience of university education in prison to start a new and highly respectable life: 'The part of me that I now value most – my identity – is irreconcilable with being the type of criminal that I was. The change was largely the unintended consequence of following a degree course; I didn't plan it and it certainly wasn't anything like we normally associate with a conversion. I decided to take a degree because it seemed to me about the best of the options to offset the corrosive effects of long-term imprisonment. What wrought my change was not any effort to reform but the process of implementing my decision. Similarly, I cannot claim any moral victory if I never return to crime, since nowadays it is not so much that I find crime repugnant as that I am more interested in other things.'[2]

As with our young delinquent, there are a great many insights in these reflections on crime, education, and reformation by this more seasoned actor. Returning to the Enlightenment values we began exploring in the first chapter, McVicar confirms that 'identity' is paramount in determining the range of social actions contemplated, in this case the adoption – at least for the time being, the tentative quality of his reflections is striking – of a student identity has replaced or shoved aside a criminal identity and in the process shoved aside crime as a reasonable activity. McVicar is adamant that the change was not planned or the result of a diagnosis. There was no 'treatment' here, the changes he observes in his sense of identity were unplanned and were gradually unveiled during the 'process' of completing his education. That decision to enrol in an education program is likewise uncoupled in McVicar's version from any intention to change – he was merely looking for the best way to do his time. Finally, proud former criminal that he is, he attaches no moral significance to the change in career and indeed announces that this too may only be temporary. He may, in fact, return to crime, one imagines, if the things he is now interested in prove ephemeral.

One should not imagine that the experiences of Geoff, John McVicar, or any of the 654 prisoner-students that provide much of the data used in this book to assess the effectiveness of prison programs can be translated into a case for a new *educational model* to replace a discredited *medical model*. Indeed, the whole notion of a *model* must remain highly suspect in the complex world of prisons, prisoners, the law, and the state. What we are looking for is rather a programmatic style or approach that is more conducive to breaking down the subject-object relationship so endemic in the prison and in the criminal justice system as a whole and programs that have an educational objective at their core seem to have the greatest potential to accomplish this. But, as we all know from personal experience, students can also easily be made into objects and when this occurs the model deconstructs itself.

The Outsider in the Prison

In this chapter we will look at prison education in some detail and in the context of the opening up of prison programs during the era of opportunities and humane containment, an example of 'letting a hundred flowers bloom, a hundred schools of contend.' During the period roughly from 1972 to 1992, prisons in North America and in England were 'opened up' to contracted services as a result of both the collapse of the treatment model and the steady tightening of budgets throughout these years with the resulting gradual diminution of prison staff. As noted earlier, it became desirable for prison administrations to contract in certain services and thereby avoid complex benefits and civil service job tenure obligations. Contracting was also more efficient since personnel and programs could be changed more easily as conditions and needs changed. Key security and administrative staff remained, but a great many of the prisoner programs were shifted to outside agencies, including in the case of education programs school districts, colleges, and universities. There were other, more 'political' benefits as well. Besides the monetary and staffing advantages, if another Martinson came along pointing out program failures the blame could be directed towards others while at the same time corrections could easily take credit for at least a portion of any successes. The great disadvantages were the increased presence of 'outsiders' in the prison and the decreased morale among corrections staff as more and more their role was reduced to security functions.

Education programs have a long tradition in modern penal history, the chaplain and teacher (early on the same person) having been part of the modern prison regime from the very beginning. Indeed they start out at the very centre of the 'penitentiary' since the study (requiring literacy) of the Bible and other moral tracts (requiring guidance) was seen as the means through which the reformation of the criminal could be effected. The idea that the prison should contain a school or at least have a schooling function was thus institutionalized from the start, marking the penitentiary off from its carceral predecessors. The ideals of hard work and discipline, which were central to this early notion of penitent schooling, are still very much alive within the modern correctional institution and in the way it is perceived by members of the public. The outcries against 'country-club prisons' are no doubt in part retributive in nature, but they may also express a persistent insight or belief that it is only through discipline, labour, and enforced reflection that these deviant individuals will have a chance at getting back on a correct and civil path. This kind of thinking betrays at once the deep impact of Calvinist thought on the modern project and our prison systems – at least in cultures formed in large part by that ideology – are Calvinist to the core.

This 'reformation of the soul' dimension of prison education was rather quickly superseded by an increased focus on literacy and training. In his musings on the penitentiary system in the 1830s, de Tocqueville admired the Quaker experiments in Philadelphia, but saw the more Calvinist-inspired and labour-driven system at Auburn Penitentiary in New York as more likely to achieve significant successes. Here prisoners were taught to read and write and work in an early version of behaviourism. The keepers and teachers were less concerned with imparting virtue than with instilling good work habits. Here one cannot help but to think of Thomas Gradgrind in Dickens's book *Hard Times*, drilling his students with facts 'nothing but Facts. Facts alone are wanted in life. Plant nothing else and root out everything else. You can only form the minds of reasoning animals upon Facts.'[3] While Dickens was offering a caricature of education, in many prison classrooms the idea that education narrowly conceived as the imparting of basic skills carried the day in the nineteenth century. Harvey Graff charts this shift from evil to illiteracy as the cause of crime and the resulting focus in the later nineteenth century on education as a central component of the corrections enterprise. Illiteracy – widespread among the imprisoned – was seen as direct evidence of ignorance and lack of schooling and 'these tabulations became the statistical foundations upon which the rhetorical house explaining criminality was built.'[4]

Unfortunately, despite the spread of education within North American prisons and a decrease in rates of illiteracy in society at large, the crime rate continued to rise. This prompted enlightened progressive thinkers to up the ante one more level by returning to the moral issue raised by the Quaker reformers of earlier times. Now the problem was seen in terms of education being too instrumental, too focused on literacy and skills acquisition while ignoring the moral dimension. Gradgrind's prescription did not work, the facts were not enough. By concerning themselves only with instrumental ends, prison educators were producing only educated criminals. The time was long past, however, when prisons could return to being 'penitent-iaries' in the true sense of that term. By the beginning of this century they were becoming huge institutions in full transition to the bureaucratic systems described by Foucault, the treatment approach already emerging in the various theories about heredity and crime, crime and mental illness, and so forth.

Still, powerful voices were raised in defence of education as the central mission of the prison, in this case education for citizenship. The U.S. prison reformer Thomas Mott Osborne in the 1920s was the most outspoken proponent for this idea that prisons should be places that through education and through participation in democratically run communities imparted increased understanding and improved intellectual ability, resulting in a more responsible human being and therefore a better citizen: 'As criminals can neither be coerced nor bribed into a change of purpose, there is but one way left; they must be educated. We must provide a training which will make them, not good prisoners, but good citizens; a training which will fit them for the free life to which sooner or later, they are to return ... Not until we think of our prisons as in reality educational institutions shall we come within sight of a successful system; and by a successful system I mean, one that not only ensures a quiet, orderly, well-behaved prison but has genuine life in it, as well; one that restores to society the largest number of intelligent, forceful, honest citizens.'[5]

One has a strong sense here of the power of the sociological approach to deviance that was referred to in the opening chapter.

Crime is clearly here a 'social' problem and the need is to somehow 'retrieve' these criminal individuals for society, a retrieval that can occur by informing or reminding them of their duties as citizens and the advantages they derive from being able to exercise those duties. Here as well is Socrates' judgment that crime stems from ignorance or error rather than from 'evil' and Rousseau's enlightenment insistence on the logical primacy of the role of citizen over that of the criminal, once one is made aware of the advantages to be derived from citizenship. The prison thus becomes the school of last resort, filling in where family and early schooling have failed.

The strength of this view became apparent during the Second World War when the Allies faced the prospect of reforming a nation of 'criminals.' Several efforts were made during the war to re-educate German prisoners of war, to awaken their sensitivities to the obligations of citizenship, and teach them the mechanics of democracy. Like Osborne, the presumption was that education for citizenship required more than classroom learning since it involved a certain spontaneity in the face of often challenging circumstances. Just as Osborne tried to implement democratic practices in the prison, in the POW camp situations were posed to the prisoners that were designed to 'arouse student participation in the debate, and to provoke the loosening up process which would prepare the men for showing initiative once they were turned back to the status of citizens.'[6] These were Jeffersonian ideals in action, a democracy based on forceful and active citizen engagement with society.

Just as German prisoners were envisaged as a spearhead in the creation of a new, vital democratic Germany, it had been implicit if not explicit in Osborne's formulations that prisoners, once properly educated, could return to society as exemplary Jeffersonian citizens. Accepting the sociological view of the origins of crime in poverty, inequality, and discrimination, prisoners were perceived to be individuals who had possessed the will to strike back – in however misguided and ill-informed a manner – in an attempt to escape the traps they had been born or thrust into. This active will could, it was imagined, be transformed via education and experience into a force leading to positive individual and social change. While these ideas were to find a powerful echo in the Black Power and Prisoners' Rights movements of the 1960s and 1970s, as we have seen earlier in this study, the idea that prisoners could be the raw material of such a notion of citizenship was not to last.

As the treatment model gathered strength in the immediate postwar years, the role of education in prisons began to shift towards 'inmate management' and away from any identification with empowerment or rehabilitation. In the new treatment prisons of the 1950s and 1960s, the school and the vocational shop became just two of many activities that were part of an overall management strategy designed to make the institution itself efficient, secure, and cost-effective while inmate reha- bilitative programs became the realm of the new treatment experts. That said, throughout this era education remained an important part of the prison regime, providing in addition to its inmate management role an upgrading service for the more high-profile rehabilitation programs. Literacy was, after all, central to many of the psychological treatments, and employment skills were still needed after release, even for the men- tally rehabilitated. Thus, in 1952, half of the 4800 men in San Quentin were enrolled in education courses, and this was typical of other juris- dictions. Even more important than the traditional adult basic educa- tion, high school, and vocational programs, however, was the appearance in the 1960s of college and university programs in prisons.

The University in the Prison

At first these new players on the prison scene were seen simply as log- ical enhancements of existing education programs and remained com- pletely separate from the 'treatment regime.' The first significant example of this was the Southern Illinois University program at the Illinois State Penitentiary at Menard in 1962. Post-secondary corre- spondence courses had been available for some time, but thanks to an entrepreneurial university extension department and a tolerant prison administration, thirty prisoners were now allowed to work towards degrees via in-person classes. In 1966 the Ford Foundation provided funds for the University of California at Berkeley to offer a full-time university program at San Quentin, and within two years over 100 prisoner-students had completed several semesters of work. In 1967, the University of Oregon started the Upward Bound Prison Project at the state prison in Salem, a program based on education and counsel- ling that was to provide the model for the NewGate Program funded two years later by the U.S. Office of Economic Opportunity (OEO).

Thus, prisons across North America began to find themselves host- ing two sets of academically bound 'experts,' the treatment staff on the one hand and university and college teachers on the other. The latter group were to play the leading role in what I have described as an 'opening up' of the prisons. This was not easy, and the relationship between these two equally parasitical visitors to the prison was complex. On the one hand their missions were ostensibly unique and the individuals involved often had little in common. The post-secondary education programs were almost always grounded in the liberal arts, a fact made necessary by the pedagogical limitations of the prison environment and made likely because it was those sectors of the university-college system that produced in greatest number the kind of social-activist faculty who might find prisoners and prisons an attractive field of educational praxis.[7] There were, as well, some problems in the form of opportunistic post-secondary institutions who saw prison programs as 'cash cows' or places to employ inferior or 'problem' teachers. In a survey of prison education programs carried out in 1979, Raymond Bell from Lehigh University found many college programs with low standards, poor faculty, and a general lack of transferability of courses to college programs outside of prison.[8]

Treatment staff, being the other cohort within the prisons who were affiliated either directly or indirectly with higher education, found their university home in psychology or the sciences and were motivated more by research interests than by any concern with social reform or 'good works.' Relations between the two sets of 'outside professionals' were not always cordial. The prison psychologist at the institution I taught in was often particularly irritated by the university program's deliberately naïve acceptance of the prisoner-subject 'as they were.' In a report on one of our students he wrote: 'Subject is presently in the university course, however, he was never tested if he is suitable for that type of program. Under the present circumstances, it appears to be quite obvious that he has not made any effort to change his personality and I believe it is unwise to train that individual as he may only become a more sophisticated criminal. It is my opinion that under the present circumstances we only compound his and our problems by allowing an individual with psychopathic personality features and a long criminal record to receive an expensive education as a gift from uncritical program makers.' Despite differences such as this, the still dominant position of the medical model and the treatment professionals linked to it within the corrections field acted as a powerful magnet for those attempting to bring innovative education and social development programs into the prisons. Initially, then, these programs tended to borrow from the treatment paradigm, to adopt research objectives, and to make claims for their efficacy in the area of rehabilitation. Despite conflicts epitomized by the above example, the objective was to work with rather than confront the treatment professionals. Then gradually, as the impact of 'nothing works' spread system-wide, these programs like others in the field retreated to a set of more conservative, traditional – and one might argue, reasonable – objectives.

The following sections of this chapter explore this process in some detail through several case studies of education and related programs that flourished in prisons in North America and the United Kingdom during the period from about 1970 to 1990 – specifically the NewGate programs in the United States, the University of California at Santa Cruz's education program at the California Institution for Women, Open University courses and the Special Unit at Barlinnie Prison in the United Kingdom, and the University of Victoria – Simon Fraser University Prison Education Program in British Columbia, Canada. While there were literally hundreds of education and related programs offered in prisons across North America and the United Kingdom during this period, the cases selected give at least a taste of the potential for variety, innovation, and tradition within the now less closed-off world of the prison. Because the case being made in this book for the effectiveness of these kinds of initiatives in both inhibiting recidivism (return to prison) and enhancing social integration and citizenship is based largely on research data from the Canadian program, special attention will be paid here to exploring the attributes of that program. It was the NewGate initiative, however, that started the process.

The NewGate Programs

After tracking the success of the prison education pilot project at the State Prison in Salem, Oregon, in 1969 the U.S. Office of Economic Opportunity provided major funding for five additional projects (Minnesota State Reformatory, New Mexico State Prison, Rockview State Correctional Institution in Pennsylvania, and Federal Youth Centers in Ashland, Kentucky, and Eaglewood, Colorado), the experiment in prisoner education going under the name Project NewGate (after the famous London gaol). Project NewGate started with two researchable questions:

1   Could prison inmates with the requisite ability benefit from higher education?

2   Could higher education help the released prisoner to achieve a non-criminal lifestyle?

While each of the sites was run independently and had several very important differences in terms of local conditions, they did share a sufficient number of key components to make the experiment possible. Each program consisted of a post-secondary education program taught by faculty from a neighbouring university and included an on-site director and support staff. The courses offered were the same as those taught on the main campus, there being no attempt to 'adapt' the content or alter the standards because of the prison context or any specifically rehabilitative objectives. Unlike many prison education programs, the NewGate model was a full-time activity for the students rather than something done after work or during the evening. Each of the programs, to the degree permitted by the prison, attempted to create a campus atmosphere through cultural enrichment programs, guest speakers, student councils, films, and any other means that might break up the prison routine.

Though it was already under attack from some quarters, the medical model was still in force in the late 1960s, and treatment was still the central mission of corrections. Unlike a comparable campus-based education program, therefore, each NewGate program perceived itself as part of the inmate's treatment program. Part of its commitment to 'helping the prisoner achieve a non-criminal lifestyle' included mandatory 'intensive therapy and counseling programs aimed toward developing and reinforcing a more secure self-concept on the part of the inmate.'[9] As part of this participation in the 'treatment' dimension of corrections, prisoners were admitted to NewGate programs not just on the basis of ability, but also on the basis of the prisoner's 'desire to change his patterns of behaviour.'[10] As part of this rehabilitative mission, each program was supposed to assist those prisoner-students who wished to continue with their education after release by providing on-campus support, including when possible special residences or halfway houses. Although all the programs made this attempt, some were more successful than others.

While mandatory counselling and admissions based on 'rehabilitative potential' were in effect backward-looking measures in the sense of their being grounded in the soon-to-be-abandoned medical model, NewGate did pioneer two important aspects of prison education that were to prove central to the success of prison programs in general. The first of these was its focus on prisoner participation in the administration of the program itself. The NewGate academic staff built on the ideas of Osborne and other radical prison reformers in insisting that internal change or growth only comes through a combination of learning and action. In NewGate programs students participated in hiring decisions, course selection and other academic matters as well as having a say through student councils in the ongoing administration of the programs.[11] The second important decision in establishing the project was the determination to follow through to the period after release. Prison programs are notorious for not having a post-release dimension, and NewGate because of the involvement of major community institutions like universities was able in some measure to overcome this difficulty. NewGate staff went to considerable lengths advising and counselling prisoner-students prior to release, helping with integration to the university community, and arranging for local on-campus housing.

In reviewing the literature produced at the time by people associated with the NewGate projects, one has a clear sense of the impact of the 'movement politics' of the era. With generous support from the OEO, the NewGate Resource Center was established with the mission of not only keeping participant institutions involved and connected, but also reviewing the whole field of prison education in the United States and assisting other correctional institutions and universities in setting up NewGate-type programs. To this end a 'model' NewGate system was constructed, and it was envisaged that many more existing education programs would join the NewGate group.

NewGate was obviously a high-profile initiative, well funded, and with support at the local prison level and at national levels as well, but it came on the scene at just the wrong time. Throughout the early 1970s prison rehabilitation programs were coming under increased scrutiny and NewGate was no exception. Conceived as an experiment from the start, a thorough evaluation of the NewGate programs was undertaken in 1972. The evaluation was funded by the OEO and included comparisons with five post-secondary prison education programs that were not part of NewGate. The reviewers found the programs to be educationally sound and of real value to the prisoner-students but, consistent with Martinson's findings a year later, no consistent differentiation was found between NewGate participants and other prisoner-students or members of control groups in terms of recidivism or 'realizing life goals.' The reviewers concluded that while they were confident that the program had a positive impact on both the prison and prisoner, measurement of that impact was too difficult because of the 'lack of sufficient methodological sophistication.'[12]

What had gone wrong? Or had anything gone wrong? Had anyone benefited from the program, or did just too few benefit? The NewGate programs did have some serious problems, that was clear. Initially prison staff in the NewGate sites had welcomed the programs, but the sudden influx of university outsiders who were interested more in education than in treatment quickly led to friction. John Irwin, one of the NewGate evaluators, notes that after the first year the 'activities of students and staff became increasingly intolerable, especially in terms of changes in prison routines.'[13] The prisoners were becoming increasingly articulate in their criticisms and demands and NewGate releasees, because they remained engaged with the prison-based program after their release, began to criticize prison authorities from outside the prison. This was, in fact, a 'worst case scenario' for the prison as institution – outsiders with no vested interest in the prison regime as it then existed had been allowed into the institution in significant numbers and were now mobilizing against the prison (or at least so it appeared to them) with the help of an equally formidable institution, the university. As a result the prison began to 'close in on the programs from several directions and take control,' with the result being a gradual shift within the education programs from innovation to accommodation.[14] Enthusiasm from both program staff and prisoner-students inevitably fell as a result, and the education programs began to appear more and more like 'prison programs.'

This is, in a sense, an 'argument from incompatibility,' that there are fundamental differences between the institutional objectives and ethos of a prison regime and a college or university and that these differences are too extreme in most cases to remain benign or below the surface. We have already reviewed the stated goals and objectives of correctional systems – security, staff morale, and rehabilitation being equally high priorities. These types of objectives – even rehabilitation when conceived of as 'treatment' – can be powerful inhibitors to any program that aims to effect the kind of liberating, self-esteem-producing, and skill-enhancing change for prisoners envisaged by the NewGate and similar programs. Instead of stability and security, such programs have the tendency to:

• Put stress on prison routines (for example, outside visitors, bringing

in equipment and supplies, requests for inmate movement, and some degree of student confidentiality)
- Raise interest in prison matters in the press and the local community
- Provide credentials for prisoners beyond the level attained by many staff
- Involve outside bureaucracies and institutions, for example, colleges and universities

While all of these developments might mesh well with the priorities of the education program and its host university, they inevitably result in increased conflict with prison priorities. At the operational levels these difficulties can become quite specific, including:

- Petty harassment of instructors and students
- Bureaucratic delays in obtaining books or the outright banning of books and other materials
- Delaying starting times for courses
- Institutional 'lock downs'
- Manipulation of space utilized by the education program
- Arbitrary rules and capricious enforcement
- Creation of new policies 'on the spot'
- Arbitrary and sudden transfers of students
- Security staff intrusion into the classroom

These are important, annoying, and in some cases crippling interventions, and for many people with experience of post-secondary programs in prison, the conflict is even more structural and too fundamental to be overcome. Jim Thomas of Northern Illinois has had experiences at Stateville penitentiary in Joliet, Illinois, which have convinced him of the essential impossibility of the task. All teachers in prison, in his view, face a 'caste system where one is forced to take sides. Everyone in prison is either identified with the staff and therefore everything they do is seen as attempted manipulation by the prisoners, or one is linked to the prisoners and seen as a troublemaker or radical by staff. Those instructors who try to steer a middle course will probably end up being distrusted by prisoners and staff members.'[15]

Morgan Lewis came to the same conclusion after attempting an innovative humanities program in a Pennsylvania prison. He argued that rehabilitation, education or positive personal growth cannot take place in an environment that 'generates a social situation that is punishing to most inmates and is characterized by continuous, but usually latent, conflict between inmates and staff.'[16] Frank Cioffi in his analysis of the issue notes that the real origin of the clash between the prison and education is in the former's focus on creating dependent individuals. The taking away of decision making and the creation of dependency 'clashes with the very ontology of post-secondary education. Infantilized by the prisons and by society, the inmate is torn between roles when he or she enters the college classroom.'[16] Owen McCullogh, operating a non-NewGate program in a Georgia state prison in 1974, saw the problem faced by higher education in an equally Manichean way: 'When a correctional institution undertakes a higher education program at least two conflicts are immediately apparent. Higher education is not status-quo oriented. It searches for truth, tolerates and welcomes diversity, challenges authority and refuses to accept pat answers. The college classroom, therefore, becomes a haven where freedom to think reigns. In a very fundamental way, its purposes and goals are antithetical to institutional policies and procedures. If the authorities of a correctional institution are not aware of this nor tolerant enough to accept it, the college program will stifle and die. This is a significant potential conflict. Only understanding and acceptance will avert it.'[18]

There are, then, at least potential contradictions at a structural and theoretical level between higher education and the prison. Do these contradictions explain the failure of the NewGate initiative? Since post-secondary education in prison has a very rich history long after 1974, one must conclude that the contradiction is not the answer. Two additional factors seem salient in the NewGate case. First, there is the confusion at the very heart of the initiative between its educational objectives and its commitment to specific rehabilitation goals. The NewGate reviewers were particularly concerned that the prisoners not confuse the rehabilitative/treatment goals of the prison with the educational/habilitative goals of the university. They recommended a form of insulation, a 'strategy that will encourage the participants to distinguish the program and its personnel from the usual prison routine and prison staff and thus prevent automatic contamination by association.'[19] We will see later that this idea of creating a 'space' between program and prison was crucial to the survival of other quite similar prison education programs. As a pioneer initiative, entering the prison when the treatment regime was still in its prime, the NewGate programs had no choice but to become closely linked to that regime with the result being confusion on the part of prisoners who thought they were signing up for education, and bitterness on the part of prison staff who thought they were admitting treatment-driven 'soul mates' into their prison.

Second, the reviewers noted their own inability to really measure just what was going on within the NewGate programs. Trapped in a world of 'it works/it doesn't work' set up by Martinson and the other critics of prison initiatives, the NewGate evaluation could only opt for one side or the other of that equation. Undoubtedly, the NewGate experience 'worked' for some prisoner-students, perhaps quite dramatically – but that information was never sought. So Project NewGate dissolved, the data on recidivism not being strong enough to warrant continued support from the federal government, especially given the scrutiny and scepticism concerning correctional interventions. Its original strength – strong backing from the federal government – meant that NewGate programs were always in the spotlight and this became its undoing.

The Office of Economic Opportunity withdrew its central funding support for Project NewGate in 1973 when the research data showed that they had not, in fact, found either a panacea or a holy grail. The individual programs stumbled on for a while, but since they were now funded only by the host prison, all the financial support for community transition and post-release integration disappeared and thus the truly innovative aspect of NewGate was gone. The universities and colleges concerned, once the federal funds were gone, also eventually withdrew support for campus-based assistance and the NewGate prison programs – those that survived – became just like all the other prison-based education initiatives.

The Santa Cruz Women's Prison Program[20]

Simultaneous with NewGate another, very different kind of prison education program was emerging in California, inspired by the potent mixture of the radical politics of the early 1970s, feminism, and the unique cultural atmosphere that characterized the Santa Cruz campus of the University of California. The Santa Cruz campus was the site of the 'history of consciousness' graduate program and was at the time on the leading edge of American radicalism as it started to shift in the 1970s from 'radical politics' narrowly defined (as epitomized by the earlier Free Speech Movement at Berkeley, the Students for a Democratic Society (SDS), and eventually the Weatherman faction) to a brand of 'cultural politics' that has become pretty much the norm in the 1990s.[21] A somewhat eclectic group of mostly women from the university made the decision in 1972 to bring education to the California Institution for Women (CIW). In the vanguard of this group was Karlene Faith (now professor of criminology at Simon Fraser University in British Columbia), whose doctoral dissertation research was based on a series of life history interviews with women prisoners at CIW. As part of this research, Faith offered a University of California extension course on 'women in society' to about fifty prisoners at CIW in the spring of 1972, an initiative that quickly became the start of a much larger program.

While contemporary with NewGate, what developed at CIW after this initial foray into the prison by Karlene Faith was a program distinctly unique from the NewGate model. From this first course there evolved a series of weekend courses and workshops taught by faculty, graduate students and others associated with the University of California at Santa Cruz and the Santa Cruz Women's Prison Program (SCWPP). The courses took place on the weekends because the prison itself was in Corona, California, about a seven-hour drive from Santa Cruz, and the instructors were all volunteers who had other weekday obligations. Clearly, this was a labour of love (and politics!), but unlike many other volunteer-based prison programs this one offered university credits with workshops taking place at least every weekend on a regularly scheduled basis. It was the 'politics' of the initiative that made it such a unique venture, indeed proof that for at least a brief period in the history of corrections 'a hundred flowers could bloom.' In this case the focus of the educational exercise was on helping the prisoner-students attain a more critical understanding of their lives and surroundings through academic courses ranging from the history of prisons to Black studies to general introductions to literature as well as through workshops on topics such as film, massage, drug use and abuse, and current events.

This was not any kind of 'treatment' that practitioners of the medical model might recognize, but in its own way it did imply a kind of treatment in the sense that the program sought to use education to 'change' the way the women prisoner-students saw the world, their place in it, and their future prospects. True to Jeffersonian sentiments, the teachers from Santa Cruz respected their students' wisdom, 'street smarts,' and insights, while at the same time presuming the need to help them transform these attributes into knowledge and behaviour that would allow them to avoid future imprisonments and engage critically with society as citizens rather than outlaws. At the same time, and completely unlike almost any other prison program, the Santa Cruz teaching staff wanted to be challenged and changed in turn in order that they too might imagine a different future. Thus, the program was intensely dialectic and reciprocal, a partnership in promoting social change. To comprehend this quite challenging objective, we can listen in on what the women involved in the program had to say about its goals, first from their public brochure from 1974. Four points are highlighted as being central to the work of the SCWPP:

1 Prisons do not prevent crime nor do they offer alternatives to prisoners, they increase the problems of living in society for people who have been locked up.
2 What prisons *do* is exist to punish and threaten the poor and to falsely reassure society in general that the state exists for the good of all and therefore deserves the power and money it appropriates.
3 The myth of rehabilitation is exploded when we realize that this economic system cannot provide jobs for those *without* prison records and *with* skills – much less an additional 1.5 million parolees.
4 The call to abolish prisons is the call to abolish the social and economic system that *produces* prisons![22]

One of the instructors, who was relatively new to the program at the time, commented during a visit to CIW that 'It seemed somewhat strange to me, a newcomer to the project, that people who were so honest about their political convictions would be allowed to enter a place which they were so critical of and which was so critical of them.' Somewhat strange indeed as anyone who has worked in or adjacent to prisons would readily acknowledge. This was southern California in the early 1970s however, and, as the instructor goes on to affirm, such access was always tenuous, often withdrawn, and, as we shall see, eventually terminated. But that is getting ahead of the story, and first we need to get a more complete sense of the purpose and structure of the program. Partly because of its grounding in the cultural politics of the time and its interest in social issues in the community as a whole rather than just prisons, the staff of the SCWPP engaged in a constant conversation about tactics and objectives, as the following from the SCWPP's 'Progress Report' of November 1974 illustrates: 'The main focus of the project is to conduct workshops within the prison on issues immediately relevant to raising the social and political consciousness of ourselves and the women prisoners ... [who] through dialogue with outsiders ... are able to develop an analysis of the social conditions which led them to prison and to develop new perspectives on their lives and goals for their futures.'

The purpose of the program is thus 'habilitative,' seeking to change the consciousness, self-image, and 'politics' of the students in order that they may re-enter society as individuals qualitatively different from the way they were at prison entry. This is quite different in a literal sense from a 'rehabilitation' program, implying as it does a 'return to a former state.' Many prison rehabilitation programs did in fact have this as an objective, desiring essentially to return the prisoner to a state prior to the assumption of the criminal role or lifestyle – hence the continual preference for remedial or literacy programs, blue-collar vocational programs, living skills programs that focused on reintegration with family, and so forth. Prisons for women, for instance, have always been known for their hairdressing vocational programs. The SCWPP's objectives were of a different order altogether, seeking not only movement up the social hierarchy through continuing university education after release, but even more important a movement up the 'critical hierarchy of understanding,' so that, in Karlene Faith's words, the woman will 'understand so well how the system functions that she will refuse to play scapegoat for the system, that she will refuse to come back and will support her sisters' efforts.'

How did all this work, and why did the prison administration allow it to work? The SCWPP was not alone in the prison. There were the usual run of vocational programs (including hairdressing), academic upgrading, and high school equivalency programs (the general education diploma, or GED), and a range of academic and vocational courses offered by a local community college. Because the SCWPP workshops took place on the weekends they were not in direct competition with these other activities, but neither were they the 'only game in town.' When functioning smoothly the SCWPP group offered two weekend workshops a month, each generally having a 'political' or 'ethnic' focus and taught by a different group of instructors. One of these weekend workshop groups is described as:

'A series of politics courses. The first was concerned with political institutions on a national level, with an overview critique of capitalism. The subsequent course focused on institutions on a local level. A psychology course offered a history and critical analysis of traditional schools of psychology, including empiricism, behaviourism, and psychoanalysis, with an emphasis on the social milieu in which they developed. This weekend also sponsors a multi-media presentation of ethnic studies. This has included guest lectures, discussions, slide shows, video tapes, and films – all concerned with Third World people in the United States and internationally. A literature course entitled 'The American Dream' examined fiction as it reflects and influences the contradictions, myths and fantasies of the dominant American culture. Special events have included a presentation on the United Farm Workers, Women's Guerrilla Theater, and special seminars on female sexuality.[23]

One other weekend a month was taken by a group of law students or recent law graduates from San Francisco who offered seminars on 'women and the law,' and the fourth weekend was handled by a group from Los Angeles who focused on art projects. Following the seminars there would often be music or other entertainment in the evenings, since the instructors were in the local town for the entire weekend and the prison was willing to accommodate the extra visiting time.

The women prisoner-students received university credit for their work in the SCWPP workshops (although this aspect of the program was always under threat from the University Extension Department since no fees were ever paid for those credits) and the experience clearly led to increased political awareness, self-esteem, and interest in personal change. In one of the project's many requests for external funding the claim was made that 'the project has succeeded in introducing significant numbers of incarcerated women to a broad array of academic and artistic concerns and skills. It has awakened their ability for analysis and has channeled their insights into more carefully reasoned perspectives of the world in which they live. It has aroused their confidence in their own abilities for academic achievement. Whereas most of the women in the initial interviewing process did not state "college" as a post-release plan, the large majority of the participants in the program do now indicate this as their immediate goal upon release.'

The group also claimed that the prison itself benefited from the program, it being a 'striking example of innovation in the penal system' and a diversion for any prisoner who might have 'thrust her undefined frustrations onto the prison staff and other prisoners [and who] may now throw her energies into her studies, new friendships and meaningful goals for herself and her peers.'[24] And, as can be imagined, the instructors were universally enthusiastic in responding to question-naires about the impact of the project on them, the interaction with the largely working-class women from ethnic minorities being intellectu-ally challenging, 'politically fulfilling,' and personally often quite intense: 'It was a dream come true ... these students gave back at least as much, really more, than they got ... they were creative, thoughtful (as in analytical) and forceful ... capable of warmth, cooperation and amazingly enough, ambition ... I really felt this to be one of the most powerful experiences of my life.'[25]

The students were enthusiastic in their praise of the workshops and the opportunity to work in more depth with individual instructors on topics that emerged from the weekend workshops. In course evalua-tions they described the program as 'meaningful,' 'exciting,' and 'rewarding' and stressed the sense of solidarity it gave them. Many students stressed how important the focus on writing had been and how they used the combination of writing and reflection to sort out problems in their lives and prospects for the future. Despite all this, by November 1974, two years after Karlene Faith's first course, the SCWPP was banned from further visits to the CIW. Given the challeng-ing and controversial nature of the academic program, it is hardly sur-prising that the prison would take such a step, but the specifics of their reasoning are instructive. There were three immediate 'incidents' that triggered the cancellation: a questionnaire about medical services in the prison distributed by one of the instructors teaching about health care; custody staff complaints about prisoners being 'massaged in a suggestive manner' by teachers in a massage therapy class; and an instance of marijuana found on one of the instructors. But these were likely resolvable through the negotiation and compromise process that had been going on for most of the previous two years. In this case the prison authorities noted issues that went deeper, such as:

1   The lack of proper screening of instructors as to motives and teach-ing abilities
2   The increasing number of instructors attending each workshop
3   The increasing focus on entertainment and refreshments instead of academic work
4   The general appearance of the instructors.
5   The lack of proper supervision of the workshops by the project coordinators

6   The presence of literature 'urging women to redefine violence as a
    tool of political liberation'

Issues of quality, style and substance were all being raised here, issues
that confront virtually any educational initiative that attempts to exist
within the prison. They are especially visible in the case of SCWPP
because the program itself, by its very nature, made them so. The coordinators tried to moderate the dress and appearance of the instructors
– arguably the easiest of the points to address – but as they were all
unpaid volunteers whose attraction to the prison teaching was linked
intimately with 'who' they were, which in those years was even more
than now linked with 'how' they looked, it seems to have been a losing
battle. The academic records of the program indicate that virtually all
students received an A for completing the workshops, a reflection no
doubt of the 'academic politics' of the time and of the unique culture of
Santa Cruz, but not something that would inspire confidence in a
much more conservative prison administration (or with other teachers
in the prison). Likewise the fact that the instructors were mostly graduate students pursuing work in the criminal justice area rather than regular university faculty may have caused some to doubt their ability to
deliver university-level instruction in the diverse fields covered in the
workshops.

Returning to an earlier discussion of the prison as institution, the
point was made that one of the primary objectives of any prison
administration is to keep the correctional staff happy, and it would
appear obvious from the correspondence surrounding the termination
of the SCWPP that this was a major factor in the prison warden's decision. The staff were deeply suspicious – as one might imagine! – of the
activities involved in the weekend workshops. To their credit, the
coordinators of the project were sensitive to this, acknowledging that
the staff 'are not sympathetic to or understanding of the camaraderie
which we enjoy with the "inmates," and they find our presence a singular and unexplainable nuisance.'[26] Here we are getting to the heart
of the issue – the nature of the relationships established between
instructors and students. Given all that we have reviewed earlier in
the discussions around prisons, Foucault, and the subject-object and
self-other nature of the prison world, any public blurring of the line
between citizen and prisoner will inevitably create significant problems. This is a problem with virtually all prison education programs
offered by 'outsiders,' but the addition of potential sexual intimacy

that was implicit at least in the Santa Cruz project made it especially visible.

The evolution of close personal ties between teacher and student in the SCWPP was not solely the result of intellectual or political bonding, or even to sexual attraction per se, but was at the very core of the feminist pedagogy being practised. Karlene Faith put the issue clearly in a 1975 SCWPP newsletter reflecting on the experience at CIW: 'In various meetings with administrators at CIW we have been repeatedly admonished against establishing "personal" relationships with the women who come to our workshops. We have in turn argued for the *necessity* of establishing personal relationships if we are to be effective as educators, much less as human beings. I think we all know that the principal reason for our "successes" at CIW is precisely our refusal (inability) to remain cool, aloof, and authoritarian in our relationships with the women who are our "students" ... An essential ingredient of our work at CIW, then, is that we do engage in a reciprocal process of sharing our selves.'

Few prison administrators understand this notion of education, and even those who do often question the degree to which it can be relevant to teaching in prison. It is, of course, quite an orthodox position in adult education if not in basic and higher education and as such should (must) be a central component of effective prison teaching. We have, therefore, a central dilemma at the core of this process and one that bedevils all such programs. It is possible, however, as we will see, to hide or mask these relationships more effectively than was the case with the SCWPP. Faith goes on, however, to raise an even more important aspect of this issue: 'Recently we have found ourselves in the middle of a troubling and paradoxical situation. For the most part, the personal relationships that have formed have been mutually valuable and positive experiences. In some cases, however, they have led to emotional involvements which have been difficult for the women at CIW to handle. This happens in human interactions anywhere. But for a woman in prison to have her hopes raised and then crushed can be excruciatingly painful and cruel ... We have to state very clearly what we can give to those relationships and what we can't give to them. Most of all, we have to be very clear in our own heads about all that; we can't go to CIW as a way to fill voids in our outside lives.'

Discounting for the sexual nature of some of the relationships being referred to in this wise counsel as being unique to this case, the issue is, in fact, a universal one for anyone engaged in working with prisoners.

The professional therapists and counsellors who operated within the parameters of the medical model were presumably trained to resist or set up barriers to such relationships, and virtually all prison administrations forbid contact between corrections staff and released prisoners, thereby inhibiting the making of promises or offers of assistance in the 'real world.' But teachers, volunteers, lay counsellors, and others who flourished within prisons during the era of opportunity models and humane containment had only austere, 'foreign,' and easy to ignore regulations to follow, and like the SCWPP group they often found it too difficult and compromising to leave their work with prisoners at the front gate at the end of the day.

Just as important was the issue implicit in Faith's observations that raising expectations that cannot be fulfilled is perhaps doing more harm than good. The women from CIW were for the most part not likely to attend college after release, and if they tried many would not succeed. The program in the prison was not substantial enough to give them the proper academic and social background, and SCWPP, unlike the NewGate programs, had virtually no community-based program to provide them with housing, financial assistance and counselling – indeed, very few prison-based programs post-NewGate have had such resources. Armed with some college credits, a glimpse into a middle-class academic culture, new critical perspectives on self and society and perhaps some roughly hewn expectations, what were these women from CIW to 'do' upon release? To their credit, the staff and instructors from SCWPP attempted to raise funds to give the program a more solid footing, hire permanent staff, and develop a community side to their prison activities, but they were unsuccessful and, having other lives and other projects, moved on when the project was cancelled.

Humane Containment in the United Kingdom and Prison Education

As might perhaps be imagined in a pragmatic and somewhat anti-theoretical culture like that in the United Kingdom, there was no unitary response within the prison services to the crisis of confidence posed by the observation that 'emperor treatment' seemed to have no clothes on – or at least was rather poorly dressed. While humane containment and positive custody became official policy, reflecting a general shift towards a concern with the criminal as inmate rather than as potential citizen, for example, the criminal as he is in prison rather than as he will be after release, treatment or a 'policy of care' continued to be a part of most prison regimes. The two examples examined here illustrate this dualism, the Barlinnie Special Unit in Scotland epitomizing humane containment in its most extreme form, and the educational activities of adult educators and various educational institutions providing evidence of a continuing concern for both a positive experience while in custody and an improved opportunity to change direction after release.

The penal system in England, Scotland and Northern Ireland is different from its counterparts in the United States and Canada in that each component of the United Kingdom has a unitary prison service. Thus, while the United States has a confusing and sometimes chaotic network of federal penitentiaries, state prisons, and local jails each run by separate administrative systems, and Canada has an often overlapping federal system and ten provincial systems, England has one prison service, as does Scotland, and as does Northern Ireland. This has resulted, many would argue, in a more professionalized prison service as well as in more universal policy direction. In the 1970s with the decline of treatment and the new focus on custody the result was perhaps even more demoralization of prison service staff than was the case in other jurisdictions, as the mission of the profession shifted away from proactive intervention in the lives and futures of the inmates. The interventions or programs that did persist in the prisons, at least in the field of education, followed either an adult education approach or an elite approach to higher education that reflected the society at large. There were no NewGate initiatives and certainly no SCWPPs in the United Kingdom in the 1970s.

The Barlinnie Special Unit

The Scottish prison service in the 1960s had a reputation as a rough place to do time, not only because the nature of the prisons and staff but also because of the tough qualities of the prisoners. The 'cages' at Peterhead Prison were notorious 'holes' in which the truly recalcitrant and violent were housed, and conditions were not much better at other maximum security sites. Glasgow slums produced a steady flow of violent, rebellious criminals who served their apprenticeship, Genet-like, in the Scottish prisons. In 1973, spurred by the advent of humane containment in England and the fear of increased prison violence resulting from the abolition of capital punishment in 1965, and built on the theories and speculations of local prison psychologist David

Cooke, the Scottish service set up an experiment in penal community living for the toughest of the tough in a small prison within a prison at Her Majesty's Prison Barlinnie just outside of Glasgow.

A small building with its own walled compound inside the main prison, the Barlinnie Special Unit was designed to allow a relaxed and flexible regime to operate within a secure perimeter. The building contained two stacked tiers of five cells each, a kitchen and dining area, common recreation and shop areas, and a small exercise yard. The yard was enclosed by a solid wall topped by concertina wire, and from the yard, looking over the wall and through the wire, one could just see the top tiers of the massive Victorian ranges of Barlinnie Prison that surrounded the unit. The Unit was initially staffed by twelve prison officers and a governor. At Cooke's suggestion, it was planned with a psychiatric treatment model in mind, but this plan was in fact never implemented given the disrepute into which such approaches had fallen by the mid-1970s. Instead, Cooke pursued a 'self-help therapeutic community' approach based on 'free expression, community and cooperative responsibility, self-awareness, trust and humanity.'[27] While it was presumed that practical experience in cooperative community living would be of some rehabilitative value, the primary motivation for the experiment was inmate management, in this case a humane alternative for men who otherwise seemed destined for death or the cages.

At the heart of the experiment was the formal community meeting held every Tuesday that all members of staff and all inmates were expected to attend. Visitors were often invited to attend such meetings, and they became a small showpiece over the years of just what could be accomplished with a bit of democracy and humane, if still spartan treatment. Each community meeting elected a chair and minutes were taken, with discussions usually concerned with internal domestic matters affecting the general management of the unit. Decisions reached by the meeting were implemented, even if the governor did not share the view of the majority – a point noted with some incredulity by the visitor from Her Majesty's Inspectorate of Prisons.[28] Personal problems and matters relating to the behaviour of individual prisoners might be discussed if the individual was present and agreed to them being raised. A flavour of the process is given in the following diary entry by one of the prisoners: 'The first staff/inmate meeting I attended was a pretty formal occasion. A chairman was elected, an inmate, and minutes of the meeting were taken by a member of staff. It seemed silly to sit there, grown men looking at each other knowing that underneath the surface we all disliked each other ... Just the idea of sitting down with a group of staff was out of this world'.[29]

In addition to this formal meeting, an informal meeting took place once a week when David Cooke visited the unit to discuss problems arising from the behaviour or attitudes of individuals or the group as a whole. Finally, a special meeting of the community could be called at any time by a member of staff or a prisoner who felt that a matter warranted immediate discussion or that a conflict needed to be resolved: 'In the claustrophobic environment of the Unit this facility is considered to be an important safety-valve but is very seldom used. New inmates to the Unit are acclimatized to the philosophy of the regime by smaller groups of two staff and two inmates.'[30]

At the start-up in 1973 five inmates volunteered for the special unit, with the average number of men at any time being about seven. They lived in single cells (10 feet by 7 feet) and during the day had freedom of movement throughout the Unit. Their cells could be decorated, they wore civilian clothing, had open, unsupervised visits, cooked their own food, and enjoyed uncensored mail. The interior walls of the unit were covered by murals, posters, and other attempts to enliven a particularly drab and claustrophobic structure. During one of my visits to the unit in the mid-1980s, it was clear that prison officers and prisoners had evolved an easy relationship, sharing space and domestic responsibilities. Despite these apparent advantages, the unit was seldom full, and given the nature of their sentences, the tenure of those who were there tended to be long term. There was one death in the unit, a drug overdose, and several requests over the years to transfer back to the more familiar regular prison system. Mistakes were made and lessons learned, and during my visits it was apparent that both staff and prisoners were conscious of being participants in an experiment, and one that needed constant defending. After all, Barlinnie seemed to run counter to every commonsensical notion about crime and punishment, with the greatest privileges being granted to the most disobedient prisoners.

As in the case of the NewGate programs and the SCWPP, the Barlinnie Special Unit was the target of constant criticism from within the prison service in the United Kingdom, especially since, as the report of the Inspectorate of Prisons noted in 1982, both 'staff and inmates are convinced that the Unit has pioneered new concepts in the treatment of inmates which could, with advantages, be introduced into the regimes of other establishments.'[31] Typical of the responses to this notion was the blistering attack by two prison officers in an issue of the *Prison Service Journal* in 1986: 'All the Special Unit has done is show that if a Unit is created for a very small number of inmates, if it is given high manning levels of specially trained staff, if the inmates on the Unit are given everything they could want, and if the success of the Unit is not measured in any rigorous way, then the inmates on the Unit will say they like it, and will tell naive, gullible, caring visitors what a wonderful, forward-looking establishment it is, and these visitors will leave believing the Unit to be successful.'[32]

Hyperbolic attacks like this were easily parried by defenders of the special unit, especially since actual conditions in the unit were far from ideal, but they did strike home in the sense that the experiment was quite modest in terms of size. By 1985, twelve years after it had started, only twenty-three men had been admitted to the unit. Of these – discounting the seven who were in residence – six had been returned to other prisons to serve out their sentences, nine had been released, and one had died in the unit. Of the nine released prisoners, only two had re-offended as of 1985, a remarkably low rate given the high-risk quality of the prisoners.

Like the SCWPP, the special unit was a classic example of the weird and wonderful world of prison regimes during the 1970s era of opportunities and openness. It served to revive interest in the 'democratic community' models of prison life that had been tried in the nineteenth century by prison reform pioneers like Alexander MacCononochie, Zebulon Brockway, and Thomas Mott Osborne, the idea that if you allow the prisoner 'some sort of say in the ordering of his daily life, give him materials to express his inner and previously untapped self, change utterly the relationship between himself and his jailers ... a new being may slowly emerge.'[33] This belief, or perhaps article of faith, was immensely popular in the non-penal world of the liberal intelligentsia, artists, and others who saw prisons as archetypes of all that had gone wrong in the era of postwar conservatism. This was reinforced in reference to the special unit because of the soon-to-be famous art work and literary publications of the prisoners. In sculpture, pottery, poetry, and autobiography the special unit proved to be a hothouse of creativity, its most famous graduate being Jimmy Boyle, author of *A Sense of Freedom*.[34] As a result, visitors flocked to the special unit to meet the prisoners, view the art being made, and in general to celebrate the possibilities it seemed to promise. This open door policy was encouraged by the unit staff as a way to 'occupy these lads in the wintertime ... in the winter it's a very claustrophobic situation.'[35]

Two elements combine to make the special unit especially important for this exploration of alternatives to the treatment or medical model approach to deviance and criminality. First, and perhaps most important, is the idea that it is through democratic and communitarian interaction that individuals grow and mature and thereby alter their beliefs, attitudes, and behaviours. Especially important here is the idea that such a process is reciprocally reinforcing, that non-criminal community norms can thrive in a penal setting. In the special unit, a particularly good example of this process, because of its size, the longevity of the prisoners' stay, and the intensive gaze of the outside, behaviours were peer monitored: 'If someone does something detrimental to the community, he has to answer to the community, and it is no secret that the hot seat can be, and is, a salutary experience.'[36] The approach is part Maoist, utilizing the powerful tools of shame and confession to forge cooperative behaviours, and part classic therapeutic community, creating a social milieu in which an individual can find acceptance, bond with a community, and develop social responsibility. The second element was educational, though not in a formal sense. The men utilized their relative freedom to experiment with new forms of expression mainly through art and writing, similar to some of the work being done at the SCWPP workshops. The principle being acted upon here was that education is not about skills or formal learning, but rather about exploration, growth, and creativity and would assume different forms with different learners. This very much reflected the 'radical' educational theories of the time and was certainly a challenge to the more traditional educational approaches common to prisons.

The special unit survived the more retributive and individualist 1980s, but it was no longer the centre-piece of public attention as it had been in the 1970s. Indeed it quickly became marginalized, and in 1995 it was shut down. As challenging to the 'system' as the SCWPP had been in California, the unit had survived in large part because of the spectacular public success of some of its alumni, most notably Jimmy Boyle and Hugh Collins (whose *Autobiography of a Murderer* was published in 1996), and because it did effectively contain extremely difficult prisoners. But the art was fundamentally dependent on the talent of individuals and that could not be programmed for over the long term. The support from the artistic community was never guaranteed to last, and as is so often the case with the media, other causes intervened to distract attention. Likewise, the unit was a therapeutic community but could not be experimentally studied without disrupting the effectiveness of the therapy, and the number of subjects was so small that no meaningful generalizations were possible – hence it was not of any significant research value to the academic community. During my visits in the mid-1980's, after its high point but while it was still a vibrant community, one had the definite sense that it needed to expand from its small base to survive, and as well needed a stronger theory to support its cost to the prison service both in money and aggravation.

Prison Education as Adult Education – the English Approach

Like the SCWPP project, the special unit by its exceptional nature can serve to illustrate more clearly important themes and issues in the area of penal interventions in the lives of prisoners. But it remains an exception, and as in the case of the SCWPP, did not manage to break out of its specific context. Much more important in terms of impact were the education programs carried on in prisons throughout the United Kingdom under the general heading of adult or higher education. There were a number of important university-based programs in English prisons and virtually all prisons in the United Kingdom had students pursuing Open University courses, but it was the general field of adult education that was dominant in terms of programming.

Adult education is a discipline in its own right and has traditions and theories that are distinct from education for young people and even higher education. Pre-eminent among these traditions and theories is the idea that adult learners are capable of playing a leading role in determining what they want to learn, how they want to learn it, and what they will do with it. In part a result of the natural respect that one might give to adults in determining such matters, this also stems from the large role that adult education plays in the field of 'training,' the delivery of specific skills or other tools that adults need to improve on or change their vocation. In the field of prisons, adult education intersects with both prisoners and prison staff, generally by educating the former and training the latter.

It is fair to say that North America has led the way in modern times in primary and secondary education for young people, raising literacy rates, and secondary school completion rates higher than those prevalent in the United Kingdom and continental Europe. Likewise, access to college and university education is much broader in North America, than in Europe, and especially in the United Kingdom. On the other hand and perhaps because of this, adult education has a much stronger tradition in the United Kingdom than in North America where it has been split between those who are more focused on literacy and training and others concerned with human development. The latter group have tended to keep away from prisons, feeling that their objective of promoting personal growth and self-actualization is in 'conflict with the mechanistic orientation toward inmates that is inherent in penal institution programs ... correctional programs seek to rehabilitate, i.e., modify and adapt behaviour, rather than maximize human potential.'[37] Thus, in the specific context of the prison, education programs in North America are more often than not delivered in traditional secondary school formats or in the traditional higher education manner via lectures and seminars. In the United Kingdom, on the other hand, education in prison is seen as 'a discipline in its own right,' part of the larger tradition of adult education.[38] While the pre-eminence of this professional cadre of adult educators in prison has been eroded in recent years by the contracting out of much educational provision, during the 1970s and 1980s they were a powerful force within the prison system.

Norman Jepson, an experienced teacher, researcher and educational administrator, has described the position of the adult educator in English prisons in terms of the insider-outsider issue raised in the beginning of this study in reference to my own stance *vis-à-vis* the prison.[39] On the one hand, Jepson argues, the professional standing of the prison adult education profession leads to a significant involvement and even identification with the Prison Service itself. Educators are involved with staff training and are often seconded to the Prison Service either in actual prison administration or in the staff college. The local education authorities (similar to North American school districts or boards), who were the direct employers of the adult prison educators, worked closely with the Prison Service in training teachers and providing resources for local staff training. The adult prison educator in the United Kingdom is thus, potentially at least, a classic 'insider' in terms of the prison.

Yet, Jepson reminds us, for that educator to be effective in working with the prisoners in the classroom it may be necessary to be an 'outsider' or, in a more invasive sense, an actual 'invader' of the total institution with all its connotation of subversion, opposition, and victory over. Basing his argument on the idea of the prison as the 'total institution' defined by Goffman, Jepson must conclude that any education or other rehabilitative or change-oriented activity that is part of or even perceived to be part of that institution will only serve to reinforce its objectives; in the case of the prison these objectives being stability and conformity.[40] This is part one of a two-part dilemma that goes to the heart of all efforts to encourage change and development with prisoners: first, 'can' it be done and, second, 'should' one even try? Jepson, like most adult educators in the United Kingdom, argues that yes, it can be done, but is less convinced that it should be done. The key to its possibility, according to Jepson, is to establish strong professional links between teachers in prison and educational institutions. Thus, while prison adult educators must work with and learn from their Prison Service colleagues they must at the same time remain independent of them. Here, then, was the strength of the system in the United Kingdom, namely the existence of a system-wide adult education network with strong bases in further education colleges and in universities.

Should adult education have as its objective the rehabilitation of its prisoner-students? Here the response in the United Kingdom was a much stronger 'no' than in North America, even given the nervousness post-Martinson concerning any linkage between effectiveness and post-release behaviour. In the United Kingdom the strong tradition of adult education being 'good' per se and having as its primary objective the maximizing of human potential overrode concerns for more utilitarian outcomes. While the more training-oriented and practical educational tradition in North America accepted the necessity of a concern for specific outcomes, even if only improved prison management, in the United Kingdom and across Europe the opposite was the case.

The European Position – For Something Completely Different

The adult education tradition had strong roots in the United Kingdom, but in fact it was less powerful there than on the European Continent. Jepson's arguments, summarized in his 1986 paper 'Stone Walls Do Not a Prison Make,'[41] found a firm echo in the Council of Europe's 1990 report entitled *Education in Prison*. That report, drawn up in coordination with the council's earlier (1987) paper called *European Prison Rules*, put the argument this way: 'It is essential that all engaged in providing education in prisons should be encouraged to see those in their classes as adults involved in normal adult education activities.

The students should be approached as responsible people who have choices available to them. In other words, the prison context should be minimized and the past criminal behaviour of the students should be kept to the background, so that the normal atmosphere, interactions, and processes of adult education can flourish as they would in the outside community. Fundamental to such an approach is that the educational programme should be based on the individual needs of those taking part.'[42]

These were sound principles of adult education, but as Kevin Warner from the Republic of Ireland, who chaired the committee, said in a recent paper, underlying the whole effort was the acknowledgment that 'prison damages people and should be used as a last resort and, where used, the suffering inherent in imprisonment should be minimised.'[43] In the effort to counteract the effect of the prison, the European report proposed a direct attack on the Foucaultean reality, with the prisoner being treated as a 'responsible subject' who may, despite the constraints of the prison, choose to take advantage of opportunities to enter a process of individual development.

In discussing the issue of prisoner motivation, the report highlights the attainment of 'a degree of autonomy for the education sector' as a crucial factor in persuading prisoners that taking part in education will not require them to 'capitulate psychologically to the prison system.' In addition to being structurally apart from the prison, teachers must have some leeway or discretion in the way they approach their work. 'Clearly, crime cannot be condoned and the futility of a criminal life may well be raised as an issue in class, but there are aspects of the prisoner's culture that the adult educator must respect or at least accept. These aspects may include a critical view of authority, anger at social injustice, and solidarity with one another in the face of adversity. As in any field of adult education, respect and acceptance of the students and potential students are crucial to motivation and participation.'[44] In Warner's paper these approaches are contrasted directly with what he calls the Anglo-American model, one based on negative stereotyping of prisoners, vengeance, and massive use of incarceration. With the Council of Europe approach, we seem much closer to the SCWPP project in California, although with a much more careful rhetoric focusing more on tolerance than on advocacy and with a determined effort to become the guiding set of principles across national jurisdictions. We have come a long way from the treatment approach of the earlier era.

The University of Victoria Program in Canada

There were several large, multi-site, sophisticated post-secondary education programs established in the early 1970s that followed on from the NewGate model. Universities and community colleges across the United States and Canada began offering credit courses in prisons in this era of opportunities, and several stand out as being particularly innovative, including the University of Wisconsin Post-Secondary Re-Entry Education Program (PREP) initiative, the Wilmington College program in Ohio, the University of LaVerne program in California, and the Boston College program. The most impressive feature of these initiatives was their attempt to go beyond a hundred flowers blooming to the creation of something akin to a garden of perennials within the prisons. In each case they were in it for the long haul and combined the central mission of teaching liberal arts university courses to adult prisoners with a concern for research and a distant but sustained partnership with the corrections service in which they operated. Some, the Boston College program being the prime example, were run by university volunteers at no cost to the prison, but most existed on annual or other short-term contracts with a corrections system. The one that seems to include the most complete set of attributes of this kind of program, however, is the British Columbia post-secondary prison education program started by the University of Victoria in 1972 and taken over by Simon Fraser University in 1984 until its eventual cancellation in 1993. Coincidentally, this program provided me in 1974 with my introduction to prisons.

When the University of Victoria first suggested offering university courses in English literature and history to selected federal prisoners in British Columbia prisons it was, like the NewGate programs, within the larger context of the medical model. In this case the university proposed to apply a specific educational 'treatment' – liberal arts courses – to a selected group of prisoners who it was speculated suffered from certain cognitive and moral 'deficits.' The following is from Dr T.A.A. Parlett whose doctoral research formed the basis of the initial pilot project at the British Columbia Penitentiary in 1972: 'There is a small but positive correlation between moral knowledge and moral acts; it, therefore, seemed reasonable to us to postulate that if we taught morality then the number of moral acts should increase and immoral acts should decrease. It was obvious, though, that an attempt to bluntly teach moral knowledge would be rejected by the inmates. Therefore, the moral implications must be hidden inside a suitable vehicle. It was decided that the most suitable vehicle would be university classes.'[45] First-and second-year literature and history classes formed the core of the experiment, with some social science courses included in response to student demand. The courses were offered 'straight,' that is, with no overt modifications designed to elicit moral debate. Nonetheless, in fact the seminar discussions did often centre on value differences among students, between students and instructor, and students and text. Although this overtly 'experimental' approach really only characterized the university program in its first 'project' years (1972–4), for some time after that staff at the university continued to probe using tests and interviews for evidence of moral shifts and cognitive growth among the students.

This probing into the effects of the university experience shifted eventually from a preoccupation with moral development, but it did continue throughout the twenty-year life of this program, thereby setting it apart from virtually all other similar programs and, for that matter, virtually all prison programs per se. From its inception the offering of courses in the prisons was linked to a research agenda focusing on the effects of education. Besides the initial doctoral research of Parlett, Ayers and Linden carried out a detailed experimental post-release study of the initial group of students complete with a matched group of non-prisoner-students,[46] Ayers and colleagues carried out a larger follow-up study of released prisoner-students in 1979,[47] and in 1996 a full-scale follow-up of 654 former prisoner-students was completed.[48] This extensive body of research data assembled over such a long time period enables us to reach conclusions about effectiveness that are much better grounded than, for instance, the NewGate evaluations or assertions about effectiveness based on snapshot samples or anecdotal reports.

The university program funded by the Correctional Service operated for the first few years in two federal prisons near Vancouver, British Columbia: the late Victorian maximum security British Columbia Penitentiary (approximately 400 inmates) and the much newer, campus-style Matsqui Medium Security Institution (approximately 350 inmates). By the mid-1980s program sites were established at two other prisons in British Columbia, William Head and Mountain Institutions (approximately 300 inmates each) and the old penitentiary's replacement, Kent Maximum Security Institution. Because the federal correctional system operated a 'cascading' system within the region, the university program was able to retain most of its students as they moved up or down the various security levels. This multi-site presence within the B.C. region was a tremendous advantage in terms of student retention and completion rates, one few other post-secondary programs could utilize.

Within these independent but interdependent programs prisoner-students pursued their studies mostly on a full-time basis, the school being considered by the prison to be a work location. Each site had a university coordinator who taught core courses and administered the program as well as instructors who travelled from the university or who were employed to teach in several program sites. The sizes of the programs varied, with an average of about forty students enrolled at each program site every thirteen-week semester, each taking two to four courses a semester. The curriculum continued to focus on literature and history as the required 'core,' but included substantial offerings from most of the social sciences and humanities departments as well as the occasional science or mathematics course. The classes were organized in lecture or seminar formats, and by 1977 advanced level courses leading to a Bachelor of Arts degree had become part of the regular offerings. Built around the theories of cognitive development (the criminal as decision maker) and moral development (criminal with moral deficits), the program saw itself as addressing fundamental student needs which, indirectly, also addressed correctional ambitions.

These correctional ambitions had not disappeared with Martinson's 1974 screed. Throughout the 1970s Correctional Service of Canada (CSC) officials, particularly those in the Education and Training Division, persisted in talking about education in prison as a means of 'moral reformation' and necessary to 'prepare inmates, upon discharge, to assume their responsibilities as citizens and to conform to the requirements of the law.'[49] These assumptions existed, of course, within the much more modest and indeed passive official correctional context of the 'opportunities model.' One can never presume, however, that policy and even paradigm shifts are total victories or even necessarily conclusive. Throughout the late 1970s and early 1980s there was a muted state of tension between the advocates of the opportunities model, who basically argued that the prison should as far as possible seek to minimize the damage it might cause and allow prisoners to help themselves if they so chose, and those stubborn advocates of a more proactive intervention in the lives (and minds and morals) of the imprisoned.

The University of Victoria program had a foot in both camps, so to speak, being clearly an 'opportunity' in that it was open to all prisoners who could qualify and, having strong links with external institutions, able to maintain some 'distance' from the prison. To that degree it was simply an off-campus program of the university. On the other hand, the program's theoretical and research agenda based on the advancement of individual cognitive and moral development (if not transformation) through education made it of more than passing interest to correctional administrators still wedded to an interventionist policy. Within the university program both camps had advocates, leading to a kind of creative tension that made the program particularly vibrant.

The decade from 1975 to 1985 was undoubtedly a low point for morale within correctional services and conversely a heady era for advocates of alternatives to the corrections agenda. The university program, while always able to cooperate with the administration of the prison system, nonetheless became subversive of this corrections agenda. Deliberately moving away from both the psychology-based 'disease' model and the disempowering determinism of the sociological model, the university program put its emphasis on understanding the criminal as a 'rational decision maker,' on individual responsibility but responsibility seen in a specific social, cultural, and psychological context.[50] Norman Jepson captured a sense of this after a visit to British Columbia: 'This is the starting point of the Canadian experiment, in which a university sought to introduce into a penitentiary a programme of study, based on the humanities, which aimed not at reforming the prisoner but rather at challenging the framework within which he makes decisions. It seeks to provide him or her with the opportunity to look and react to situations in a variety of frameworks rather than exclusively within the framework to which he has been accustomed.'[51] The key notion here is that of 'framework' or the context for decision making, the words implying not just a social dimension but also a cultural, cognitive, and ethical dimension. Implicit here is the recognition that social environments and economic realities can restrict the range of choices open to individuals, but need not be determinative of specific choices.

Several threads contributed to the dynamic notion of decision making that came to characterize the university program's approach to the prisoner-student. The commitment to creating a radically different alternative cultural milieu within the university program was informed in part by Luria's observations that 'sociohistorical shifts not only introduce new content into the mental world of human beings; they also create new forms of activity and new structures of cognitive functioning.'[52] Thus, while other voices were developing arguments that it was the cognitive ability of the prisoners that needed addressing rather than the content of their thinking, the university program was placing primary emphasis on the content and on the socio-cultural context in which the thinking took place.[53]

The work in moral development theory and praxis by Lawrence Kohlberg, Jack Arbuthnot, Peter Scharf, and others provided additional support for the crucial role of the context within which work on decision making could take place. They argued that to achieve development or growth in both the cognitive and moral domains one must create an educational setting that is isolated from the remainder of the prison in as many aspects of daily life and governance as possible, and which allows for practice in translating one's highest level of cognitive skills into thinking about very real, everyday conflicts or dilemmas, a conclusion very similar to that arrived at by the evaluators of the New-Gate programs: 'We would argue that experience-based activity involving conflict resolution, problem-solving, participation in decision-making and role taking opportunities beget compliance and independence of more than an uncritical law and order sort. Educational experiences of conflict and participation extend the human's capacity to differentiate and integrate and to contemplate different points of view, in other words, to develop principles for evaluating 'right' and 'wrong' and perfecting a sense of responsibility, obligation, law, and justice.'[54] Just as persuasive was research into the effects of higher education which argued that 'the most important contribution to a student's intellectual and moral development comes not from the curriculum, but from the realization of community.'[55] If 'campus climate' in fact plays the 'crucial role in changing the values and attitudes of students,'[56] and if the 'two most powerful determinants producing change in the students are their roommates and the intellectual atmosphere and traditions of the college'[57], and if prisons are the authoritarian 'cognitive slums' that 'teach dependency, not self-reliance or personal growth,'[58] then something had to change if university in prison was to be in any way successful.

For the university program, constructing an alternative community within the prison meant experimenting with democratic decision making within the program, offering classes that focused on controversial subjects, creating a fine arts and theatre program with opportunities for performance and role-taking, and importing into the prison as many personalities as possible from the university community. Accomplishing this required from the prison a degree of autonomy that in many respects was unprecedented in its liberality and cooperativeness. The results were impressive. Research in 1979 into the post-release lives of the seventy-three prisoner-students who had been released and who met certain minimum criteria for inclusion in the study showed a recidivism rate of only 14 per cent, high rates of employment, strong evidence of social change and social satisfaction, and increased personal stability.[59] The response of the men to the opportunities offered in the program was what one might have expected: 'One of the most important aspects of the SFU prison program is the atmosphere of mutual respect that develops as the students and the professors struggle together to accomplish the task of learning. Real learning is not about indoctrination or intimidation so often used in prison; it is about discovering the truth, finding it, testing it and using it to develop the tools to better understand and operate in the world. Rehabilitation really means expanding the awareness of choice that we each have as individuals within society so we are not doomed to repeat old patterns.'[60] During this period of relative stability and quiescence on the part of corrections, the university program struggled to keep centred on this dimension of education and mutual respect, fending off the potentially corrosive effects that direct engagement with student personal development, and excessive concern about post-release behaviours could have on the commitment of the program to education per se. Asserting that 'education is seductive, socialization therapy is not,' the staff of the program insisted that 'while it is admittedly important from the perspective of society and corrections that this program help reduce recidivism and change lives, this can only be accomplished by offering a credible education program.'[61] But, just listen to how two criminologists more interested in rehabilitation than education described what was 'really' going on:

UVIC challenged educationalists to de-emphasize the three Rs and to focus on cognitive restructuring, moral development, and problem solving in the interpersonal and social skills necessary for the prisoner to function prosocially in society. These goals were taught in undergraduate humanities courses, a direct but subtle method of teaching social cognitive skills. Professors, employing small groups and Socratic dialogue, served as role models and presented information not as a 'treatment' of personal deficits, but for the purposes of working toward a university degree. This latter strategy was important, as many of the participants were older high-risk offenders with long and serious criminal histories, who might resent a traditional authoritarian approach.[62]

So, Norman Jepson on a visit from England saw the program as delivering traditional university education, instructors perceived their activities as at least slightly subversive, students saw a forum for growth and mutual respect, and the criminologists saw a hidden process of treatment and rehabilitation. At least four schools of thought were contending here, and probably more, and that no doubt accounts in large part for the success of this endeavour and others like it. In the presence of a policy vacuum, the penological amateurs who found themselves in charge of a large, complex prison education program ended up in a kind of theoretical and policy anarchy, taking action in a multitude of areas and in a multitude of directions, dependent in part on the mix of staff and student interests – but all the time sustaining the solid core of the educational program.

What was that 'sustaining core'? In virtually all of the post-secondary programs operating in this period the curriculum was grounded in the classic liberal arts disciplines, often with a strong focus on the humanities. There was an explicit assumption operating in all these prison education initiatives that 'knowledge' rather than, for instance, 'work' or even 'insight' can lead to freedom. There was an assumption of there being a link between learning and action in the world, and this assumption was central to the conviction that these programs could change peoples' lives in the sense of helping them to remain free of crime and hence of further imprisonment. This notion has its roots in the Socratic tradition that evil (inevitably seen as unfreedom) flows from ignorance and that freedom means 'enlightened choice ... action in which habit, reflex or suggestion are superseded by an individual's fundamental judgments of good and evil ... action whose premises are explicit ... action which proceeds from personal reflection and integration.'[63] To be free, to exercise enlightened choice, requires an awareness of possibilities as well as the *skills, abilities,* and *will* to *recognize* and *act* on those possibilities.

While the program-as-program provided a context for individual growth or maturation much like any schooling situation, and while teaching staff acted as role models and through their efforts at enriching the educational experience no doubt enhanced the prospects for change and development among the students, it was the curriculum itself that carried the primary burden. Some social science and more 'practical' courses were included in that curriculum, but its strength was never in its potential for direct application to future employment. Instead, it had more esoteric ambitions. In assessing the impact of liberal education in general Winter and his colleagues note the depth inherent in such a standard question in a history examination as 'Compare and contrast the Renaissance and Reformation.' Such a question calls for the 'integration of an enormous amount of confusing and conflicting material ... it requires knowledge of a wide range of historical facts [and since] there is no single correct answer or set of facts – a good answer depends more on how the facts are selected, arranged, organized and interpreted.'[64] Forster, in his assessment of an English prison education program run by Leicester University, notes that the notion of a long-term payoff which is part of any university education helped the prisoner-students moderate their tendency to desire immediate gratification.[65] In Heath's study of the impact of higher education on student values he singles out literature courses as decisive in stimulating 'the largest range of maturing effects,' enabling students to 'think more clearly and logically, to express themselves concisely, and to write efficiently and quickly.'[66] These skills and abilities are crucial aspects of the Socratic quest for freedom, but the more crucial set of changes are deeper and more fundamental, involving, as George Steiner claims, a new way of seeing, acquiring a new set of lenses through which paths of action in the world are illuminated:

A man who has read Book xxiv of the *Iliad* – the night meeting of Priam and Achilles – or the chapter in which Alyosha Karamazov kneels to the stars, who has read Montaigne's chapter xx and Hamlet's use of it, and who is not altered, whose apprehension of his own life is unchanged, who does not, in some subtle yet radical manner, look on the room in which he moves, on those who knock at the door, differently, has read only with the blindness of physical sight. Can one read *Anna Karenina* or Proust without experiencing a new infirmity or occasion in the very core of one's sexual feelings? ... He who has read Kafka's *Metamorphosis* and can look into the mirror unflinching may technically be able to read print, but is illiterate in the only sense that matters.[67]

Idealistic stuff, one might say, and question its usefulness in prison.

But there are two important points here. First, the instructors in these university programs, based as they were in the universities and in their disciplines, believed in Steiner's point – they believed in the transformative power implicit in literature, history, philosophy, sociology, or geography – and in so doing presumed that they could pass it on to their students. Second, Steiner is acknowledging that the transfer is not automatic, that concentration camp or gulag guards also read Goethe and Tolstoy, and that many prisoner-students would remain 'illiterate in the only sense that matters.' The liberal arts were not seen as a panacea, a magic bullet that would defeat the lure of crime, but rather as providing the first steps into a new way of thinking about oneself in relation to others and to society.

All this was, of course, incredibly complex and thus all but incomprehensible to correctional bureaucrats – not because they were in any way incapable of such comprehension, but rather because they needed simpler, more elegant explanations to satisfy both politicians and the public. The educators attached to the University of Victoria program like the activists within the SCWPP program, the creators and participants of the special unit at Barlinnie and all the other programs described and alluded to here had constructed exceedingly complex systems within which equally complex processes of change, development, maturation, and transformation were taking place. As mentioned earlier in respect to the post-secondary program, for these complex processes to occur successfully the individuals concerned had to be exposed to at least the following:

- An awareness of the possibility for individual change or development, for a different way of living a life that did not start from a premise of personal inadequacy or deformity – that it was possible and perhaps even desirable to build a life within the parameters of the law that incorporated one's history, personality, and ideology rather than necessitated starting anew, that one did not need, in the words of the Council of Europe's report, to psychologically capitulate to the prison in order to lead a virtuous life.
- The basic skills and abilities necessary to embark on this new path, such as literacy, numeracy, communications, and the personal and social skills necessary in putting them to use. Just as important as the acquisition of such skills and abilities was the presence of an environment in which they could be nurtured, tested, and sustained. Enhanced abilities in areas of the personality such as self-

control, tolerance, confidence, and even communications are acquired most effectively in practical situations rather than artificial therapy settings, classrooms, or private study.

• The will to recognize and act upon these new possibilities, to employ the skills, abilities and insights acquired 'inside' in real life situations on the 'outside.'

Such a complex and potentially fragile process of personal development may have remained largely hidden from public view and anathema to the understandings of many corrections professionals, but as long as corrections services remained unsure or at least undecided as to their missions or objectives, subsets of corrections like the university program could prosper by carving out their own 'space' while serving a variety of masters. Thus, the university program contributed to institution management, provided a high-status educational opportunity in a setting relatively aloof from the prison, maintained a research program that supported the possibility of positive change in prisoners, and by its institutional links became involved with community corrections. Throughout much of the early 1980s this condition of bureaucratic neutrality (or paralysis) within corrections generally contributed to the steady growth of programs like this. Even a threatened cancellation because of fiscal restraint in 1983 was overturned thanks almost completely to the strength of the program, the energy of its staff, and the quality of its supporters in the community. In a world in which very little of a positive nature seemed to be happening in prisons, experiments like this seemed worth keeping.

A Word about Recidivism

What are the possible outcomes when an individual is released from imprisonment? Or, in other words, what might it mean to say that an effort to change or transform that individual has succeeded or failed? There are six possible outcomes:

1 Full integration with society and no return to criminal activity of any sort
2 Return to criminal activity without detection by the criminal justice system
3 Revocation of parole or other term of release because of a technical rule infraction

4   Rearrest for a new crime, but no conviction
5   Conviction for a new crime but no re-incarceration
6   Reincarceration for a new crime

Outcomes (1)–(5) could all be interpreted as successes – (1) clearly, and at least in statistical terms (2) as well; (4)–(5) imply at least a lesser crime than the initial conviction, and (3) is often more a temporary set-back than a failure.

As to the actual rate of recidivism taking into account (4)–(6) above, the data in North America are remarkably consistent, as is shown in the following studies:

1   Study of 108,580 individuals released in 1983 from 11 states:[68] rearrested, 62.5 per cent; reconvicted, 48.8 per cent; reincarcerated, 41.4 per cent
2   Study of 1,806 U.S. federal prisoners released in 1970:[69] rearrested, 62.5 per cent; reconvicted, 41.6 per cent; reincarcerated, 40.8 per cent
3   Comparison of two groups of prisoners in Florida:[70] rearrested, 78.6 per cent; reconvicted, 55.8 per cent; reincarcerated, 44 per cent
4   Juvenile parolees (aged 14–15 years) released between 1978 and 1982 in the United States:[71] rearrested 69 per cent; reconvicted, 53 per cent; reincarcerated, 49 per cent

Some Evidence

In retrospect there is strong evidence that prison programs like the one in British Columbia did 'get it right.' If the NewGate programs were too schizophrenic in their lingering attachment to the therapeutic, the SCWPP-type initiatives too iconoclastic and confrontational to survive, and the Barlinnie-type experiments too small and claustrophobic to live outside their hothouse of origin, those programs employing the breadth of technique epitomized by the University of Victoria example offered here not only survived, but more importantly in the process of surviving changed people's lives, both prisoners and teachers. We know this in more than an anecdotal sense because of the extensive research that has been done on the men who participated in the British Columbia program over the period 1973 to 1993.

The 1979 follow-up study of participants in the University of Victoria program had created a sensation and been decisive in persuading the Canadian government to continue the program despite the fiscal constraints on the recessionary years of the early 1980s. In 1984, the contract to deliver post-secondary courses to prisoners in British Columbia shifted from the University of Victoria to Simon Fraser University, but the program and personnel remained essentially the same. In 1993, coincident with the decision of the Canadian government to finally close down the program as part of a general process of government spending cutbacks, the Social Sciences and Humanities Research Council of Canada funded a three-year follow-up study designed to assess the program's effectiveness. Thus ironically, one hand gave while the other took away.

The program had expanded considerably in the 1980s, and after twenty years in operation it had a significant group of 'alumni.' In recognition of the fact that education takes some time and engagement to have an impact on an individual, only those prisoners who had completed at least two courses and been enrolled over a minimum eight-month period were considered eligible for the study. As well, they had to have been out of prison long enough to have potentially remained free for three years. This resulted in a sample of about 800 men and of these complete biographical and follow-up data were collected on 654. The sample was matched against the Correctional Service of Canada Inmate Profile and found to be a fair representation of the kind of men found in Canada's federal prisons.

Utilizing a recidivism prediction device developed by the Correctional Service of Canada (the SIR, or Statistical Index on Recidivism), the predicted post-release behaviour of the group was compared with what actually happened to them after release. The SIR predicted a failure rate of 42 per cent for the group of 654 former prisoner-students (meaning that 275 of the men should have been returned to prison for a new offence within three years of their release, about average for North American prison systems), but in their actual post-release lives only 164 of the men were returned to prison, a failure rate of only 25 per cent.[72]

Detailed analyses of the results of this research are described in Chapter 7, but the 'global' results are significant enough to warrant an examination here. The follow-up data, after all, provide important evidence of what was occurring within prison programs during this era of the opportunities model in corrections. Although the results are specific to one program, there is sufficient corroboration from other studies to make a strong case for the general effectiveness of the approach epitomized by the post-secondary program in British Columbia.

Measuring Effectiveness – Methodology and General Results

In measuring the effectiveness of the B.C. post-secondary program the research team employed a 'realist' methodology that starts from the premise that in searching for the roots of program effectiveness the central starting place is theory; the set of suppositions behind the program being evaluated, the theories, ideas, and practices that might account for or explain its success.[73] These theories stem both from the experiences and insights of the practitioners within the program itself as well as from the literature and research in the relevant academic fields, in this case primarily higher education, criminology, psychology, and sociology. Because programs are inevitably complex, these theories concerning 'what works for whom in what circumstances' will necessarily be multiple and diverse. Nonetheless, they form, the basis for specifying how the various *program interventions* are expected to trigger *varying causal mechanisms* within the *varying contexts of an initiative* and so generate a *range of outcomes*.

In the case of the prison education program, it was assumed that a higher education program *could* inculcate change in prisoners' economic or personal or cognitive or moral outlooks, but whether such development or change *actually* takes hold also depends on their criminal history, their family background, and their educational and social achievements, as well as the myriad other circumstances of their imprisonment and the varying nature of their post-release environment. Programs thus offer a series of potential pathways for different subjects and, through detailed examination of the progress of subgroups of prisoners, it is for the evaluator to determine what was it about the education initiative that worked for which types of offenders in which prison context and that survived through which parole and release circumstances. In the case of this research there were three specific 'realist' questions fundamental to the project:

1 Outcomes – Did recidivism decrease?
2 Mechanisms – What did the program actually do to bring about change?
3 Context – Where, when, and with whom did the mechanisms work best?

Our first methodological task was to find the yardstick by which we could measure success, both in absolute and in relative terms. We opted to use recidivism, choosing the definition used by the Correctional Service of Canada, a recidivist being someone returned to prison for an indictable offence within three years of being released on parole. To be a 'success' in terms of outcomes, therefore, the former prisoner-students must remain out of prison for a minimum of three years.

There remained, of course, the issue of self-selection (the idea that a high percentage of men 'fated to succeed' selected themselves into the education program) and the corresponding need to measure the actual success (or failure) of the students against some standard or set of expectations. Both of these issues were dealt with by the use of the SIR recidivism prediction device as a central component of the research. The SIR score is a numerical value assigned to an individual offender. It is calculated using indicators of risk levels such as marital status, type of offence, number of offences, and age at first arrest. For example, as common sense might suggest, an offender who has stronger ties with his family, does not have a lengthy criminal record, and has a decent employment track record, constitutes less risk for re-offence than a long-term, transient, habitual criminal. The system has now been in use for fifteen years, and recent validation exercises have found it to be 'temporally robust ... retaining much of its predictive efficiency.'[74] The Correctional Service of Canada concluded in 1989 that 'the device has demonstrated an ability to forecast the post-release recidivism of federal inmates [and] the stability of the SIR over time and with different samples of offenders also appears to be established.'[75] The SIR has been used within the CSC to assess the success of a variety of programs from cognitive living skills to vocational training and has been described as being 'central to sound correctional practice.'[76]

The important point about systems like the SIR, however, is that they were not designed to predict individual behaviour. The SIR presents a historical pattern of the post-imprisonment record of former inmates *in the aggregate*. It is derived from an aggregate multi-variate analysis of risk factors and thus is intended to generate probabalistic predictions of the behaviour of prisoners within a particular SIR category. There are five such categories, ranging from A – low risk to re-offend – to E – high risk to re-offend. The SIR puts the case positively, so that of any group of A category offenders, 80 per cent are predicted not to re-offend within three years of release compared with any group of E category offenders, of whom only 33 per cent are predicted *not* to re-offend.

The SIR, then, provided a means of calculating the predicted post-release behaviour of the former prisoner-students and in follow-up research that prediction could be compared with their actual post-release behaviours. As well, the SIR provided a means of comparing the distribution of the student group across the SIR risk categories with the distribution of the Canadian prisoner population as a whole, thereby addressing the issue of self-selection at least in terms of risk-assessment categories. If the distribution was the same or close to the national norm, it could be argued that self-selection was not a major issue. Indeed, Blumstein and Cohen argue convincingly that when instruments like the SIR are used the self-selection factor is in fact negated and 'the incremental effects of the treatment alone can then be estimated.'[77]

The next component of the research design involved selecting the subjects who were to be followed up. In the twenty-year span of the university prison education program over 1500 prisoners had been enrolled as students and several hundred more had completed high school equivalency or university-preparatory courses within the program. The operative 'folk wisdom' within the program put great stress on education needing some time to take effect, that it was not a 'quick fix.' As well, the staff felt that there needed to be some evidence of commitment on the part of the student for the educational experience to have any real impact. It was decided, therefore, to include in the student group to be followed up only men who had completed at least two university courses for credit over a minimum of two semesters (eight months). After reviewing all 1500 university transcripts this resulted in a 'student group' of about 800 subjects. Of these, approximately 700 were eligible in terms of the timing of their parole (they must have been paroled by September 1993 in order to possibly complete three years without incarceration by 1996, the termination date for the research) and complete correctional service files were located for 654, which then became the 'total group.'

The starting point for the analysis of the data was a set of hypotheses generated in discussions with program staff and in a review of the literature in the field. These hypotheses were of two types, those which focused on 'types' of subjects (for example, high flyers, improvers, second chancers, or high-risk men attached to the criminal subculture) and those which focused on program 'mechanisms' (for example, engagement, self-esteem, or breadth). As will become clear, the more productive path into the data was through the first group of hypotheses, those that focused on the various types or groups of students

Table 5.1.   Sample profile of prison population (n = 654)

	n	(%)
Born in B.C.	236	36
Married / common law	255	39
Education:		
≤Grade 10	297	45
Post-secondary	142	22
Juvenile offender	217	33
Substance abuser	508	78
Violent offender	402	61
More than 3 convictions	438	67

found within the program, with the mechanisms being particularly useful in identifying sub-groups of 'SIR-beaters.' No particular mechanism turned out to be a central factor in student success per se, but several different mechanisms were found to be particularly effective with different groups of students – just what the methodology was designed to discover.

The first task, however, was to establish some baseline data, to get a picture of the total group of 654 subjects. Table 5.1 reviews some of the data collected on the fifty-three variables associated with each subject. In an attempt to place the total group within the larger context of the prisoner profile in Canada, a criminal history comparison was made with the 1993 Correctional Service of Canada Sentence Profile (Table 2). The comparison is inherently problematic, of course, because the national sample is from a single year and the prisoner-student sample is compiled from individuals in prison over a twenty-year period. Nonetheless, assuming some degree of consistency in crime, it does indicate comparability. Table 5.3 compares the SIR rankings of the total group of prisoner-students with the national distribution of SIR rankings as of 1990.

There are some interesting differences between the total group and these 'snapshots' of the Canadian prisoner profile. In part the differences may stem from the fact that the total group is a composite drawn from twenty years and hence reflects changing offence and sentencing patterns. As well, there are important regional differentiations within Canada in terms of both offences and sentencing, with the West Coast having a much higher number of drug offenders, a category that tends in the SIR system to be rated as lower risk. That said, there is no doubt

Table 5.2.   Comparison of total group to Canadian prisoner profile (%)

	1993 Canadian sentence profile	Prisoner-students
Offence		
Homicide	18	12
Sexual offences	14	15
Other violent offences	7	8
Robbery	24	28
Other non-violent offences	15	7
Break and enter	14	13
Drugs	9	23
Sentence length (years)		
1 to 3	27	25
3 to 6	34	35
6 to 10	14	20
≥ 10	25	20

Table 5.3.   Comparison of SIR distribution (%)

SIR category	All federal offenders 1984	Total group of 654
A	25	32
B	16	17
C	17	17
D	21	15
E	21	19

SIR = statistical index of recidivism.

a self-selection process is at work here as well, with the university program attracting a slightly disproportionate number of prisoners from the lower risk categories, including, for instance, older prisoners with long sentences who saw the program as a stable place in which to spend several years, sexual offenders who comprised the entire prisoner population at one program site, and younger offenders incarcerated on relatively minor drug offences. For the total group this results in a higher than average predicted success (Table 5.4).

Table 5.5 breaks down this pattern of success by SIR category, showing the importance of risk levels in measuring success. The almost per-

Table 5.4.   Post-release success of total group of 654 (%)

SIR predicted rate of success	Actual rate	Difference	Relative improvement over prediction
58	75	17	30

fect post-release success of the lowest risk prisoners (SIR category A) is less impressive statistically (and perhaps politically!) than the more modest successes to be found in the higher risk categories which accounts for the greater importance in this research of the percentage of 'relative improvement' – relative to risk.

Once ranked by the SIR 58 per cent of the total group of 654 prisoner-students were predicted to remain out of prison for at least three years after release on parole. Given that the mean SIR prediction for the Canadian federal system is for a post-release success of around 50 per cent, it would appear that the self-selection factor has produced a group with somewhat better odds of rehabilitation or at least successful avoidance of further imprisonment than would have occurred with a random selection of prisoners. However, as shown in Table 5.2, when the parole files of the 654 men were examined it turned out that 75 per cent of the total group were in fact successful in remaining free of incarceration for three years after release, a difference of 17 per cent over their SIR prediction or a 'relative improvement' over SIR of 30 per cent.

While encouraging, this global figure tells us virtually nothing about the effectiveness of specific mechanisms within the education program nor about the circumstances that might have contributed to individual successes and failures. At this level of analysis the program remains a 'black box.' In attempting to get a better look inside this box, the total group was examined using fifteen different variables, including a set of academic variables, community engagement variables, release process variables, and biographical variables. In doing so we were looking for sub-groups – for instance, high achievers, intensely engaged students, or younger men – who would improve over their SIR prediction by significantly more than the 30 per cent attained by the group as a whole. The results were predictably unsatisfactory for such a large and amorphous body of subjects, the variables revealing only minor shifts within the total group. The exercise did provide some important clues about what kinds of variables might produce more significant results when more coherent groups were examined. For instance, within the

Table 5.5. Predicted and actual rates of parole and/or release success for total group (%)

SIR category	Number in category	Predicted success rate	Success rate	Actual difference	Relative improvement
A (4 out of 5 will not re-offend)	214	80	98	18	23
B (2 out of 3 will not re-offend)	110	66	82	16	24
C (1 out of 2 will not re-offend)	108	50	73	23	46
D (2 out of 5 will not re-offend)	98	40	57	17	42
E (1 out of 3 will not re-offend)	124	33	45	12	36

Table 5.6.   Grade-point average (GPA) comparison in total group (%)

Subgroups (n)	Predicted	Actual	Difference	Relative improvement
GPA declines (146)	57	73	16	28
GPA stable (389)	59	75	16	28
GPA improves (119)	57	77	21	37

five academic variables utilized it was clear that 'more was better,' those subgroups of students with more credits, more semesters, more consecutive semesters, higher grade point averages, and improving academic performance in every case outperformed their SIR prediction at a higher rate than their peers. While the variations at this level of analysis were not great, they did indicate possibilities. The most impressive of the academic variables was the comparison of academic performance (grades) at the start of courses and the end. Here, as Table 5.6 shows, the 'improvers hypothesis' seemed to show considerable promise. Remembering that the total group improved over its SIR prediction by 30 per cent, this 7 per cent increase on the part of the improvers indicates that factors such as improved self-esteem or self-confidence, possible by-products of success at academic work, could be important mechanisms in the education program. The subgroup of 119 improvers were generally younger than their peers in the other two subgroups, were enrolled for more consecutive semesters, had higher grades, and were judged to be more intensely involved in the academic program. They became (see Chapter 7) a group worthy of further study in order to locate subgroups within the improvers who surpassed SIR by even greater margins.

Because the university program made such a point of stressing the 'community of learning' established in the various program sites, the level of student engagement with that community was seen as a potentially powerful indicator of success. To explore this 'engagement hypothesis' with the total group, three variables were utilized: the degree of formal involvement in program affairs or activities, the level of 'intensity of engagement' as judged by staff and student records, and the degree of participation in extracurricular activities – in this case the theatre productions associated with the university program. Again, the 'more is better' trend continued but without the emergence of any outstanding subgroups. As Table 5.7 shows, those students seen to be more intensely engaged with the program did improve slightly

Table 5.7. Intensity of engagement in total group (%)

Subgroups (n)	Predicted	Actual	Difference	Relative improvement
Below average (63)	55	59	4	7
Average (284)	57	74	17	29
Intense (206)	57	76	19	34
Very intense (101)	62	84	22	35

on the performance of the total group, but perhaps more significant was the dismal showing of the sixty-three students who were seen to be virtual non-participants in the program. Once again, some promising potential subgroups emerge from this look at the total group – particularly the sixty-three underachievers in terms of engagement. As well, the intensity measure emerges clearly as an effective variable for differentiating levels of engagement within the student body, with the relative size of each subgroup being what one might expect in a 'residential' and community-oriented adult education program.

Turning to the process of release from prison and the period on parole, long recognized in the literature as being the most crucial factor in successful reintegration with society, four variables were brought into play: type of release (parole or statutory release), the gap in time between program participation and release, proximity to previous residence, and enrolment in further education. Neither type of release or the gap between program participation and release revealed any significant or very interesting subgroups, but as the literature suggested proximity of parole destination to previous residence did prove important. Those men released in locations fifty or more kilometres from their previous residence beat their SIR prediction by 39 per cent, compared with only 24 per cent for men who returned to locations closer to their previous home. This was expected. What was not expected was the number of subjects from the total group who completed education or training courses after release and their rate of success (Table 5.8). Once again, some interesting subgroups emerged from these data. The sixty men who enrolled in further education but withdrew before completing any classes were a much higher risk group according to SIR, and their post-release success fell far below that of the total group. Staff from the program noted that some students had defaulted on student loans after release and that there was some concern that a minority of men were using the possibility of enrolling in further education after

Table 5.8. Participation in further education – percentage of total group

Subgroups (n)	Predicted	Actual	Difference	Relative improvement
No further education (378)	57	71	14	25
Enrolled and withdrew (60)	52	55	3	5
Further education (213)	61	87	26	42

release only as a means of acquiring these loans. On the other hand, the 213 men who did complete courses after release, even though they comprised a lower risk group, still improved on their SIR prediction by an impressive 42 per cent, 12 points higher than the average for the total group. As will be shown, for many groups examined in more detail further education after release was to prove a particularly vibrant identifier of successful subgroups, in most cases at rates much higher even than the 42 per cent for this group.

The strength of this further education variable led the research team to develop a working hypothesis that some kind of non-correctional institutional affiliation after release might be an important contributing factor to successful avoidance of crime and incarceration, and that colleges and universities, particularly those in which the former prisoner could locate a supportive person or office, were well suited for this role.

Finally, in applying several biographical variables to the total group another assumption found in the literature and represented in this research by the age hypothesis seemed to be confirmed. Table 5.9 breaks the total group into five subgroups based on age at current conviction; the hypothesis that SIR beaters will be found at the lower and upper ends of the age spectrum appears to be confirmed. The most encouraging item in this set of data was the success of the highest risk subgroup, the group aged 16–21 years, who far surpassed their predicted rate of success. On the other hand, the success of the subgroup of men over 36 was anticipated by SIR, as was the rather dismal performance of men in their twenties. It was clear that as the literature and the program staff anticipated, these age differentials were to be important variables in the examination of subsets of the total group.

These examinations of the total group of 654 subjects had established a norm for the group in terms of beating the SIR prediction in that the group as a whole showed a relative improvement over SIR of 30 per cent. For any subgroup of prisoner-students to stand out in terms of

Table 5.9. Total group by age at current conviction (%)

Subgroups (*n*)	Predicted	Actual	Difference	Relative improvement
Age (years)				
16–21 (65)	52	75	24	46
22–5 (127)	54	66	12	23
26–30 (174)	55	67	13	23
31–5 (132)	58	74	16	28
≥36 (156)	67	91	24	36

success it would need to exceed that standard by a considerable margin. Likewise, any subgroup that fell well below that 'standard of success' would be of interest not necessarily in terms of program failure, but rather as indicative of a type or category of prisoner for whom this intervention was not particularly effective. The next task in this research was the search for subgroups within the total group which stood out in some way. The analysis of the total group data provided some important clues as to how such subgroups might be located by pointing towards specific variables such as further education, academic improvement, intensity of engagement, and age, but that search will continue in a subsequent chapter.

Because the post-secondary education program that these men participated in was catholic in its admissions policy, making no pretense at sorting high risk from low, or receptive students from unresponsive, the subjects of this study were simply fellow students along with at least 1500 men who also enrolled in courses from 1973 to 1993. They self-selected initially by choosing this program over others in the prison and then self-selected again by successfully becoming part of the 654 men who completed at least two courses and remained in the program at least eight months. In these two decisions, by taking specific actions while in prison, these men set themselves apart from peers who shared their history of family chaos, poor schooling and juvenile crime. These qualificatory steps in gaining admission to this study are, in fact, a dramatic emblem of how programs like this worked. What followed was a whole series of further choices and selections – Should I stay with the program for a year? – and then a further year? – Should I slog through the course on the base of a poor start? – Should I choose the theatre course? – Should I try for further education after release? It is the sum total of a myriad of such decisions that adds up to the big choice – Should I quit crime? Here lies a vital and uncomfortable message for policy-maker and evaluator alike – it is not programs that work, but their capacity to offer resources that allow subjects *the choice* of making them work. It was in this decisive sense that initiatives like the university program in British Columbia exemplified the best attributes of the opportunities model approach to corrections.

All of the programs reviewed here were unique but shared elements of a common core, a focus on the prisoner first and foremost as an individual, a learner, and a subject. Each example offers insight into the difficulty of sustaining this common core in the face of the authoritarian imperatives operating in the correctional system. The NewGate programs perhaps did not go far enough in forcing the issue, while the SCWPP in California clearly went too far. The Barlinnie project only survived as long as it did by literally walling itself off from the prison. The British Columbia programs and their post-secondary counterparts in U.S. jurisdictions struck the best balance and survived the longest. Other prison programs certainly had the capability to achieve the same kind of success at building reciprocal relationships with their prisoner-clients, but there is no similar record of success at putting this into practice. Indeed, even most so-called education programs had no measurable impact on the lives of their charges.

Programs like this – and by 1981 the head of the Correctional Education Association could assert that 'almost every state prison system now offers some formal college program for inmates'[78] – heralded a genuine renaissance in the possibility of prison becoming an agent of individual transformation. Not just for prisoner university students, but for men and women pursuing literacy or adult education, vocational training, social skills and other aspects of individual development. By opening itself up to the complex variety of developmental tools available in the larger community, prison systems in the late 1970s began to move out of Foucaultean world they had created for themselves. But at a cost, the cost of giving over to others, to outsiders, the direction of activity within the prison with a corresponding loss of prestige for the professional class of prison staff, experts, and advisers.

CHAPTER SIX

The Return of the Criminal as 'The Enemy Within'

This is a modern miracle. The one we live in. A culture that not only worships itself, but assumes it is greater than any culture in time and history. This is a culture of decomposition, bursting apart with the screams of the routed millions who have been shattered by their efforts of work. They lie tattered along the roadside, worn out by the war of attrition between culture and time-splitting diversions that pound away inside their heads as if the brain was made of pieces of vermilion atoms ... The exhausted life-worlds lying at the roadside ditches are reproduced in the communications model, a middle class system which has no inner life. The hope that one day the unfulfilled potential of bourgeois subjectivist culture might be realized is gone forever; gone into the future which, like the technological process itself, becomes a culture of symbols, rules.[1]

Jery Zaslove, 'Ten Fables for the Heroic Future' (1988)

When Martinson and Morris issued their call to abandon the treatment regime it seemed to be a simple empirical issue. The regime was ineffective in that the illness (crime) continued to infect the body (the criminal) after treatment, the evidence being consistently high rates of recidivism irrespective of treatment. In fact, however, much more was going on here than a simple empirical discovery. There were already claims being made in the mid-1970s that modernity itself – the universalizing Enlightenment culture in which the medical model was born and bred – did not 'work' and that we needed to move on and confront a postmodern era characterized by a celebration of uncertainties, relativism, and difference. Foucault, as we have seen, helped pave the way for the application of this critique of modernity to the world of corrections (along with many other worlds), thereby undermining even the possibility of its 'correctional' claims being credible since the root 'to

correct' was hopelessly 'modern.' Suddenly the extravagant and catholic claims, advanced in the name of modern culture and society, that
poverty could be eliminated, diseases wiped out, crime cured, and
peace of mind attained all were called into question. After 1975, in corrections at least, it was no longer possible to think about 'it' working or
even to consider that there could be an 'it' given the general questioning of all universalisms that characterized postmodern thought or, for
that matter, to accept that there could be simple dual categories like
'working' or 'not working.'

The institutions of society did not, of course, all become 'postmodern' as a result of these new cultural insights, far from it. As Jery
Zaslove hints at in the opening quotation, the various programs, treatments, cures, and solutions that lay in the roadside ditches were dor-
mant, but not dead. Institutional operatives continued to hope that the
mood would pass, and they would once again be able to operate in the
realm of surety in systems, but in the meantime they dared make only
modest and specific claims. Some programs did achieve successes – the
education programs reviewed earlier being prime examples – and they
could be talked about, albeit carefully. The public, having caught on to
only the cynical side of postmodernism but at the same time sensing
the general cultural instability of the times, was in no mood to hear
again the exaggerated claims of the scientists, experts and 'fixers.'

The New Fear of Crime

The era of humane containment did not, however, work out that well.
In those prison systems or individual prisons where there existed progressive, innovative, and therefore – as I have argued – habilitative
programs, these were for some the best of times. The heavy hand of the
treatment model was gone, public expectations of reformation were
minimal, and prisoners had greater opportunity to interact with people from other than penal kinds of institutions. These were, however,
the exceptions not the rule. The combination of neo-conservative governments and accompanying fiscal policies, the early 1980s economic
recession, and a general lack of public interest in prisons and corrections (stemming in part from their disillusionment with past promises)
all meant less money, fewer resources, and a weaker political presence
for corrections in Canada, the United States, and Britain. At the same
time, the earlier advice of Martinson and Morris concerning shorter
prison sentences was not followed, in fact, quite the opposite hap-

pened and the new under-resourced prison systems quickly became overcrowded warehouses, especially in the United States where the incarceration rate increased by nearly 150 per cent between 1975 and 1989. In 1980, one in every 453 Americans was incarcerated, that number had increased to one in every 189 by 1993.[2]

Part of the problem had to do with crime itself. The liberal, anti-prison ideas put forward in the mid-1970s by Martinson, Morris, and others had, as we have seen, been firmly grounded in a critique of a system gone awry. Opting for simple non-intervention or avoidance of incarceration whenever possible would only prove effective, however, if the energies and funds that had previously been misspent on 'treatment' could be quickly shifted to prevention or community corrections. Not only was such a quick shift difficult in terms of the fiscal and operational systems concerned, in the conservative 1980s it was just never in the cards. There were to be no champions of 'just societies,' 'new,' or 'fair deals' in this decade, no mobilization of society for a 'war on poverty.' Instead there was a pervasive 'war on crime' that has lasted well into the 1990s, spinning off parallel 'wars' on drugs and sexual deviance. As a result the prisons quickly began to fill.

Causation is difficult to sort out in all this. Each in their own way the United States, Canada, and Great Britain were all becoming increasingly authoritarian and militarized. For the United States the Cold War was reaching yet another climax in the 1980s with defence budgets ballooning and 'star wars' projects becoming part of popular culture. Great Britain was wallowing in the glory of the Falklands victory and engaged in a steady hot war in Northern Ireland. Canada, the most peaceful of the three, was nonetheless preparing itself once again for a life-and-death struggle with Quebec separatism. All these efforts had an economic cost, and the early years of the decade were years of recession, restraint, and economic constriction that in turn reinforced the conservative, cautious cultural and social predilections of members of the middle classes who perceived themselves as bearing the brunt of these economic changes. For those on the margins of society, which included many full- and part-time as well as some-time criminals, these were particularly difficult years, and many turned to crime out of economic necessity. Finally, the increasing hedonistic individualism of the 1980s – with Margaret Thatcher insisting that there was no such thing as 'society,' only 'individuals' – reinforced an ethic of 'looking out for Number One' as well as an increasing intolerance for those who did so and got caught. Avaricious evangelists and capitalists alike were heroic media stars until they were clumsy enough to be seen to be doing what common sense said they must be doing, and then they became objects of scorn. In this sense they took over a populist role fulfilled by criminals from the time of Robin Hood, thereby pushing crime and the criminal off the moral horizon into a realm formerly reserved for pariahs and communists.

These changes in the public perception of crime were undoubtedly fueled by an actual increase in criminal activity during the 1980s, coupled with an increasingly strident fear of crime and condemnation of the deviant, indeed a conviction that crime was out of control. For instance, in 1981, *Newsweek* magazine ran a not atypical feature entitled 'The Plague of Violent Crime,' complete with gory photos, charts demonstrating perilous increases in all types of crime, and dismal predictions of the future.[3] By the end of the decade some commentators were declaring it a 'state of emergency' in the United States, especially with crime among young people and within the inner city.[4] It would appear that the rate of crime increased in the 1980s and then began to level off and in some instances decline, but the 'actual' rate of crime is an elusive thing to measure, being subject to, among other things, changing criminal law (that is, the naming of what is illegal), the rate at which crime is reported, socioeconomic conditions that may produce crime even in the face of more intensive law enforcement, and the varying potential for apprehension and conviction.[5]. The causes of the increase varied, but undoubtedly demographics played a role along with economic dislocations, the dramatic spread of drug use, and, thanks in large part to the efforts of feminists and victims of sexual abuse, greater public interest in crimes related to sexual deviance.

While there seems to be a consensus that the increasingly sensationalist and powerful media have played an important role in transforming what seem to be modest and temporary fluctuations in the total amount of crime in these three countries into a virtual state of emergency, there are nevertheless good reasons for people to be concerned. Just as important, there has been a dramatic reduction in public tolerance for 'crimes' like schoolyard violence, higher rates of reporting for spousal and sexual assault, and a widespread movement of hard drug use from the inner cities to the community as a whole.[6] The spread of these kinds of criminal activities coupled with steadily reduced resources for both police and the court system has resulted in lower arrest rates and fewer convictions, thereby fuelling public disquiet about safety and justice. Despite the myths displayed on television and in the movies, people sense that most criminals are neither caught nor convicted, and they are right – the Home Office in the United Kingdom, for instance, estimating recently that 'only about 2 per cent of offences of which victims are aware (which may itself only be a tiny proportion of all offences) result in a conviction.'[7]

Finally, the public perception that crime and deviance are 'out of control' and the desire, indeed demand, that strong steps be taken in response can also be seen in non-rational terms. Some might argue that with the end of the war in Southeast Asia and the collapse of the Soviet Union in 1989, the cultural (and political) need for an external threat was simply transferred to an internal enemy: the criminal. Much like communist spies and infiltrators were feared to be infecting the body politic in earlier decades, now drug dealers, sexual perverts, and common criminals were corrupting youth, ruining the economy, and challenging authority.[8] Or, taking a more Freudian tack, one might argue along with David Garland that criminals represent a threat because their behaviour often 'expresses desires which others have spent much energy and undergone much internal conflict in order to renounce.' As a result crime can provoke a 'resentful and hostile reaction out of proportion to the real danger that it represents.'[9]

For a public increasingly influenced by sensationalist media, destabilized and morally wearied by the frenetic pace of modernity, and still suspicious of claims about winning wars on drugs, crime, or poverty – for this public crime has become one of the indications that perhaps Karl Marx was right about modernity after all when he warned us that all that seems solid will eventually melt into air.[10] While many despair at this prospect, others perceive this as a period of breakdown leading perhaps to collapse, but more likely to renewal either in a reborn modernity or a renaissance in some postmodern formulation. In either case, collapse or renewal, the symptoms of the breakdown require a response.

These symptoms include the 'crisis' of the family, the spread of addictions, the collapse of community, and the growth of authoritarianism and moral absolutism, and they are as manifest in the world of the criminal and the prison as they are in society at large. Indeed, as implied throughout this book, the realm of crime and prisons does not consist of a collection of 'aberrant' individuals or of people characterized by 'aberrant' behaviours – rather, it is filled with 'extreme' examples of behaviours and personalities that are pervasive in a culture undergoing the process of breakdown and response outlined above.

This view, of course, requires that we reject the psychologically driven perspective that prisons are filled only with 'special' people – the learning disabled, the psychopaths, the morally depraved, and the professional deviants. Instead, the prison becomes a home not just for these special cases, but for the weakest, nastiest, or unluckiest of a variety of social types, including opportunists, hedonists, materialists, and the desperate. We may, therefore, be able to gain important insights into this current crisis of modernity by examining some of its symptoms in their most extreme manifestations – the prison as laboratory, as a panopticon we enter not, this time, to gaze upon the criminal but rather to gaze upon ourselves. This possibility was first noted in Max Horkheimer and Theodor Adorno's work in critical theory when they posited that: 'Man in prison is the virtual image of the bourgeois type he still has to become in reality. Those who cannot manage outside are forcibly held in a terrible state of purity in prison.'[11] The criminal and penal world may be more a reflection than a mirror-image of the conventional world: the breakdown of the family being more complete there, the addictions more visible and pronounced, the collapse of community already transformed into contempt for it, and the moral absolutism – though narrowly conceived – complete.

Just as important as this use of crime as a lens through which we can look into the larger culture, a close examination of specific criminal or 'deviant' responses to the perceived crisis or breakdown of modernity reinforces the case made in Chapter 4 that criminals and prisoners do not need treatment as much as they need to acquire the resources necessary for pursuing a legitimate response to the manner in which that breakdown manifests itself in their lives. The focus on community reintegration, education and skills acquisition, and diversity that epitomized the more effective prison programs would seem, therefore, to be what is required – a 're-fit' rather than a 'cure.'

With weakening family and friendship patterns, on constantly shifting moral ground, and faced with the lure of addictions everywhere, the life of the criminal on the margins of the culture shares these desolations with that of her or his peers at the centre of the culture. One can refer to these crises, breakdowns, and attempted renewals in the abstract for only so long before one begins to ache for the particular, for what George Steiner refers to as a 'chronicle of small desolations,' the task normally assigned to the novel.[12] To move towards this sense of the particular a series of fictionalized biographies of criminals can illustrate in some detail how these symptoms of cultural breakdown when transformed, as they inevitably must be, into criminal behaviours helped fuel the sense of general breakdown and crisis within the culture. The biographies are derived from the extensive review of criminal history files undertaken during the research into the effectiveness of the university prison education program in British Columbia.

Drug Addiction – Albert's Story

A great many current prisoners began their deviant careers in the 1960s and 1970s as participants in what was perceived at the time as a 'counterculture,' an inevitable and to many welcome, alternative to what seemed to be a conventional culture at once stifling and collapsing. In addition to politics and style, the use of drugs became one of the means employed by participants in this cultural movement to set themselves in opposition to the norm. For some, over time the drugs became an end rather than a means, and in response the state adopted Draconian drug laws and thereby helped precipitate a wave of criminal careers. Albert's story is part of that history.

Albert is dead now, victim of a heroin overdose at age forty. He was a sharp, bright, good-looking young man when I first met him in prison in 1975. He was also smooth, a bit too smooth most of the time, evasive, manipulative, and in his own way both endearing and frustrating. By the time I met him, heroin had come to dominate his life, although at the time I had no idea what that really meant and to some degree still do not know. The oldest of three siblings, Albert was born into a military family in 1950. The family moved often because of the father's career in the military. Both his parents were described in Albert's correctional files as alcoholics. Albert ran away from home at age sixteen, following an open break with his father, but later returned to complete high school and then join the army himself. During his two years in the service he began to experiment with drugs, got married, and fathered a child.

An intelligent, sophisticated, brash, and well-travelled young man, Albert's first brush with the law occurred in 1970 when, fresh out of the army, he was arrested for possession of a narcotic and given a month in jail. Moving more heavily into the commercial side of the 'drug scene' of the West Coast in the early 1970s, Albert was arrested in 1972 with a large amount of marijuana and cocaine and given a two-year sentence for trafficking. In prison he found himself in frequent conflicts with staff and with institutional rules and was described by staff as 'refusing to work or fails to work at the best of his ability ... is indecent, disrespectful or threatening in his actions, language or writing toward any other person.' Nonetheless, Albert was paroled eight months later.

Speculating from the biographer's vantage point, we can see that Albert begins life the victim of addiction, in this case the alcoholism of his parents. As well, he is in a sense denied a strong sense of community thanks to the constant movement of the family. He reacted in a more extreme manner than most to adolescent pressures by openly breaking with his family, only to return and attempt to locate a community in the only one he knew of, the military. He then attempts to 'connect' through marriage and fatherhood, the West Coast 'hippie' community of the early 1970s, and finally, addiction, all of which fail in part because he has no successful patterns to follow. In a world where drugs are simply part of everyday life, indeed a crucial component of community, crime becomes part and parcel of that same daily life. Pulled out of society Albert became a 'problem prisoner,' already no doubt seeking a form of community or family amid his fellow prisoners.

The next three years were spent nurturing an addiction to heroin acquired while in prison with intermittent stays in jail on minor theft charges, leading in a few years to his full emergence into the criminal and penal world with a ten-year sentence for a series of bank robberies. Now began the 'long march through the institutions,' correctional and educational, as well as the 'long march through his soul,' as Albert's intelligence, deviousness, and addiction did battle with his keepers and his teachers. Imprisoned in British Columbia, he discovered the university program almost immediately and found it a safe haven as well as a challenge. In his first two years his marks were miserable but he kept at it and discovered in the program's theatre activities a flair for acting. After three years of steady work his grades began to improve, and he began to formulate plans for an early release on parole.

Here is Foucault's description in action, a lawbreaker by choice to be sure but a criminal created by the system his lawbreaking forces him into. Albert acquired a lifelong drug addiction and learned, albeit poorly, how to rob banks. Once imprisoned, his talents led him to the most advantageous activity he could find, in this case school. Albert was a 'hard slogger' as a student, bright but poorly disciplined, verbally adept but easily distracted. He found in the university program in the prison a tolerant version of community that he could thrive in, and while never a 'leader,' he nonetheless became an active participant in the life of that community.

With Albert one was never on firm ground in the struggle between reality and rhetoric, between intention and outcome. His first campaign for parole took eight months and was based on his discovery of academic interests combined with a flair for acting and theatre production, two facets of a 'new' Albert who, in his own words, will prove a 'wiser and more thoughtful individual as well as a capable and responsible citizen.' These hopes were supported by teachers and correctional staff; their letters of reference to the Parole Board stressed the 'rather considerable changes' Albert had gone through, his success at 'becoming a university student within the prison,' and his acquisition of a 'positive attitude towards life.' (I, for instance, supported him 'without reservation.') Stressing his work on the student council and in the prison theatre group, Albert insisted that these experiences had given him a 'totally new perspective.'

There are hints, however, of a Mr Hyde in Albert's other activities in the prison. After three years of aggressively ignoring corrections staff in the living unit, he now sought their advice and shifted parole plans several times during the year, apparently responding to what he perceived various authorities wanted to hear. Having separated from his wife at the beginning of his prison term, he began a passionate liaison with a woman met through a prisoners' rights group and was charged several times with visiting rules violations. The Parole Board, concerned that Albert stubbornly refused to acknowledge his heroin addiction, reminded by the police about the seriousness of his street activities, and feeling that he lacked 'insight into his behaviour,' deferred any decision pending a psychological evaluation. Their concerns seemed to be confirmed by Albert's 'smart alec attitude' following the hearing, prompting his parole officer to describe Albert as 'adversarial,' as unable to work with those who are trying to help him. Meanwhile, during the months of parole negotiations Albert's grades suffered, and he lost the possibility of an unescorted temporary pass when his new girlfriend was caught smuggling drugs into the prison.

A psychological review concluded that Albert was immature, rebellious, egocentric, and bright – a 'belated adolescent beginning to move toward awareness and adulthood' – but was deteriorating fast while in the prison environment: 'I greatly fear that needlessly prolonged incarceration will continue to elevate the obvious psychopathic tendencies

... he is learning deviance right now ... [Albert] is a very torn, polarized individual who is just slowly beginning to stir and become aware of an undiscovered adulthood in him.'

Thus, Albert at age twenty-eight, heroin addict and bank robber, three years into his ten-year sentence, was described as being immature, cocky, aggressive, and rebellious – like so many of his mid-twenties prisoner peers, essentially a teenager in an adult body. Yet unlike many of those peers, Albert was seen by teachers and psychologists to be 'ready' to start a new life, to begin constructing an adult identity through further education. Corrections staff on the other hand saw only a manipulative con, someone who 'attempts to sway to his opinion with verbiage, abuse and ridicule.'

A year later the parole process started anew. Albert's teachers argued strongly that he was 'more than ready' to make the transition to the community and would make an excellent university student on campus. He was plagued, however, by the firm view of parole and correctional staff that he was manipulative and that he used the verbal skills mastered in school and on the stage to mask his lack of insight concerning his drug addiction (he still claimed not to have a drug problem). Over the next year Albert's teachers and an increasing number of corrections staff continued to support his release plans, and finally in November 1980 he was transferred to a minimum security camp as a prologue to day parole. In a letter to one of his instructors written from the camp Albert referred to himself as an 'illegal hostage of the Parole Board' and complained that the delay in his release was making him increasingly cynical and angry and quoted W.H. Auden's line about 'those to whom evil is done do evil in return.'

Released to a halfway house in September 1981, Albert was employed in sales work and enrolled in classes at the university and was doing well at both until he was laid off at work in February 1982 in the midst of a severe economic recession. With economic pressure came his 'old and familiar crutch and the deterioration was swift.' He was suspended once in June 1982 but quickly returned to the halfway house on the advice of his parole officer. But a month later he was apprehended with a known drug trafficker and returned to prison for a much longer stay, once again joining the university program.

Albert was just one of many men on parole at this time whose return to prison seemed linked to the economic recession of the early 1980s. In Albert's case one had a sense of moral fragility or an excessively weak will to remain free of crime (and drugs), so that the first sign of social or economic difficulty could lead immediately to a return to familiar territory.

In June 1983, in the seventh year of his sentence, Albert was released on mandatory supervision and once again enrolled at university. He started off well but complained that 'the summer is a difficult time to concentrate on studies,' and his grades suffered accordingly. He was nonetheless determined to 'commit myself to completing the degree this year.' Once again, his teachers in the prison program supported his efforts, praised his dedication and hard work as a tutor in the school, his leadership role within the education program, and his integrity.

A few months later Albert was back in prison, this time for theft under $200. While under the influence of drugs and alcohol, he had grabbed a handful of bills from a grocery store till, what he later described as a 'spur of the moment crime ... an instance of momentary stupidity.' He was given another year and spent much of his time sulking in prison, refusing to return to the university program, and refusing any dealings with corrections staff. The drug dealer turned bank robber turned addict became an uncontrollable petty thief, stealing impulsively for quick cash to supply a drug need that was never acknowledged as an addiction. A year later his parole officer's predictions were suitably pessimistic: 'He has no offers of employment and a vague plan to become involved in theatre. He had $100 cash and student loan debts of $8500 and was unable or unwilling to provide the name of anyone in the community who can assist him. Thus, he starts a three-year term of Mandatory Supervision with no residence, employment, funds or community resources.' Six months later Albert was back in prison charged with robbery, this time attempting to steal methadone from a druggist. An additional three-year sentence gave him a time to be served of five years and four months.

Here the addict seemed to have hit bottom, the crimes now completely integrated with the habit. Previously Albert stole for money in order to purchase drugs and other 'necessities' of a heroin-driven lifestyle such as expensive clothing, automobiles, travel, and so forth. Now he had to simply steal the drug or a version of it directly.

Albert now executed an about-face, volunteering for any prison program he could find that addressed drug addiction. He attended Alcholic Anonymous and Narcotics Anonymous meetings and his case management team responded enthusiastically, noting that to this point Albert had put his academic education before his addiction rehabilitation but that now he had reversed the order: 'He is, in common with many heroin addicts, a very intelligent person who has in the past utilized this gift for manipulation of people and situations; this time he appears to be using it to help himself ... The Case Management Team did not view [Albert] as a criminal but rather as a victim of his addictions.' A year later, while denied day parole, Albert was allowed to live in a special halfway house for addicts two days a month and then transferred to a minimum security camp. Six months later, in March 1987, he was granted day parole in acknowledgment of his 'acceptance of his own limitations.' In the 'treatment dance' that had occupied the past ten years of Albert's life the state had now come round to Albert's original self-diagnosis – that *he* was the victim. This came about as a quid pro quo because Albert during this last period of incarceration had finally abandoned his determination to engage with education and abandoned his 'war with the state,' or at least shoved it out of sight.

For the next eight months Albert was in a revolving door, being suspended four times for drug use, violation of halfway house rules, and associating with known addicts. He was argumentative, drank to excess, gambled, violated curfews, annoyed other residents, made constant demands, and 'in many respects is like a needy teenager' (he was now thirty-six years old). He had intermittent employment as a film extra and began to talk about returning to university in the new year but was sent back to prison when he failed to return to the halfway house because he knew he could not pass the drug test. A few months later he was released again, now on mandatory supervision (year thirteen of a sentence that began in 1976) and once again rejecting the idea that he had any kind of drug problem. Miraculously, Albert completed this period of mandatory supervision with only one minor shoplifting charge. The Parole Service had more or less given up, acknowledging that Albert 'will succeed or fail almost independent of our influence.' In the closing report, the parole officer noted that Albert was 'a long time hype who seemed to be trying to limp out of his criminal lifestyle ... he is a bright guy but has a long way to go.'

Albert was not one of the more 'successful' products of the Canadian university prison education program, even though he did technically complete his period on parole. That 'successful' parole was more a result of the parole service simply giving up and letting him remain out of prison as long as he did not commit any serious crimes. In fact, they likely knew that Albert's propensity for serious crime was long past. He was too old, too burnt out, too much the 'hype' to do more than nuisance crimes and would more than likely turn to alcohol or die of an overdose. Albert died because his particular form of addiction was so dangerous, but had he turned to alcohol, or successfully managed methadone, or found some other less lethal chemical he might very well have persisted within society as one more of the victims of social and familial carnage, exaggerated expectations, and the dependency producing habits of our intervening institutions.

Anyone who has experience with crime, criminals, and drugs will recognize Albert and acknowledge that men like him are hard to fathom. Outwardly they seem to hold great promise, largely because they possess so many of the social skills that we recognize and value – they are highly verbal, present themselves well, and appear to place a high value on sincerity. Yet, beneath that social veneer lay a set of troubles that the non-addict can only guess at, troubles that manifest themselves as a predisposition to fool themselves and those who work with them. To this day I have no idea how to judge Albert's sincerity during the several times when our paths crossed, and I supported his plans for personal reformation. But many of those who knew Albert in prison in the mid-1970s persist in the belief that there was a brief time when he was salvageable, when the changes in self-esteem and life chances offered by his success in school could have been translated into a productive and crime-free life. In this view the delays in his release, the reluctance of the system to credit his claims, were like an early frost on the bud, and he used this as a means of taking the easy road of giving in to the addiction at every opportunity.

Money, Morals, and Crime: Bill's Story

The link between economics and crime is complex, and certainly almost never linear. Jean Valjean goes to the galley for stealing a loaf of bread to feed his child, but that is the exception far more than the rule. Still, the connection is there, and the economic rollercoaster that is modern capitalism combined with a materialist, hedonistic, consumption-driven culture plays a central role in persuading or pushing people into crime. Even more to the point, the cycles of a modern capitalist society in their down side affect most radically the entrepreneurs on the margins, often persuading them to cut corners and engage in illicit activity, which in turn can lead to arrest and the start of a criminal career. Dickens put it starkly in the words of his unforgettable Mr Micawber: 'Annual income twenty pounds, annual expenditure nineteen nineteen and six, result happiness. Annual income twenty pounds, annual expenditure twenty pounds ought and six, result misery. The blossom is blighted, the leaf is withered, the god of day goes down upon the dreary scene, and – in short you are forever floored.'[13] Money, the lure or lack thereof, is a major factor in the process of becoming both a criminal and a prisoner. Jean Harris was convinced after her own immersion in the penal world that for most of her fellow inmates money was the key factor in their offence: 'She may have been hungry or frantic or angry or frustrated or just plain greedy, but money touched the offense in some way.'[14] She reminds us as well that it cannot be simply a 'great cosmic coincidence' that prisons are peopled by the poor and almost never by the rich.

The rejoinder is obvious, however; not all the poor nor all those who are 'forever floored' become criminals. Some find a way out of the morass of poverty and others stay in it while the lives of still others hover about in frustrating indecision. Bill's story may help illuminate one criminal pathway out of economic difficulty, one based on striking back decisively. Bill ended up in prison at age twenty as a first offender with a ten-year sentence for the combined offences of armed robbery, kidnapping, unlawful confinement, and possession of a weapon. Bill came from a middle-class family and had what he described as a 'happy' childhood. There was a divorce that, according to his father, led to some 'emotional problems' for Bill and his two siblings, and there were a couple of moves during his school years that were socially disruptive, but not apparently in a serious way. Bill reports getting on well in high school, playing several sports, making friends, and having a good relationship with his new stepfather. There is no record of any juvenile delinquency. So none of the major warning signs of a 'criminal in the making' were there, although there was evidence of some soft drug use (it was the mid-1970s), and Bill did decide to drop out of school after grade 11 and start working.

There are indications that the school-leaving was motivated as much by friction with his mother as by the desire for money, and certainly after age seventeen he rarely visited his parental home. Bill started modestly by working in restaurants and gas stations and then obtained work in the construction industry and was doing quite well until the recession of the early 1980s. He had purchased a car and was enjoying a 'somewhat extravagant lifestyle,' not that difficult for a young man on his own, when the bottom began to fall out, and he faced Micawber's prophecy of being 'forever floored.' He edged towards crime first by selling stolen property on behalf of some acquaintances and then, being intelligent, entrepreneurial, and strong willed, decided to eliminate the middle man and obtain the goods directly. He began alone but soon acquired a small gang of accomplices, specializing in robbing store employees who were making bank deposits. The robberies, which took place over the course of a year, enabled Bill to sustain a lifestyle based on free-spending, treating friends well, and accumulating possessions. Bill fits perfectly the pattern of the 'stickup man' described by Jack Katz, the criminal for whom money, lifestyle, and crime are intricately interconnected:

> By dissipating the proceeds of their crimes, stickup men, regardless of the social position from which they start, create an environment of pressures that guide them back toward crime ... That is, high living would produce poverty and the need to rob; at the same time, an inclination toward spontaneous robberies underlay fast spending, which would produce dire need, which would produce stickups ... The causal relationship through which high spending produces economic pressures that produce stickups is lived by persistent offenders in the details of various lines of illicit action ... In one sense, then, high living indicates that the threat of impoverishment, or economic determinism more generally, is never the cause of persistence in stickups. But given the diffuse and relatively constant economic pressures created by his diverse debts to a cross-cutting extensive social network, the persistent offender's stickups are always a response to economic pressure.'[15]

What sounds like circularity in Katz's argument is really quite linear. It is the desire to live a certain life, not poverty per se that produces the need for crime in order to deflect or deny the reality of poverty that sometimes intrudes on life. And, of course, the high living that is the cause produces poverty which produces more crime, and so on. Bill was certainly caught up in this cycle.

There was something else as well. The police, psychologists, and prison officials were unanimous in their reports on Bill that he was 'without conscience,' that he had absolutely no concern for or interest in his victims, that he was ruthless in dealing with his compatriots, and once apprehended showed no sign of remorse. Worse yet, in a perverse kind of way, there was no indication that drugs were a factor in his crimes, leading to the conclusion that he had 'freely chosen' his actions rather than been pushed into them by drugs, alcohol, or chemicals. The psychologists in the prison logically concluded that he suffered from a personality disorder, in Bill's case characterized by 'weak internal controls, impulsive behaviour, resentment of authority, and limited frustration tolerance.' Luckily for Bill, he was in prison during the post-medical model era when such diagnoses carried less weight than they had before (or would again – see next chapter). Nonetheless, the label 'personality disorder' does follow Bill through the system, blunted in the end by the refusal of two consulting psychiatrists to enhance the description by labelling him a psychopath.

After serving seven years in prison Bill was paroled, reluctantly to be sure since he remained uncooperative to the end and, in the eyes of the experts, unchanged. He had enrolled in the university program and done well but had refused all psychiatric intervention and remained aloof from efforts at counselling or other interventions. It was presumed that either the prospect of more time in prison would serve as a deterrent or that he would launch on another, more violent crime spree. In fact, he married, started his own business, and completed his parole successfully, his parole officer describing him as a 'mature and responsible individual ... determined to avoid further criminal involvements and to lead a low profile lifestyle.' One might posit here that the three years he spent taking university courses in prison may have simply given him a means of insulating himself, his actual 'self,' from the deleterious effects of imprisonment and immersion in a cultural milieu of bitterness, anger, and criminal skills training. More optimistically, if he really was without conscience the liberal arts courses may have awakened some latent moral sense, thereby helping Bill return to society older and wiser but otherwise much the same ambitious, hard-working man he had been before incarceration.

Despite the attempt to attach a sociopathic label to Bill in order to 'understand' his deviance and defiance, his version of crime is perhaps the most straightforward of all and the one least in need of labels. In a culture with rapidly collapsing ethical rules governing individual economic advancement – which certainly characterized the 1980s – Bill interpreted what rules there were in the most liberal and self-advantageous a manner possible. He was hard-working, clever, intelligent, and entreprenurial – and he was out of work. His needs, skills, and individualist ethical system impelled him, as it were, towards the easy money to be made by theft. That there were few internal stop-gaps between 'need' and 'take' certainly fueled the fire. Reminded eventually of the penalty to be paid by the non-professional, non-connected criminal once apprehended, Bill set about mobilizing the same skills to achieve his ends in other ways – significantly, without ever addressing in a visible way the moral or ethical issues intrinsic to his original choices. In the *choices, skills and abilities*, and *will* triad referred to earlier, Bill used his time in prison to broaden his entrepenurial options and acquired some new skills and abilities through education, but his will no doubt remained as ruthlessly dedicated to self-interest as it had been in his criminal career.

Crime and the Family

Crippled by their upbringing, they cannot escape the prison of themselves.[16]

The family is the most obvious yet hidden battleground in the breakdown of modernity. The geographical fluidity forced by the modern economy, the postwar double income imperative, and persistent high levels of periodic unemployment often lead within the family directly to alcohol abuse, physical abuse, divorce, abandonment, and to crime in the next generation. We have no shortage of iconic happy families against which to measure our own lots in life – one thinks of the Cratchits surviving even the meanness of Scrooge and the perils of Tiny Tim's pending demise, of the Baileys' irrepressibly wonderful life, the Nelsons' irremediably peaceful if claustrophobic life, and the Waltons' benign mountain existence. To see the toxic side of these ideal images one only has to peruse the files of a random collection of the imprisoned. Here, for instance, are samples of men who one might argue were virtually born into delinquency:

1   Father an alcoholic and died when subject was two years old – lived with grandmother and various aunts most of his life and was unable to get along with his stepfather who was physically abusive and described as a 'perfectionist who has shown little understanding or interest in the subject' Frequently ran away from home, becoming a ward of the Superintendent of Child Welfare at age 12 and described as 'an extremely aggressive youngster [who] feels rejected by all adults.' After numerous foster placements, was deemed 'incorrigible' and sent to a juvenile detention centre at age fourteen and a year later found himself in jail, where he was described as a 'poor worker and a constant custodial problem.'

2   Oldest in a family of five children in a family described as being
'debilitatively negative in influence.' Subject's father is an addict
and his mother an alcoholic . They divorced when subject was two
years old, and his mother remarried to an alcoholic who turned out
to be physically abusive to the subject. Convicted of wilful damage
at age twelve and put on probation and then convicted for car theft
at age fifteen. Subject not told about his real father until he was sixteen years old, at which time his mother returned to the original
marriage. Subject began drinking at age fourteen, left school at sixteen after completing grade 10, incarcerated in juvenile institution
at age seventeen for auto theft, and by age eighteen was a heroin
addict along with one brother and a sister.

3   Father an alcoholic and mother a drug addict and prostitute aged
sixteen when subject born. When he was fourteen, mother killed by
a customer and father committed suicide a year later. Subject subsequently lived in foster homes where he claims both physical and
sexual abuse. Dropped out of school at grade 8 and attempted suicide. Between ages 15 and 19 he admits to being 'out of control,'
expressing his anger in physical violence towards men and women
indiscriminately.

4   Parents divorced when subject four years old. Placed in foster home
with younger brother because mother an alcoholic. Left school and
declared a ward of the court at age nine. Sent to 'training school'
when mother failed to appear in court to claim him. Ran away from
the institution several times and, after conviction for auto theft at
age sixteen, sent to a reformatory. By age seventeen he was a heroin
addict and in a maximum security penitentiary. In reflecting on all
this later he says, 'I'm only what you made me.'

In cases such as these it is hard to contest the idea that these individuals are, in fact, 'merely what we made them.' Not all such crooked
timber that emerges from flawed families and catastrophic youth
engages subsequently in a life of crime, and it is not unreasonable for
society to expect one to rise above or learn to cope with such disadvantages. But certainly in tolerating such circumstances we increase the
odds that many such individuals will fail in these efforts and that
therefore we will, both individually as victims and collectively as citizens, suffer the consequences. Charles Dickens warned us about this
just as we were making this modernity, and as far as we know Oliver
Twist was the only one of Fagin's group of young thieves to escape a

life of crime and that only because of extraordinary and serendipitious connections denied the likes of the Artful Dodger.

All criminals, of course, do not spring from such obvious origins – hence the intractable complexity of crime and deviance. For some, the quite normal rebelliousness of adolescence may, for instance, run headlong into a particularly recalcitrant parent whose style of discipline forces a break with the family and, if no other support systems are present, a descent to the street and then possibly – again, only if circumstances are right – to crime. A case in point is James, the oldest of four children from a thoroughly middle-class family with two professional people for parents and the only one to 'turn out bad.' James had some difficulties in school as a result of some childhood medical problems and failed in competitions with his younger brothers. He became a discipline problem at home, and his father admitted that James 'definitely received more *lickings* than his brothers and that he was very difficult to discipline.' The father, a former policeman, had great difficulty showing any emotion or affection towards his children, explaining that 'his own father behaved similarly and he did not experience the feeling that his father did not care for him as "James" apparently does.' A psychologist later concluded that 'there seems little doubt that his father was extremely physically abusive and psychologically cruel' to James, as was his mother. By age fourteen James had begun to drift into the local drug culture (the mid-1970s again) which only served to escalate the conflicts at home. By age seventeen he was injecting heroin and using LSD. On three occasions his father phoned the police to have him picked up when he brought drugs into the family home, the last occasion resulting in a jail term. Within a few years James was trafficking in heroin and using firearms in armed robberies aimed at maintaining his drug habit.

In reviewing James's file one can almost feel the pressures within his in most ways quite average middle-class childhood home, the competition among the siblings for achievement in sports and in school, the need for discipline in order to maintain a complex household run by parents with career pressures, the heritage of an earlier generation of middle-class disciplinarians, and even, reading between the lines, a sense of the pleasures derived from the dispensation of discipline. These were the mechanisms at work within the household, and under normal circumstances they might have 'worked' as planned, but there was a new context which James had access to, the drug culture and its doppelgänger, the criminal culture. James could move easily, even at fourteen years old, into a world of drugs, theft, and pleasure that had previously existed only among the marginalized but that by the 1970s had come to pervade the culture as a whole. The existence of this alternative context within which one could live a life produced only further frustration and discipline at home, to the point of calling upon the state, Brutus-like, to gather up the young rebel for the benefit of the whole.

The issue of discipline and rebellion knows no class boundaries. Greg grew up in a family with similar rules, but from a solid working-class background. Greg and each of his siblings left home at age sixteen, as soon as they were able, all because of difficulties they had with their father. His mother insisted that her husband 'cares about his children but has difficulty communicating with them.' Greg agrees, and describes his father as 'restrictive and authoritarian,' a man who no doubt cared about his children but 'it got lost in the issues of control and discipline.' While his three siblings managed to engage with work and family after leaving home, Greg turned towards drugs and delinquency by age fourteen, was convicted of breaking and entering by age sixteen, and by age nineteen was in prison for a 'senseless' murder.

If our first group of examples suffered from too little family, the second set suffered from too much. Particularly disturbing for the culture as a whole is the clear knowledge that the breakdown – some would say collapse – of the family is a direct cause of not only social chaos but also individual pain, coupled with the growing insight that we can do little about it. In the more than 800 files reviewed in the evaluation of the prison education program in British Columbia, the researchers early on singled out what they called 'toxic families' as a central theme in the life histories of the subjects, the toxicity stemming from either collapse of the family or from a too desperate attempt to stem the tide of collapse. The cultural insight of our time may be, if the postmoderns are correct, that the presence of 'exhausted life-worlds lying at the roadside ditches,' has its origins at the very core of human society, the family, and the cultural energy and creativity needed to address the breakdown of such a fundamental component of our collective being just may not be present within the 'modern.'

Sex and Crime – The Final Frontier

All these treaties one makes with passion are purely imaginary:
like all true tyrants, it is either enthroned or in chains.[17]

If the medical model and its correlate the application of treatment to the phenomena of deviance had come upon hard times in the 1970s, its time in the wilderness was soon to end. A revolution was occurring in the wider culture that was being spearheaded by the feminist movement, a movement that demanded an end to sexual violence directed at women and children. After much campaigning, new laws were passed and all aspects of the criminal justice system began to be sensitized to the importance of taking more seriously a range of behaviours that in the past had been too often ignored or minimized. By the late 1980s a powerful consensus had been reached that not only should such behaviours as rape, sexual assault, incest, and child molestation – among others – be the subject of severe judicial action, but also the criminal justice system should be mandated to treat such offenders, by coercion if necessary. Here was the opening for a resurgent medical model and eventually a new medicalization of corrections. The objections of Morris and others that linking treatment or rehabilitation with coercion was both wrong and doomed to failure was specifically and deliberately cast aside in the new moral crusade against sexual interference of any kind.

Quickly the proponents of treatment, including correctional staff who had long been chafing under the restrictions of opportunity models and humane containment, moved to expand the notion of sexual deviance requiring treatment to include *any* crime of a sexual nature. Thus, perpetrators of incest, serial rape, violent sexual assault, sexual touching, molestation, and attempted sexual assault were all labelled 'sexual offenders' and thereby destined for treatment. The long-standing distinction between sexual deviants, who always seemed different from ordinary criminals, and men who commit violent attacks on women was blurred or in some cases eliminated. Likewise, career criminals who may have specialized in theft or drugs but who added a sexual assault to their repertoire were more often than not also given the new label of sex offender. The result, inevitably, was a vast expansion in the number of sexual offenders, in Canada a 40 per cent increase from 1990 to 1995.[18] The massive shift back to a revitalized and reformed medical approach to corrections in the 1990s, triggered in effect by this new preoccupation with sexual deviance, is the subject of the next chapter, but by examining in detail a few cases from the 1980s we can explore its early gestation.

To see how this worked in practice we will examine three cases: Raymond, convicted of attempted rape in 1981 and sentenced to five years; Allen, convicted of two counts of sexual assault in 1988 and sentenced to six years; and Glen, convicted of sexual assault and indecent assault in 1988 and sentenced to four years. Each case takes a quite distinct course despite the similarity of origin, and the variations can tell us a lot about the operation of the correctional enterprise. It is, of course, a commonplace among prisoners that the punishments meted out for similar crimes vary wildly, but in these cases it is not the punishments or sentences that are of interest, but rather the process and pace of release that is revealing.

Raymond's Story

Raymond had a nasty youth starting with parental divorce, stepfather problems, delinquency, training schools, crime, and drug use – the usual. He went through two common law marriages by his early twenties, fathered a child, and continued his increasing involvement with drugs. Between the ages of eighteen and twenty-three he was convicted on eight separate occasions of robbery, theft, narcotic possession, breaking and entering, and assault causing bodily harm, each carrying short sentences, fines, or periods of probation. Raymond was in most ways a typical small-time criminal with addiction and drug abuse problems.

Then, after two years free of offences and with no indication from his record that it is coming, he committed, or attempted to commit, a rape. After a bout of heavy drinking in a city bar, Raymond confronted a woman on the street, shoved her into an alley, and sexually assaulted her, the actual rape being interrupted by passers-by and the police. In court, Raymond used his drunkenness as an excuse, complained that he never intended to 'really' hurt the woman, and that it was a one-time-only incident related to circumstances and his state of mind at the time. The court saw the situation otherwise, and in sentencing the judge recommended that as part of his sentence Raymond be sent to a psychiatric prison for treatment. The criminal justice system had shifted gears in a dramatic way in dealing with Raymond, alerted now to (a) a serious escalation in violence in a long-time offender, and (b) commission of an act for which psychological motives are seen as paramount instead of economic, subcultural, or addiction motives. From this point on it would not be enough for Raymond to avail himself of opportunities such as education, be a good inmate, demonstrate personal growth, or address his drug problem, he would now be asked to admit to an illness and accept treatment.

Raymond's offence occurred in the early 1980s, when the power of the treatment forces was blunted if not defeated. Raymond refused from the start to admit that he had a 'sex problem,' was uncooperative at the psychiatric centre, refused to participate in therapy groups with other sexual offenders, and persistently demanded transfer to a 'normal' prison in order to continue his education. As a result, at his first application for parole he was deemed to be 'basically untreated' and told to return to the psychiatric centre to 'gain understanding of what motivates your criminal actions.' The officials at the psychiatric centre, on the other hand, wanted no part of Raymond because 'he still insists he is not a sex offender.' By resisting the label, Raymond was preserving for himself an identity as 'criminal' rather than 'sexual deviant,' but at the same time paying the price of serving more time in prison. Two years into his sentence his Correctional and Parole Service management team dismissed his success at completing a high school diploma and taking university courses as well as his participation in a narcotics addiction program, saying neither will 'promote insight into his underlying hostility and anti-social sexual behaviour.' He was subsequently refused his last chance at early parole and forced to remain in prison until his date of mandatory supervision (at completion of two-thirds of sentence). When the Parole Board members insisted on probing once again into his offence and his 'failure to confront his problems,' Raymond bolted from the interview exclaiming, 'I don't have to sit here and take this.' And he was right!

Three months later Raymond was released on mandatory supervision, his parole officer rejecting the board's suggestion that he be subject to 'special parole conditions.' Raymond had difficulties during his year and a half on parole, but there was no evidence of serious drug use and no further sexual offences. He managed, despite the nature of his offence, to avoid accepting the label of sexual offender, and while that cost him some additional time in prison, it was minimal compared with what he would have faced had he been in Allen's situation a few years later.

Allen's Story

Allen started out his life as inauspiciously as the others recounted here. He left school age fourteen, began to drink heavily, used a variety of drugs, ran away from home, and reported several incidents of sexual abuse first by girls and then for a prolonged period by an older man. His criminal record started at age sixteen when he was convicted of breaking and entering, but he remained primarily a transient labourer and showed few signs of any commitment to a criminal lifestyle. Then, in 1988 when age twenty, he committed a serious sexual assault, though as in Raymond's case the actual rape was interrupted by the intervention of several witnesses. In Allen's case he 'picked up' the woman in a bar following an evening spent with her drinking and dancing and the assault followed a 'disagreement' over supposedly promised sexual favours. There is no question of guilt in the case, but what may be at issue is 'guilty of what'? Was Allen a psychopathic sexual predator who will assault and rape again or an alcohol-driven young man with massive confusion about his sexuality and low sense of self-worth because of chronic underachievement? For the crime he received a sentence of six years, and in his case he served the full sentence.

Sent for psychiatric evaluation at the start of his sentence, Allen was described as emotionally immature, likely to act without attention to consequences, and suffering from confusion and conflict about his sexuality. After arrival in prison he eagerly participated in education programs and in activities designed to provide occupational training, but resisted participation in counselling or psychological programs. His case management team at the prison were encouraged by his determination 'to make his sentence productive,' but unhappy with his refusal to participate in psychotherapy and insisted that he needed to 'overcome his acquired distrust and develop a trusting relationship with a counselor or a psychologist so he can explore his troubled childhood and through treatment develop emotional sensitivity and empathy for others, especially his victims and women in general.'

Three years into his sentence, Allen was persuaded to enter an experimental aversive-therapy program for sex offenders, partly in response to pressure from his case management team and partly because it involved a transfer to a lesser security institution. The therapist described Allen as an 'undercontrolled powerthrust offender type' and began working closely with him, within two months concluding that he was 'highly motivated to rehabilitate himself and has demonstrated a commitment to treatment.' As a result Allen was recommended for transfer to even lower security so he could be included in a different therapy group. Once that transfer was completed, however, things began to go awry. Allen fell in with a religious group and decided to withdraw from the therapy program in favour of attending a program for alcoholics and a life skills program. The therapist reversed course and concluded that Allen was manipulative, exploitative, and likely to re-offend: 'If the subject's risk of re-offending is to be reduced it is essential that he continue in treatment for an indeterminate period of time and be closely monitored upon release in the community.'

Things had changed since Raymond's time. The Correctional Service in Canada now had the power to 'detain' a prisoner past the mandatory supervision date and force him to serve the full sentence in prison. The therapist and a consulting psychologist both recommend that Allen be detained. In its report, his case management team now referred to Allen's offence as a 'brutal rape' and recommended detention. Only the parole officer assigned to the case recommended against detention, citing Allen's accomplishments in prison, his willingness to consider treatment, and the lack of any overt indications he would re-offend. Five months after withdrawing from the therapy program and four years into his sentence, Allen was detained. He subsequently withdrew from all programs and became a grounds worker in the prison. As an 'untreated sex offender' he was not eligible for transfer to lesser security and at one point was described as a candidate for maximum security because of his being a possible escape risk – and this when he had less than two months to serve.

After the first year of detention Allen refused to attend the Parole Board's hearing concerning his case and the detention was continued for a second year. His works supervisor described him as a reliable worker, and his case management team expressed concern that Allen seemed to be 'waiting until his warrant expiry date and will decide without the correctional service's assistance exactly where he will go and what he will do.' Needless to say, there is no indication of irony in the team's statement of concern. As a final gesture, the prison denied him access to the recreation and craft areas in the two months prior to his release. It was still possible, then, as late as 1991 to stubbornly 'do your time' and resist any attempt to reach into the soul. As this is being written however (1999), there are calls from pressure groups and from within the corrections service for additional powers to detain prisoners who refuse treatment beyond even the terms of their original sentence. Raymond and Allen resisted, paid a price but in their own ways 'won.' What happens if one cooperates? Glen's story offers some clues.

Glen's Story

The product of a turbulent childhood that included the death of his mother when he was young, a stepmother who physically abused him, a father who was 'distant,' and older relatives who engaged him in sexual activities, Glen was seemingly fated to have difficulties imagining, let alone living, a normal sexual life. He was twice married, each marriage ending with indications of violence as a contributing factor, and only intermittently employed. He was convicted in 1988 of sexual assault and indecent assault on children from each of the marriages, activity that in each case lasted for several years while the children were aged seven to sixteen. He was sentenced to four years.

From the start Glen's story is different from that of Raymond or Allen. He cooperated fully with the prison psychiatrist who noted that Glen 'accepts responsibility for his marital failures and sexual offences.' No psychiatric disorder was identified and he was not diagnosed as a pedophile, but rather as someone with a 'tremendous sense of personal inadequacy' who at times of stress falls into a feeling of helplessness. The prison psychologist put great stress on his childhood problems, including a reported sexual assault by a man when he was twelve, beatings by his stepmother, and inappropriate sexual play with a cousin over an extended period of time. He did express some concern about Glen's sincerity and worried that it is still possible that he does not accept that his actions were really wrong. Tests, however, such as the Minnesota Multiphasic Personality Inventory (MMPI), the California Psychological Inventory (CPI) and the Sixteen Personality Factor Questionnaire (16PF) showed no serious psychopathology.

His case management team was impressed with Glen during his first year in prison. He enrolled in the university program and did very well, joined a therapy group as well as a drug and alcohol counselling group, and completed the prison life skills program. He was described as 'sincere and motivated to continue to work on his problems. He is very open and able to discuss his crime cycle and verbalize good insight.' Within sixteen months of entering the prison, Glen was released on day parole to a halfway house. While his parole officer worried about Glen's ability to 'spout the therapese quite easily,' he attended therapy sessions regularly and showed what the psychologist called the 'appropriate emotions ... and very good understanding' in discussing his 'offending cycle and steps that must be taken to avoid re-offending.' Eight months later, after completing only half of his sentence, Glen was granted full parole. The Parole Board complimented Glen on his progress, noting that: 'you have an excellent understanding of what led to your offending ... you appear to accept responsibility for the offences and to understand the harm done to the victims. You have endeavoured to ensure such behaviour will not be repeated by undertaking programming and counseling ... You appear to have benefited from incarceration.' Glen was clearly a success, having taken full advantage of programs, grown cognitively and morally, accepted responsibility and shown evidence of remorse.

To compare the three cases is not really fair to the corrections service because Glen's offence is clearly of a different order than either Raymond's or 'Allen's. Glen falls into the category of 'sexual deviant,' men (primarily) who are generally neither aggressive nor violent and who as a general rule are willing to admit that they have sexual problems for which they need help. Raymond and Allen, on the other hand, fall into a category typically called 'sexual assaulters,' younger men from the lower socioeconomic stratum who are likely to have extensive criminal records and who definitely do not consider themselves psychologically abnormal.[19] The point here, however, is not that all three 'should' have been treated the same, but rather to illustrate how in the later 1980s the Correctional Service of Canada in this case had begun to collapse the categories into one sexual offender package and to show how this worked in terms of individual offenders. The analogy in other jurisdictions would be to so-called political criminals and the determination of some states to deny one access to that category and instead insist on the common label 'criminal' or 'gangster.'

The Response of the State

In the 1980s public attention became focused intently on issues related to sexual assaults against women and the finer distinctions that at one time surrounded these offences, including the idea that the context might indicate some measure of reciprocal responsibility, were being set aside. Offences against children, however, were still seen in an essentially medical framework, a situation that would not change until the 1990s when offences against children began to receive comparable attention. In both these cases, offences against women and against children, their high profile in the community provided the impetus for a reinvigorated medical model to once again begin to pervade corrections, at least in North America.

Returning to a more philosophical perspective on the shifts in public policy that come to characterize the state's response to both public pressure for order and increasing signs of a breakdown in public safety and conformity to the law, the current tensions can be seen as stemming from a new version of the fundamental conflict in modernity between Kantian universals and Humean particulars. The public in North America and in Great Britain, in a desperate attempt to cling to a modernity they feel is collapsing in on itself, are becoming increasingly Kantian in their demand that universal notions of justice, of right and wrong, be applied in the criminal justice system. In Kant's formulation there are moral imperatives involved in actions in the world, including criminal actions, and there need to be specific and precise social responses to those actions.[20] This 'eye-for-an-eye' approach, where punishments match the crime and in which there is an overwhelming moral dimension to evil or deviance has tremendous appeal to a populace feeling under siege by both social disorder and by an intellectual culture drifting towards postmodernist conceptions of 'privileging' difference, including sometimes deviant difference. This public mood is allowed particular free rein in the area of crime and prisons because of the almost universal categorization of the criminal as 'other,' a categorization increasingly difficult to sustain in parallel areas such as mental health, race relations, or gender differentiations where the boundaries between 'other' and 'us' have become hopelessly blurred.

The criminal justice system, on the other hand, is rooted in a Humean contextualism and a Benthamite utilitarianism, complicating its mission by beliefs in the importance of – among other things – deterrence, individual backgrounds, the contexts in which actions occur, and the moral climate of the time. Prisons and the criminal justice system as a whole are seen as places where discretion is necessary, meaning that actual punishments almost always involve a compromise, a compromise mediated through and administered by 'experts' in 'corrections.'[21] As we have seen, in particular in the analysis of the three sexual offenders, while the crime itself still forms the basis of the judgment and the punishment, the criminal justice system is really more concerned with the passions, instincts, anomalies, infirmities, and maladjustments that accompany the crime. As Foucault argued, aggressiveness is punished along with acts of aggression – rape is punished but also perversions – murders are punished but also drives and desires – all in an attempt to 'determine to what extent the subject's will was involved in the crime.'[22] Thus, we see the diminution of the act itself in favour of discovering the shadows behind the act.

The result of these conflicting views of crime and punishment is a kind of stand-off, a 'high noon' confrontation between the public as the angry lynch mob heading for the local jail to administer justice, and the sheriff holed up in the jail protecting the offender in the name of a law embedded in contextualisms. In the movie version the sheriff is almost always right, and the populace learns its lesson. In real life in the 1980s the issue was no so simple.

In the first place, the public was increasingly aware that the experts themselves were not convinced that criminals could be helped, reformed, or rehabilitated. Worse yet, some experts claimed that prison programs – not just prison per se – actually made things worse.[23] Second, research carried out in the late 1970s introduced into public discourse the notion of the 'career criminal,' the idea that crime is actually the practical and pragmatic 'work' of a relatively small number of individuals who are essentially incorrigible and their removal from society would result in a significant drop in the level of crime. Thus, a RAND Corporation study of career criminals in California reported that 8 per cent of 624 felons in five state prisons committed more than sixty crimes each year in the three years prior to their incarceration.[24] The data were at times spectacular, with in one case only forty-nine 'armed robbers' accounting for over 10,000 individual crimes (3620 drug sales, 2331 burglaries, 1492 car thefts, 995 forgeries, 993 grand thefts, and 855 instances of robbery).[25] This idea, reinforced in countless movies and other media, convinced people in the United States and the United Kingdom – less so in Canada – that incapacitation of large numbers of these career criminals would be worth the cost, both in economic and social terms.

Further evidence for incapacitation was provided by the different experiences during the 1980s of two of the largest prison systems in the United States, the Texas and California state systems. Texas had opted for decarceration and enhanced parole opportunities during the 1980s, while California, which had already abandoned parole as an option, went on a prison-building spree. When the data were in they showed clearly that property crime in California had decreased while it had risen substantially in Texas.[26] Despite there being a number of possible alternative explanations – specifically, quite different economic conditions in the two states during this period – the more obvious lesson was learned, and Texas subsequently shifted with a vengeance to a massive prison-building program, attaining by 1996 the highest incarceration rate in the United States (659/100,000 people) and their lowest crime rate since 1973.[27]

The result of these policies of incapacitation was a dramatic increase in the prison population, increasing by 150 per cent in the United

States during the 1980s. The increase could partly be attributed to a rise in the rate of crime, albeit more slowly than people imagined, and improved arrest rates as part of a general 'get tough on crime' ethos, but the real cause was a 50 per cent increase in prison admissions, longer sentences, and fewer paroles. Parole, in fact, became the greatest casualty of the era since it was widely reported that rates of recidivism were increasing throughout the decade. The system of parole had always acted as a 'safety valve' in the criminal justice system, but now it was increasingly being blocked by legislative fiat and public scrutiny.[28] The detention system referred to in Allen's story was introduced at this time in Canada as a means of blunting parole and various kinds of 'dangerous offender' laws were passed enabling individuals to be held without parole or for indeterminate periods of time.

The Three Strikes Movement which began in California in 1993 and quickly spread is perhaps the perfect manifestation in this response to crime. The outcome of the brutal murder of a young girl, Polly Klaas – a statistically rare offence – became for the North American public symbolic of all crime and a vehicle through which to vent their frustration. Samuel Pillsbury, a California law professor, in reflecting on the Three Strikes Law that followed the Klaas murder, saw the power of the case in its narrative quality, the 'story' of an innocent child, an evil man, and an incompetent legal system. The resulting legislation is a public victory in the sense that it imposes an absolutist, Kantian-derived imperative – three strikes and you are out – on a contextualist and utilitarian system, a marriage not made in heaven. Pillsbury estimates that in California alone the effects of the law will result in 80,000 additional prisoners by 1999, 149,000 by 2004 and 274,000 by 2026 at a cost of billions of dollars. Worse yet from the professional perspective, the 'three strikes law cannot be reconciled with any generally accepted punishment theory. It violates basic utilitarian principles: Instead of using the minimum amount of punishment necessary to deter the worst wrongs, the law creates an often haphazard penalty scheme, inflicting a great deal of pain on many offenders who have committed relatively minor offenses. It terms of fiscal policy ... it requires the state to distribute one of its most precious resources, long-term prison space, to offenders who have committed non-violent offenses and to violent offenders who are likely at the end of their violent criminal careers. Meanwhile, the law flouts the retributive principle that the most serious offenses receive the most serious punishments.'[29] The Three Strikes Law epitomized the state of crisis that the criminal justice systems of North America and Great Britain were in. Having abandoned rehabilitation as a singular objective as it had been in the peak era of the medical model, but not having abandoned the conviction that 'something' could work, the system had fallen back on gross incapacitation, isolated pockets of openness, and experimentation without commitment, and finally, it been forced to abdicate responsibility and simply warehouse those who 'struck out,' were swept up in anti-crime campaigns and drug wars, or who fell victim to the latest variant in the new policing of sex. All this occurred in the context of shrinking resources, deteriorating staff morale, competition from private prison entrepreneurs, and massive overcrowding (California was at 182 per cent of capacity in 1995).

To repair this situation would require a new belief system, a new faith in the positive mission of the correctional enterprise, and as well a new set of scientific tools – a renaissance of rehabilitation in other words. The basis for this renaissance was being readied throughout the 1980s by a collection of Canadian criminologists and psychologists working closely with colleagues within the Correctional Service of Canada as well as corrections professionals in the United States and was to burst on the scene in the 1990s sweeping all before it – including most of those still-blooming hundred flowers.

CHAPTER SEVEN

A Cold Wind from the North –
The Medical Model Redux

There are few presumptions in human relations more dangerous than the idea that one knows what another human being needs better than they do themselves.[1]
Michael Ignatieff, *Needs of Strangers*, 1984

By the late 1980s it could be well and truly said that corrections and prison systems in general were facing a crisis. The growing political consensus around the idea of incapacitation that had grown out of the coupling of criminal career research with the growing public obsession with crime as a menace on a par with communism was leading to massive overcrowding of prisons, a court system in gridlock, and parole and probation services unable to cope with expanding case-loads. Available public monies were being consumed in prison construction, leaving inadequate resources for staffing, institutional programs, or after-care. Given the central political role that wars on crime and wars on perversion were coming to play in the culture, the fixation of the media on crime, and the growing obsession with the need to pay off the massive public debt accumulated after forty years of Cold War, it was clear to all involved that neither the overcrowding nor the fiscal situation was going to change in the near future.

A Resurgence of Corrections

Inside the prisons the individuals and groups that had been allowed in through the era of opportunities and humane containment – universities, colleges, school districts, contractors, volunteers, church groups, and so forth – were hard at work in a myriad number of programs of varying quality and effectiveness. Since they were outside the formal system, however, they were the first to take the 'fiscal hit,' constantly being asked to do more for less. Particularly frustrating for the correctional bureaucracies and their government watchdogs was the lack of consistency and lack of order implicit in this cacaphony of programmatic activity within the prisons. Various groups were offering literacy programs, living skills programs, counselling efforts, employment skills training, and education programs – each with its own set of standards, objectives, and values. Efforts were made, of course, to standardize reporting in order to ensure that contract and system goals were being met, but in the absence of central control such standardization was impossible to achieve. The correctional administrator had to somehow make sense from afar of a literacy program that might report hours spent in individual tutoring, a college reporting grade levels achieved, a vocational program specific skills acquired, and a university the number of credits completed.

There were the inevitable conflicts over authority, privacy, and jurisdiction. Universities, for instance, would often refuse to release prisoners' academic records to the prison authorities, some contractors would resist or not take seriously certain security measures like taking the daily counts of inmates, and volunteer tutor-counsellors would often form close bonds with their charges and be persuaded to break minor rules about contraband. As well, there was the constant stream of outsiders coming into the prisons as the outside agencies sought to enrich their offerings, rotate their staffs, and respond to shifting priorities. Worst of all, the correctional system could not be sure that all these outsiders shared any of the prime goals of corrections, namely, the peace and good order of the institution, security of containment, and rehabilitation. In fact, often the more entrenched they became the more the contracting parties openly rejected these goals. Even more disturbing, in many cases these outside groups carried with them the influence of community-based groups and institutions. Thus, admission of a post-secondary program into a prison introduced at the same time a college or university-as-institution into a carceral world that had formerly been under the sole scrutiny of the prison as institution. Likewise, the admission of a Black Muslim counselling group, a literacy lobby group, or an artists' or writers' workshop into the prison brought with them, implicitly if not explicitly, the scrutiny of their affiliates in the community at large. We have seen the impact of this in the story of the demise of the SCWPP and the Barlinnie programs.

As an interesting adjunct to the changes in offender programming that had taken place most correctional systems had experienced a parallel change in the nature of their senior administrative staff. During the era of the medical model corrections administrators had been expected to have direct involvement with programs for offenders. Education programs in prisons had tended to be administered by prison officials with backgrounds in education, therapy and counselling programs by prison officials with backgrounds in psychology, and so forth. By the late 1980s a new generation of corrections administrators was in place, experienced and more professional managers who had no particular subject or service area expertise but rather were expected to make the system more accountable while cutting costs wherever possible.

In terms of organization, morale, and sense of purpose, prison systems were in disarray by the mid-1980s. From being professionally run security and work-oriented institutions throughout most of the twentieth century they had shifted first towards a medical, almost hospital-like mission in the 1960s, and when that collapsed in the mid-1970s shifted once again, this time towards an increasingly open and deprofessionalized system with multiple missions, a vast array of programs, and little sense of common purpose. While it may be a stretch to attribute this situation in any direct way to the rise of a postmodern intellectual culture, the sense of self-doubt, the multiplication of interest groups, the increasing fragmentation of the inmate population by race, class, and even type of offence, and the erosion of authoritarian decisiveness in the system's response to these and other challenges bore an uncanny resemblance to the challenges being faced at the same time by other mainstream institutions.

The response was not long in coming. Two national task forces, one in Canada and the other in England, came to remarkably similar conclusions in 1985 following their assessment of the state of correctional programming, staff morale, and system-wide purpose. The author of the English report, Ian Dunbar, visited correctional systems in Sweden, the United States, and Canada as well as undertaking a thorough review of prisons in the United Kingdom. His report, *A Sense of Direction*, called for a new focus within the English Prison Service on objectives, communication, and staff training.[2] The English system had not gone nearly as far down the road of contracting out for services as had the systems in Canada and the United States, and following several prison riots and the adoption of the humane containment policy, the prison system was perceived to be drifting without clear direction. Dunbar identified the failure of the earlier treatment approach as resulting from the practical impossibility of its objective, that is, reducing recidivism. No single component of the criminal justice system could be charged with that task, Dunbar argued, it was too complex an outcome. At the same time, he worried that a prison system without treatment, one that only contained, however humanely, could only lead to the deterioration of the prisoner and the demoralization of the service. In this age of post-Martinson minimalism, treatment still did not 'work,' but it remained an essential part of the prison regime because it arguably prevented things from getting worse and, Dunbar asserted, improved staff morale. Above all, Dunbar's report clearly enunciated the demand from corrections professionals (Dunbar was a senior prison governor) that something be done to stop the drift: 'the aims of the prison system cannot be allowed to ebb and flow in an unpredictable way and some clear statement is called for, if the vacuum which I have already described is not to become the aim of the system.'[3]

In Canada, a *Review of Offender Support Programs* completed in 1985 under the direction of T. Sawatsky on behalf of the Correctional Service of Canada came to quite similar if more specific recommendations. The Sawatsky report opened with the declared ambition of creating some order out of what was seen as the 'eclectic ... trying to be all things to all people' approach to programming that had come to characterize Canadian corrections from the 1960s to the present.[4] More than just a recognition that efficiencies were required in light of reductions in resources, Sawatsky condemned the spreading of programs across institutions, the erosion of the linkage between security level and program accessibility, the absence of a required connection between prescribed inmate need and program access, and the refusal of the system to recognize that change in inmate behaviour 'demands a capacity to provide meaningful positive and negative consequences.'[5] The medical model was not so far away after all given this clear behaviourist rhetoric, and indeed Sawatsky signalled the end of the opportunities approach by voicing what most corrections staff had felt for some time: 'The "opportunities model" is a primary contributor to the instability [in correctional programming]. Because this model assumes the offender to be responsible, the staff have, regrettably, all too often seen their responsibility as being only to ensure that the offender is afforded program opportunities of his choice. The result of this orientation has seemingly created a "window-shopping mentality" where inmates "wander" or "drift" in and out of programs without addressing key areas of need or seeing a particular program through to its completion.'[6] Now here was the 'bold truth' finally being spoken. Not only was the system 'adrift,' but as a result the poor inmate was drifting as well, suffering under the delusion that he or she is 'responsible,' can make 'choices,' and decide which of his or her needs might require being met. The empowering of the prisoner, a very real effect of the opportunities approach, had never set well with corrections staff. The Sawatsky report called for a clear identification of 'core' programs after which funding and access priorities could be established and inmates channelled into those program areas that the corrections professionals decided were important.

Change was clearly on the way, but what kind of change? What kind of direction? Before that could be determined there were some important missing pieces. The system had to acquire more information or insight about who to keep locked up – that is, who were the really dangerous offenders in need of treatment? This was important because decreased overall resources meant that all prisoners could not receive treatment. There had to be a way to determine who among the increasing number of the imprisoned should be receiving treatment. Who, for instance, was a high risk to re-offend, a potentially violent offender, a repeat sex offender?

Two things were required to put into effect the ambitions of a rejuvenated but still unsure correctional service. First, the efficacy of treatment as a primary objective and purpose of corrections had to be re-established – rehabilitation had to undergo a renaissance. Second, a means of prediction had to be established in order that these new, and inevitably expensive, treatments could be imparted only to those who 'needed' them. The next five years, from 1985 to 1990, were to see the successful accomplishment of both of these objectives.

Thinking and Crime – The Cognitive Panacea

With the illness metaphor in at least temporary disrepute, analyses concerning the nature of the criminal had shifted in the 1970s towards the idea of purposefulness, the criminal as decision maker. In line with other pressures in society pushing for the empowerment of the disadvantaged and formerly disempowered (for example, women, gays, ethnic minorities, and the mentally challenged), the idea of the criminal as decision maker fit well both with a radical or materialist image of the criminal as responding to structural injustice and inequality, as well as with the more conventional idea that the criminal was simply a poor decision maker, or a maker of poor decisions. As we have seen, the first approach fit well with the opportunities approach to corrections, imagining the apprehended criminal entering the prison and choosing from among a range of rehabilitative opportunities. In addition, as the Sawatsky report pointed out quite bluntly and Dunbar's review more indirectly, this notion of the prison as 'cafeteria' soon became anathema to corrections professionals who observed early on that the prisoners did not choose those programs that the professionals felt or knew they needed – sex offenders resisted therapy, thieves rejected vocational training, and drug addicts insisted it was the system not them that needed fixing.

What did fit perfectly with the ideas and interests of the corrections professionals was the second dimension of the criminal-as-decision-maker analysis, namely, that the prisoner made poor decisions (that is, first crime and then refusing proper help) and did so because he or she was either lacking or deficient in the requisite skills, abilities, and attitudes that were essential for properly informed decision making. In an indirect way, we returned to Socrates and Plato and the idea that crime, evil, or deviance springs from ignorance rather than ill will. But – and this was an important qualification – it remained an open question whether the ignorance stemmed from lack of information (education), improper or deviant values, or missing or underdeveloped components of the cognitive apparatus. For a few years all three of these possible understandings of the link between thinking and crime were kept in play through explorations into the nature and effect of formal education, moral learning, and cognitive development, until finally the latter emerged as dominant and a new medical metaphor was born. Crime – evil behaviour in Plato's language – did not stem simply from not knowing, from ignorance, and neither did it result from improper or insufficient moral training. Rather, crime was the outcome of insufficiently or unevenly developed rational or cognitive capacities – criminals did not know how to know!

It is important that we explore in some detail just what is meant by 'cognitive development.' We first encountered the cognitive approach in the discussion of 'insight' in Chapter 2, with Spivak et al. explaining in their 1976 text that successful problem solving (another variant of decision making) depends on *how* one thinks through the problem rather than on *what* ones knows, and that this 'how' is in turn built on a base of cognitive skills. This 'how one knows' – cognition – is no simple process, involving as it does the 'systematic interpretation and reorganization of the information that is received as a result of interaction with the environment.'[7] Cognition is a process of 'development' starting at birth or before and continuing through to adulthood, leading, if all goes well, to the refinement of perception and memory, the ability to select key stimuli, and the creation of the structures needed to code experience. The work of Jean Piaget on cognitive development in childhood played a particularly important role in the application of cognition to criminal behaviour. For Piaget the 'normal' person was fully mature in a cognitive sense by late adolescence, having by that time combined the physical maturation of the nervous system with both direct life experience and with ideas acquired in social interaction. In doing so the individual, according to Piaget, passes through four developmental stages:

- Stage 1 – sensory-motor (birth to two years): The individual is tied to immediate, concrete events that she or he perceives.
- Stage 2 – preoperational (age 2–6): The beginnings of anticipation and expectation of objects and events even though they may not be perceived. The concept of cause and effect emerges, and language is developed to impose order and structure on the environment.
- Stage 3 – concrete operational (age 7–11): The ability to understand cause and effect, to form hypotheses about likely consequences of actions, and to begin to grasp the organization of events that render the external world coherent. Insight into the 'facts' of the surrounding world is still derived primarily from direct concrete experience.
- Stage 4 – formal operations (age 12–15): The abstract principles out of which concrete facts arise are grasped and events understood in terms of their symbolic meaning. Theoretical possibilities can be weighed without the necessity of them actually taking place and behaviour can be attuned to theoretical possibilities that may never happen.[8]

The distinction between the last three stages is often illustrated by the example of the row of standing marbles, the first marble being hit by another marble that causes the last marble in the row to move (the desk-toy version has the marbles suspended by a string). A four- or five-year-old child thinks that the first marble somehow magically moved around the row and hit the last marble, even though such a movement could not be observed. Around six, the child thinks that each marble moves, tapping the one in front until it comes to the end of the row. By eleven, the child no longer needs to think that each marble moves – it is the force of the first one that passes through all of them and is transmitted to the last one.[9] In cognitive development theory these stages are built on 'capacities' in the mind, capacities that appear through maturation. In that sense we are all capable of full formal operational cognitions after about age fifteen, but we may not all realize that capability, or may do so 'unevenly.'

> These capacities manifest themselves in a set of skills and abilities that in turn enable us to achieve the appropriate stage of cognitive development. These skills are described variously, but generally include at least the following:
> - Self-reflection – the ability to assess one's own thinking in a critical manner
> - Empathy – being aware of the feelings of others and having the ability to put oneself in their position
> - Means-end reasoning – the ability to articulate the means necessary to solve a problem
> - Field awareness – the understanding that actions have social consequences and are socially derived[10]

There are four components to cognitive development theory: first one's nervous system has to mature sufficiently and fully enough to attain the *ability* for cognition; then we develop specific *capacities* through the interaction of these biological abilities with the physical and social world; these capacities give rise to a range of *skills*; and finally these skills manifest themselves in definite *stages* of cognitive development. It is a complex process with many pitfalls along the way. Physical damage can occur and affect one's ability for cognition, capacities can be inhibited by severe or harmful childhood social experiences, skills can be acquired unevenly or not at all, and one can remain stuck at an earlier stage in all or in some aspects of one's thinking.

In applying this notion of cognitive development to the world of crime and criminals it was the potential of uneven development that was so appealing, the possibility that in the maturation process something could go wrong and the individual could end up with cognitive 'deficits,' missing or underdeveloped capacities or skills. Because the deficits are developmental rather than innate, the door is opened for repair and renewal, for education, counselling, therapy, or other interventions to restart the developmental process. The existence of such a respectable final product – the fully socialized abstract thinker – had obvious appeal to a corrections ideology that needed to posit a conflict- and contradiction-free society into which it could release its reformed charges. Piagetian theory and its offshoots in moral and political theory (Lawrence Kohlberg at Harvard, for instance) now seems hopelessly 'modern' in its universalizing tendencies, its failure to acknowledge let alone celebrate difference and contradiction, and its optimism that deficits need not be pathologies – that everyone could somehow 'fit in.' For corrections this was a much more comforting approach than a postmodern eagerness to 'live with, thrive upon and eventually take pleasure in the contradictions' that comprise life in society and life in body.[11]

The moral dimension to developmental theory had an obvious attraction to the corrections enterprise, though not in the sense of moralizing, exacting remorse, or passing on a particular 'bag of virtues.' The idea that there was a moral end-point, a principled morality, was embedded in the Enlightenment tradition of Kantian theory brought up to date by John Rawls, Kolhberg's colleague at Harvard. Already in the 1980s, however, it was becoming unfashionable to hold such universalist positions. The idea that if people were just rational enough they would like what they ought to like and be able to argue themselves out of mean or evil behaviour was running into resistance from theorists more interested in identifying differences in ends rather than similarities. For the prison context, however, this was not troubling, because few in corrections had any illusions or, indeed, desires for their charges to reach the final, principled stages of development, stages in which decisions about actions in the world are based on the individual's understanding of the principles behind the rules. Rather, for corrections the goal was to move criminals towards the 'conventional' moral stages, the levels of development that lead to 'conforming and upholding the rules and expectations and conventions of society or authority just because they are society's rules, expectations or conventions.'[12]

This perspective on corrections was set out in a coherent fashion first in Canada in the late 1970s, becoming a central theoretical underpinning of the Correctional Service of Canada's (CSC) education and training effort and as well a major component in several prison education programs, most notably the University of Victoria program in British Columbia. In Ottawa the head of the Education and Training Division, Bill Cosman, and his colleague Douglas Griffin sponsored visits by the Israeli learning theorist Reuven Feuerstein,[13] touted the controversial work of Yochelson and Samenow on the 'criminal personality,'[14] and encouraged the work of University of Ottawa criminologist Robert Ross on the link between thinking and crime. In British Columbia, Douglas Ayers and Tony Parlett introduced Kohlberg's research on moral development into the mix.[15] All of this work had as a central premise that the criminal was less a victim of circumstances, either social or emotional, than a decision maker albeit a poor one. More importantly, they presumed that arrested development rather than skewed development was the problem, leading to an educational rather than a therapeutic solution. With appropriate and sometimes aggressive training the criminal could simply grow out of these deficiencies.[16]

It was not difficult to draw a commonsensical link between specific cognitive deficits and crime. For instance, these deficits were seen to manifest themselves in a lack of comprehension of detail in perception, lack of a proper distance between impulse and action, insufficient ability to compare long-versus short-term outcomes of any given decision, deficient analogical ability (comparing one thing with another) leading to an episodic grasp of reality with resulting poor planning. There were obvious connections here with the apparent weakness of deterrence with most criminals, given that such cognitively deficient criminals would have difficulty thinking of the future, connecting past behaviour with future consequences, or imagining that something as abstract as a future apprehension could relate to present behaviour. I was first exposed to these ideas soon after hearing in prison a hilarious tale of a bank-robbing team who had failed to agree ahead of time on who was to drive the getaway car and were apprehended in the back seat arguing the point. The theory seemed to make sense, especially since one might conclude that criminals with such deficits would logically self-select into prison in greater numbers than those who did not.

Another incident, recounted to me soon after that, made an even more compelling case for the combination decision maker and cognitive deficit argument. Two friends, both with long criminal histories but with no pending charges, had left the city to attend a party in a town about eighty miles away. After leaving the party late they discovered that they had missed the last train home and would not be able to report to work in the morning, thus risking losing their jobs. After considering their situation, they decided to steal a car from a nearby car dealer's lot and drive home. After breaking in, taking the car, and proceeding down the road they soon ran out of gas in the middle of the countryside. They began walking and hitchhiking only to be picked up by the police who had earlier found the abandoned stolen vehicle. A few weeks later one of the men, while out of jail on bail from the car theft, proceeded to work his way across the country as an armed robber. Finally, being confronted in the street of a small town following a botched midday grocery store robbery, surrounded and faced with surrender or a shoot-out, he surrendered. He then successfully plea-bargained and avoided both extradition back to face the car theft charge and on a technicality had his armed robbery charge reduced to simply robbery. The first decision in this long chain, to steal the car, was taken because he 'could see no other alternative.' Thus, from the concern about losing a job, a decision is made to steal a car, followed by a decision to jump bail, followed by a decision to become an armed robber, and concluding with a decision for self-preservation. Along the way there were bad judgments, poor planning, and the serious moral difficulties associated with the use of lethal weapons in public places. One thinks here of Aristotle's example of drunkenness and responsibility (see Chapter 1) in that the responsibility for the catastrophic series of events starts with the first poor decision that seems grounded more in a character flaw than in either ignorance or circumstance.

The other aspect of cognitive development theory that seemed to resonate well with the experiences people had in working with criminals and prisoners was the crucial importance of role-taking or empathy. The ability to put oneself in the place of another is clearly an ability tied to human development since children are notoriously unable to do so, the world and themselves being in effect an undifferentiated whole. The opposite of empathy, egocentrism, tends to remain a dominant trait throughout childhood and only ebbs with the expansion of one's social horizon in adolescence, but even then the linkages remain limited to an immediate and like-minded social group. In Yochelson and Samenow's research on their patients at St Elizabeth's Hospital for the criminally insane they observed that 'every criminal regarded himself as totally unique.'[17] Daniel Claster in his work on perception concluded that criminals 'suffer from a delusion of exceptionalistic exemption from the laws of cause and effect,' a kind of magical belief in their own cleverness and luck, even when in obvious conflict with reality.[18]

And in a study comparing delinquents with non-delinquents, Chandler concluded that 'in contrast to their better socialized counterparts, a substantial proportion of the chronically delinquent subjects tested demonstrated a marked developmental lag in their ability to successfully adopt the roles or perspectives of others. These discrepancies persisted despite controls for the differences in socioeconomic and intellectual levels which characterized these groups.'[19] While expected in children, unbridled egocentrism in young and mature adults can be difficult and dangerous. Taken collectively, the argument for cognitive deficiency seemed a potentially powerful replacement for the illness approach of the medical model and at the same time an effective antidote to the anarchism of the opportunities model.

Nothing, of course, is ever quite that simple, and from the beginning the emerging cognitive model had to be qualified. Robert Ross, who was to become the best-known proponent of this model with the development of his Cognitive Living Skills program, insisted from the start that 'not all offenders evidence such deficits and ... few offenders evidence all of these deficits. Many offenders evidence not the slightest cognitive deficits; their criminal acts are perfectly rational, well planned ... and profitable.'[20] This, of course, fit well with the need within corrections systems to target interventions on the basis of need in order to make the most effective use of dwindling program resources. From the opposite side of the fence, Kohlberg's research showed clearly that, using the Piagetian system, at least half of all Americans never reach the final stage, that is, 'never develop the capacity for abstract thought.'[21] Luckily for Piaget, he had never claimed that adolescents actually reach that stage, but rather that they were only capable of abstract thought during or after adolescence.

Most citizens seem, in fact, to function quite well at the concrete operational stage or in between that and the next level up, using abstract thought in some aspects of their lives but not in others. For example, at work one might employ formal operations, in everyday business transactions concrete operations, and in artistic activities perhaps even preoperational thinking.[22] There can be vast areas of uneven development within a single person in the cognitive as well as the moral domain, and the cause of that unevenness, the theorists posit, is the environment – the social interactions that comprise our biographies. So now we return in a neat circle to the issue of life context – the nature of friendships, childhood experiences, schooling experiences, and parental treatment – as the central trigger for cognitive development. Thus, in the example of the car thief turned armed robber, that series of decisions was decisively affected by the fact that he had acquired in his life the skills needed to steal a car, to acquire a gun, to carry off a robbery, and to know how to manipulate the justice system. Without those skills his decisions would have been necessarily quite different.

The problem, therefore, is not cognitive uneven or underdevelopment per se – both are endemic in society – but rather the combination in some individuals of these deficits with a set of socially acquired skills and predispositions, a combination that seems to lead almost inevitably to criminal decisions. The impact of parental discord, schooling failures, early delinquency, labelling, incarceration, and the myriad social connections made along the way works to retard, skew, or freeze what might otherwise have been a normal process of cognitive development, resulting in a criminal fully formed with a functional repertoire of skills, predispositions, and mental frames. The most powerful point the cognitive theorists made in outlining this theory to corrections jurisdictions was that while little could be done to alter the social or psychological past of the criminal, the cognitive structures could be changed through various forms of education and training, a dissonance thereby created between mental outlook and habit, with the result being a process of change, maturation, or 'habilitation.'

Embracing 'Cog Skills' – The Corrections Response

Before theories of cognitive development could be of value to corrections they had to be operationalized and that was the task undertaken by a group of Canadian academics and corrections administrators during the latter half of the 1980s. This was a two-track process, undertaken on the one hand by prison educators seeking to ground their traditional knowledge transmission craft in a stronger and more applied theoretical tradition, and on the other hand by criminologists and psychologists seeking to shift their treatment focus from therapy to learning.

The educators' initiatives were spearheaded by staff from the University of Victoria and later Simon Fraser University Prison Education Program in British Columbia, as well as key figures in the Canadian Association for Adult Education and the U.S.-based Correctional Education Association. The latter group in particular – which by the late 1980s had strong links with Canada, Australia, and Western Europe –

provided these researchers with a public voice through its journal, yearbook, and annual international conference. My own contribution to this process included several articles in the CEA's *Journal* and other publications and talks at conferences in Canada, the United States, and England. Colleagues associated with the B.C. experience such as Douglas Ayers and Tony Parlett contributed to this academic discussion, as did those involved in similar programs elsewhere such as Lucien Morin in Quebec and Thom Gehring in the United States. By 1990, Gehring was able to refer to the existence of a 'Canadian Correctional Education Paradigm' built on the research carried out in the 1980s and consisting of cognitive instruction, participatory decision-making, moral education, and a focus on the humanities.[23]

The prime mover behind the academic criminologists' work with cognitive development was Robert Ross at the University of Ottawa, along with his colleague Elizabeth Fabiano and fellow researchers Paul Gendreau and Donald Andrews. In the early phases of Ross's work he insisted that there were no real distinctions between the teaching of 'cognitive living skills' as they were coming to be called and more traditional education programs that focused on developing critical thinking through education in the disciplines, the university program in British Columbia being a case in point. Indeed, it looked for most of the 1980s that this alliance of teachers and researchers was engaged in a common project rather than working at cross-purposes, as had been the case earlier between university teachers and the academic and professional psychologists and social workers.

Ross and Gendreau had carried out an exhaustive examination of corrections programs in an effort to reassess Martinson's 1974 conclusion that 'nothing works' and in the process had come to some quite different conclusions.[24] It was clear from their research that some programs did work in reducing rates of recidivism, and others did not. Those programs that were effective, Ross and Gendreau argued, were based on teaching rather than therapy and focused on 'modifying well-defined behaviours, changing anti-social attitudes, correcting faulty thinking or inappropriate social perception, and developing social competence.'[25] Above all, effective programs included techniques devoted to having an impact of the offenders' thinking – their impulsivity, empathy, notions of cause and effect, problem-solving skills, and reasoning skills.

This was indeed good news for corrections and, if true, potentially for society as a whole. While resigned to Martinson's gloomy conclusions about rehabilitation, no one was really comfortable with the idea that we were incapable of making something 'work,' even in prisons. It violated some deep-seated belief held by most North Americans, at least, that no one should really be held beyond redemption or totally devoid of any goodness.[26] Here at last was someone with evidence that something worked – indeed Donald Andrews, at Carleton University in Ottawa, showed that 40 per cent of treatment programs reported positive effects, supporting the conclusion that 'some service programs are working with at least some offenders under some circumstances.'[27] By 1985 Ross and Fabiano had published what became for many a kind of core text for theory and practice in this new field of thinking and crime; it was entitled *Time To Think: A Cognitive Model of Delinquency Prevention and Offender Rehabilitation.*[28]

The more the cognitive model became transformed into a 'cognitive living skills' *program,* or 'cog skills' as it came to be called within corrections in Canada, the United States, and eventually Western and Eastern Europe, the more it seemed to grow distinct from the educational approach that had been present at its creation. Post-secondary programs in the liberal arts had been for Ross virtually ideal case studies of cognitive development in action. He had evaluated the University of Victoria program in 1980 and referred to it as an excellent example of a multifaceted program which, if it did not address cognitive skills directly, certainly did so effectively in an indirect manner. Such programs, however, were increasingly on shaky ground in the world of corrections. In the United States they tended to rely on federal government grants to individual prisoner-students (Pell grants) and these were constantly under threat of elimination by a government bent on getting 'tough on crime and criminals' while at the same time cutting spending. In Canada the threat had been bluntly issued in the 1985 Sawatsky *Review of Offender Support Programs.* In that report postsecondary programs are referred to in passing as useful to long-term and/or maximum security inmates 'who seem to find it ego-gratifying' and thus use it to 'constructively occupy time,' but while it is perceived by some staff to be a 'nice program to have, it is not essential – not "core" and could be reduced if necessary.'[29] The stage was being set for the return of rehabilitation and, just as important, for the repatriation to the corrections professionals of the control of rehabilitation.

By 1989 Ross was arguing that 'correctional education can be not only educational; it can also be correctional,'[30] a direct contradiction of the beliefs of many prison educators that education's effectiveness rested, in fact, on its distancing itself from any correctional objective. The two approaches were growing apart despite or perhaps, being like rival siblings, because of their common origin. But the contest was never an even one given the attractive qualities to corrections of the cognitive skills model over the educational approach.

Particularly appealing among these qualities was the suggestion that cognitive skills programs such as anger management, life skills, and critical thinking could be taught by corrections staff after a period of short but intensive training. The programs were being designed by Ross and Fabiano as 'packages,' preprogrammed modules that could be easily adapted to varying prison conditions. With cognitive skills prison officers and custody staff could become 'teachers' and 'trainers,' giving them a tremendous boost in morale and at the same time lessening the dependence on 'outsiders' for program delivery. Education programs from literacy to university, on the other hand, were externally accredited activities and required certified, professional staff who in many cases were affiliated with community-based institutions or organizations rather than corrections. Even more important from the point of view of the prison as institution, the cognitive skills program aspired to involve all the prison staff in the process of imparting these skills, which was in marked contrast to education and other activities that sometimes deliberately sought to remain aloof from the prison and especially its custody staff.

Cognitive skills programs also were much more overtly 'correctional' than education programs. While improving literacy, earning a high school diploma, or even university credits might be seen to have some connection with correctional objectives, they were no where near as direct as the targeting of specific 'criminogenic needs' by cognitive skills, needs that were seen to be directly rather than indirectly related to rehabilitation. As delineated by the proponents of cognitive skills, these criminogenic needs included:

- Antisocial attitudes, feelings and peer associations
- Familial affection
- Identification with anti-criminal role models
- Increasing self-control and self-management skills
- Development of prosocial skills
- Reducing chemical dependencies
- Shifting the density of rewards and costs for criminal and non-criminal activities[31]

With modules being designed to deal with each of these 'needs,' and systems being put in place to diagnose the specific needs of each inmate, cognitive skills had the advantage of a solid theory and an even more solid suggested practice.

Perhaps the most attractive aspect of the cognitive skills model, however, was its employment of the 'risk principle.' Education programs in the prison tended to be open in their admission policies, following long-established principles of adult education. Cognitive skills programs, on the other hand, were designed for high risk offenders, high risk, that is, to re-offend. Andrews and colleagues set out the principle in 1986: 'According to the risk principle, intensive controls and services are best reserved for higher risk cases, while lower risk cases are best assigned to lower levels of service and control. The principle suggests that higher levels of supervision may reduce the recidivism of higher risk probationers but will have no such effect on the recidivism of low risk cases. Indeed, the principle suggests that, at best, the assignment of low risk cases to intensive service is a waste of scarce resources. At worst, assignment to service may be criminogenic for low risk cases.'[32] Education programs – considered here as 'treatment' – might according to this theory be doing actual harm in their easy mixing of high- and low-risk offenders into one program. If not, they were certainly an inefficient use of scarce program resources. According to Andrews and colleagues, low-risk offenders, who were no doubt in the majority in most prisons, were best left alone or provided with only minimal services in order that attention could be given to where the need is greatest. While rejecting any idea that this was a return to a medical model, it does not take a great leap of the imagination to impose the notion of 'medicine' on 'services' and see the logic of this being a classic case of 'old wine in a new bottle.' Carrying on with the medical analogy, criminal tendencies are here like a cancer, requiring intensive chemotherapy, specialized care, and invasive, sometimes dangerous drugs. For educators crime was much more like an outbreak of influenza, to which one responded with mass inoculation for the well and some chicken soup and aspirin for the ill.

In Canada cognitive skills had become the national policy of the Correctional Service of Canada by 1990. A new commissioner of corrections with quite liberal views based on his Scandinavian background introduced a set of 'core objectives' for the Canadian corrections service and with them came the requirement that the prisons structure offender programs around these objectives. Core objectives therefore came to require core programs such as the following list developed in the British Columbia region of the CSC:

- Individualized substance abuse programs
- Native life skills
- Living without violence living skills
- Family parenting skills
- Community-based substance abuse bridge programs
- Counseling program for family violent offenders
- Native substance abuse
- Native spirituality program
- Cognitive skills training
- Leisure education life skills
- Anger management life skills
- Native awareness training for staff

By 1991 this had been further codified into four areas of core programming
1   Cognitive skills training
2   Personal and interpersonal development
    - Living without violence
    - Family life/parenting skills
    - Anger/emotion management
    - Leisure education
3   Prerelease programming
4   Substance abuse – primary and secondary intervention

Noticeably absent in all these lists is any mention of education, whether literacy, high school, vocational, or university. These programs, once flagships during the days of opportunities, were now being slowly starved for funds and, worse yet, bureaucratically ignored in the new burst of rehabilitative fervour. But if education was now out of favour, learning itself was still the key to the new objectives, indeed the corrections service claimed that it 'has adopted the cognitive, social learning approach to personal development programming. The model ... attempts to teach offenders how to think logically, objectively and rationally without over-generalizing blame.'[33] The cognitive skills advocates were adamant in denying that their program could in any way be considered 'treatment,' the offender being considered as a 'person who must be *taught* rather than *treated*'[34] (emphasis in original). In an interview with Ian Benson, chief education officer in the English Prison Service, the coordinator of the cognitive skills program explained the distinction between cog skills and education by asserting that: 'Education is about teaching people *what* to think; cognitive skills is about teaching people *how* to think.'[35] Needless to say, educators would raise serious objections to such a distinction and, in fact, after a close look at the cognitive skills program might even suggest reversing the order.

By 1991 the advocates for cognitive skills were beginning to put more distance between their approach and the traditional approach of education. In schools across North America the notion that 'critical thinking' and other cognitive skills should be taught directly, as subjects in their own right instead of attributes of disciplines was riding a powerful wave of instrumental thinking. Elizabeth Fabiano, by this time the most outspoken proponent of cognitive skills in the field of corrections, stated the case bluntly: 'The challenge for all educators, particularly correctional educators, is for us to move away from the assumption that cognitive skills will develop as a natural consequence of an individual's exposure to various parts of the school curriculum, particularly reading, writing, math, and science. In order to effectively impact on an offender's ability to adjust in a prosocial manner it may be necessary to teach thinking skills in an explicit and direct manner.'[36] In a letter to Simon Fraser University in 1992, the regional Correctional Service of Canada outlined the new realities, announcing the 'comprehensive and fast-paced' nature of the implementation process: 'The Correctional Strategy is based on the concept that offender needs should drive programs and service delivery in the CSC, and that programs should focus primarily on successful reintegration of offenders into the community.' The strategy starts from the premise that 'Good corrections is, in effect, the successful reduction of the risk of recidivism' and this is to be accomplished by:

1   Assisting the individual offender in addressing needs relating specifically to his or her criminal behaviour so that the likelihood of recidivism is reduced
2   Investing in programming to this end and providing incentives for offenders to participate in order to correct their criminal behaviour
3   Such programming to focus on changing beliefs, attitudes, and behaviours that relate to criminal behaviour

Thus, all 'programming must be directly linked to meeting offenders' needs, and particularly those needs which if addressed will result in pro-social behaviour ... All programs should have a correctional orientation and correctional goals [and] the assumption that existing programs will meet the offenders' needs must be avoided.' Even more alarming to the recipients of this message was the admission that the new correctional strategy was being implemented at a time when the government was in an era of restraint and that therefore reallocations of resources would be necessary if these new programming initiatives were to succeed. A year later the university program in British Columbia was cancelled by the Correctional Service as a cost-cutting action.

The alacrity with which the correctional service in Canada adopted cognitive skills as *the* core activity with offenders was striking. In a few years the nightmares caused by the humiliating demise of the medical or treatment model were forgotten, and officials from the Correctional Service of Canada began to spread the new gospel into the United States and Europe. At a speech to colleagues in the United Kingdom in 1993, Roger Cormier from the CSC could state without flinching: 'Reducing re-offending by changing offenders from criminal to law-abiding lifestyles is a central theme in corrections in Canada ... the Canadian correctional system is predicated on the assumption that offenders can change from a criminal to a law-abiding life style.'[37] In a 1995 feature article in the CSC's in-house research publication it was further spelled out that this process of change was possible because the research associated with what was by now a cognitive skills 'movement' had led to the creation of a coherent and proven rehabilitation system based on the following:

1   Offenders have needs that directly cause their criminal behaviour.
2   We can diagnose these needs accurately.
3   Appropriate intervention is available.
4   Intervention will reduce these needs.
5   Reduced need will diminish criminal behaviour.[38]

One might, were one so jaundiced in matters like this, accuse the authors of taking rather too seriously the logic lessons from Philosophy 101 in their outlining of this tight little paradigm, but by this time the Correctional Service of Canada only had room for 'true believers' so such a comment would have fallen on deaf ears.

The juggernaut that became 'cog skills' received its impetus in part from its adoption by a newly invigorated research operation with the national headquarters of the Correctional Service of Canada. As part of its effort to become more efficient and cost-effective the CSC had expanded its internal research operations in the 1980s. Researchers from that office ended up working especially closely with Ross at the University of Ottawa and Andrews at neighbouring Carleton University, eventually hiring Ross's graduate student and colleague, Elizabeth Fabiano who was subsequently put in charge of both implementing and evaluating the cognitive skills program. These kinds of almost 'incestuous' relationships are seemingly endemic to centralized systems, reminiscent of similar links in Washington, DC, between various government departments and the local universities.

The logic inherent in the cognitive skills system was a powerful incentive for other jurisdictions which were having little success with alternative approaches. In the United States, still wedded to a massive 'get tough on crime' agenda driven as much by politics as by need, record numbers of criminals were being 'incapacitated,' new prisons were being built, and 'tougher' laws and programs encouraged. A 'no frills' prison section was added to the Republican-sponsored Take Back Our Streets Act of 1994, the State of Alabama re-introduced chain gangs, Pell grants for prisoner-students were eliminated thereby crippling post-secondary education in prisons, and, typical of the political mood of the times, the governor of Massachusetts was on record as wanting his state's prisons to be a 'tour through the circles of hell' where prisoners would learn only the 'joys of busting rocks.'[39] Hardly fertile ground for cognitive skills, one might suppose, but even in this Draconian atmosphere corrections professionals were looking for more positive solutions.

Early favourites of the 'get tough' era were falling on hard times by the 1990s. Boot camps, for instance, were fine image-builders for those wanting to score points with the public or relive their halcyon days in basic training, but they were being shown to be ineffective in reducing recidivism. Nevertheless the State of Georgia had space for 3,000 offenders in boot camps by 1994, and the State of New York had expanded its boot camps to 1,500 spaces. Researchers claimed, however, that what few successes there were among the boot camp operations seemed more the result of the treatment programs they hosted than the discipline and military drill they built their image on.[40] By 1996 Arizona, Florida, and Maryland were scrapping or scaling down these operations. In Michigan the governor proudly noted a dramatic reduction in recidivism and claimed that tough Michigan prisons proved that good old-fashioned deterrence was the key to crime reduction. In fact, while the reductions were real they were more likely the result of a 50 per cent increase in the number of parole and probation officers in the state and the creation of special community detention centres for technical violators of parole.[41]

While the federal Prison Service and several states moved towards mandatory literacy and even high school completion, the U.S. correctional landscape was too fractured by the dominance of the state systems to allow for the kind of wholesale adoption of a single approach as had happened in the Canadian federal system. Cognitive skills was, however, high on the list of programs being examined, and several states had pilot projects running by the early 1990s. By this time Elizabeth Fabiano had formed a private consulting firm with the sole purpose of selling cognitive skills and was being sought out by corrections systems across Europe and North America. The program looked simple to use, relied on existing corrections staff, was modularized so that it could be shaped to almost any context, and it had a solid research base. Even more, 'preliminary' research results released in 1990 seemed to indicate that it was effective in reducing recidivism. By 1996 the cognitive skills program had been institutionalized in Canada, was present in American and English prisons, and was being marketed in systems from Brazil to Latvia as a twenty-first century key to the problem of repeat offending. Education programs were neutralized, eliminated or transformed into service programs for cognitive skills, vocational and industrial programs were marginalized, and the decision-making prisoner of the opportunities model was reduced once again to the dependent inmate first described by Foucault.

Cognitive skills in many ways embodied the ideal of the 'modern,' the enlightened, rational, universal, theory-driven formulation designed to be applied to social problems that had become pervasive since the nineteenth century but were being challenged by the weight of their own contradictions, the scepticism of a disillusioned public, and the critiques of postmodernist thinkers. Its originators, and Robert Ross in particular, had insisted that cognitive skills was not a panacea, that it was really only effective when used in conjunction with traditional education and training activities, and that its real strength was more in the area of preventing delinquency rather than rehabilitating the offender. But such complexity does not survive once immersed in the cauldrons of modern bureaucracies where such a mix is immediately boiled down to its simplest formation: 'it works – everyone should have one.' Even the cautious originator, as is so often the case, becomes swept up in the marketing maelstrom that accompanies an innovative success, and in a culture governed by trends and new ideas cog skills was a sure winner.

There were some problem areas in the system that needed scrutiny and illumination, however, problems that were embedded in the Enlightenment core of the cognitive skills initiative, in its 'science,' its progressivist implications, and its empirical claims. Cognitive skills was inextricably linked to the policy of 'selective incapacitation' which in turn was dependent on accurate prediction techniques and systems. As well, since cognitive skills was, in fact, a range of interventions, it was dependent on an accurate diagnostic system if it was to identify the particular needs of the inmates who had been selectively incapacitated in order to apply the appropriate cognitive skills intervention. All of this, of course, was driven in large part by the fiscal crisis of corrections in general, the determination of the state to make its deepest deficit-reducing cuts in the places it least feared negative voter reactions – prisons being at the top of that list.

It may be significant that a system that is dedicated in so profound a manner to the issue of understanding should in turn settle on 'cognitive' interventions as the primary means of 'treatment' in corrections. Its own need to understand is thus imposed or transposed onto the object of its examination – if I need to understand you then you need to understand you too! Like the Socratic dialogue, the desire to have the object understand itself manifests itself in the form of a deception – the real desire is to have the object adopt the understanding of itself that has been prescribed by the examiner. After all, did any of the companions of Socrates really have a chance in one of his dialogues? Presumably the revered status of Socrates had the effect of diverting the irritation one would have felt at being led down one of his paths, but the same status cannot be claimed for the prison. Hence, the deception is both transparent and despised. Only the weakest willed take on the self suggested by the state, the clever wear it only as a veil, and the stubborn resist as best they can.

Prediction and Diagnosis – The Science behind Cognitive Skills

The imprisoned men and women, corrections and prison staff, various contracted and volunteer personnel working with the penal system, members of parole boards, and probation, parole, and community volunteers are locked in an embrace that is at once structurally antagonistic and yet unified in its opposition to the dangerous proposition that 'nothing works.'[42] The language used by all the participants in this macabre dance of prisoner and keeper, patient and doctor, sinner and saint is built on a predictive foundation that in turn is based on an epistemology – a theory of the nature and scope of knowledge. When a prisoner is given a particularly harsh sentence, denied parole, detained in prison, or singled out for special conditions after release it is most often because he is deemed 'likely to re-offend.' Such a statement, such a conclusion, is made at the end of a long process of evidence gathering, analysis, discussion, testimony, and comparison, a process based on certain beliefs about the possibility of knowing given the use of a proper methodology (research process). Great care is taken to consult a variety of 'experts,' to collect and codify all the records, to gather systematically all the impressions of the subject, and to rely on proven statistical and psychological instruments. Thus, the vast bureaucratic system of observation, recording, and reporting described by Foucault is not merely for purposes of 'control' – though it does serve that purpose admirably – but also for prediction.

There has been a long-standing belief in the social sciences that variables such as violence or re-offending can be predicted with 'reasonable' accuracy given the proper tools. This has been the special hallmark of psychological approaches to criminal behaviour. Thus, while a sociologist may predict in a general sense that crime rates will be high in poverty-stricken communities or among people suffering from racism or other forms of discrimination, they insist that one cannot predict which individuals in these situations or contexts will participate in crime. Within the psychological approach to crime there are those who argue strongly that such individual predictions can be made – some based on biology and others on psychology. They would hold that the process of prediction done properly is a 'science,' no different in theory than attempting to predict the behaviour of certain microbes or combinations of chemicals. The fact that the results are so often wrong is commonly attributed to the crudeness of the instruments (we need more money for research!) or the poor access to data (we need more compliant subjects!). Chance, accident or perversity in this view merely indicate our (temporary) inability to discover the complex links between all the causative factors.

The operational problem of prediction starts with the foundational

cultural insight of Western culture which places the start of all understanding at the task of 'knowing thyself' – gaining insight. This self-
understanding is arguably the only knowledge that is truly possible,
and we know post–Freud and Marx that even this is severely limited
by psychological tricks and social biases.[43] Nonetheless, our Enlightenment tradition tells us that a degree of self-understanding is possible
and that self-understanding combined with the nurturing of empathy
can lead to sufficient fellow-feeling that a limited understanding of
others can follow. If Adam Smith could declare in the opening of his
Theory of Moral Sentiments that through our imagination we can share
the feelings of 'our brother upon the rack,' then surely an enlightened
modern expert can enter into the mental world of the criminal and
thereby begin to understand.[44] There is also a supposition that the
examiners of the offender are working from facts, that they view the
offender 'as he is' both historically and presently. They dispassionately
weigh the crime, the sentence, the biography, the post-incarceration
activities, the personal statement of the offender, and, increasingly, the
political context of the times, and then make their decision. This decision is thus seen as having been rooted in both 'empathy' and 'science'
within the accepted limitations of those words.

There are two problems with this process of prediction. First, there is
the issue of observer bias or the impossibility of an 'objective' assessment of the offender. According to quantum physics, there can be no
such thing as an independent observer – no clear boundary between
subject and object – 'We are sensuous participants in the very world we
seek to describe.' Because consciousness is part of the measurement,
so-called reality (that which is measured) will always be blurred and
indeterminate. What we see is not nature, but 'nature exposed to our
method of questioning.'[45] This constitutes one of the more direct
attacks – whether it is 'postmodern' is open to question – on positivism, which in turn is one of the central pillars of modernity and its science. All observation now ceases to be dispassionate or neutral and is
instead theory-laden, all perception is conditioned by the perceiver,
and 'the line between data and theory [is] hopelessly blurred.'[46]

These questionings of the possibility of an empirical path to the truth
(if only we had more data!) ring of postmodern sensibilities but also
harken back to a fundamental issue at the start of modernity. David
Hume, the eighteenth-century sceptic, insisted that there was no necessary connection between cause and effect, that what we call causality is
ultimately only chance, and what we see as 'laws' are really just cus-

tomary conjunctions between events. We predict the sun will rise each morning in the east because it has done so for as long as we can recall and because we determine through language the notion of 'sun' and 'rising' and 'east.'[47]

Second, it can also be argued that any prediction of individual behaviour, whether of self or others, based even on such insight-driven understandings, is impossible. Dostoyevsky's perverse Underground Man and our secret knowledge of our own actions are always before us, warning us that to pretend that behaviours can be moulded or predicted through knowledge or understanding is futile, regardless of the instruments we use or the access we obtain. It is possible, however, both to understand and predict the behaviour of groups. Norval Morris argues this in his work on prediction theory, saying, 'The epistemology of prediction provides no grounds for predictions of individual behaviour; it refers by nature to predictions on the behaviour of defined groups of individuals ... The individual in question always belongs, by virtue of certain stated and previously tested characteristics and circumstances, to a group with a given likelihood of violent criminality.'[48]

This idea is supported by chaos theory in physics which tells us, for instance, that while we can predict weather patterns we will never be able to predict precise weather occurrences. Using chaos theory, an individual must be seen in terms of a *dynamic system*, akin to a natural system. We can, then, look at a person in essentially ecological terms. In current thinking about such systems there is emerging agreement that linear approaches based on cause and effect are of little value and that therefore traditional predictive approaches bear little fruit (for example, 'nothing works'). The behaviour of these dynamic systems (for example, weather patterns or human beings) are just too complex to be susceptible to such analyses. Likewise, traditional segmented analyses based on Cartesian fragmentation or Newtonian mechanics will not give satisfactory results. Unlike clocks, complex dynamic systems do not behave in linear, predictive ways. What we can look for in such systems in place of cause and effect data are *general patterns*. Thus, in the micro-world of individual persons indeterminancy is the rule – there are no predictive devices that work with a system as complex as an individual person. However, according to Werner Heisenberg, the uncertainties that are so significant in the micro-world disappear in the macro-world – in the macro-world the phenomena *are* deterministic, predictable. Thus, while the Newtonian perspective would insist that small changes would have small effects, thereby enabling one to study a phenomenon (for example, a person) in isolation, in the world of chaos theory 'minute fluctuations are amplified into dramatic large scale changes.' Thus, a small event, a chance encounter, a serendipitious thought in the life of a prisoner could have dramatic consequences akin to the butterfly wing causing a cyclone, but we cannot 'know' that and certainly we cannot 'predict' it.

We are left, therefore, with the dilemma that while we can know and affect other individuals, we can only predict the behaviour of groups. In the context of criminal justice this on the one hand frees us from the hubris of the scientist or saint claiming to save individual souls while allowing us the freedom to claim generic change, but leaves us helpless before the futures of individual selves.[49] Michael Ignatieff makes this point in reminding us that it 'is a humbling indication of the limits of modern social science ... that the most analytically sophisticated account of criminal motivation ever written is Dostoyevsky's *Crime and Punishment* ... an account of one case.'[50] Having used that novel in several courses over the years, I had anticipated that the story of Raskolnikov would be useful in this exploration of crime and criminals, but it is indeed so 'particular' as to be of limited use in exploring the general.

This reality of the limitation of the individual case is driven home by the statisticians who insist that there is overwhelming evidence that favours actuarial over clinical predictions. In the practice of making predictions there are three basic ways to proceed:

1   Anamnestic – This is how the person behaved in the past when circumstances were similar. It is likely he or she will behave in the same way now.
2   Actuarial – This is how people like him or her, situated as he or she is, behaved in the past. It is likely that he or she will behave as they did.
3   Clinical – From my experience of the world, from my professional training, from what I know about mental illness and mental health, from my observations of this patient and efforts to diagnose him or her, I think he or she will behave in the following fashion in the future.[51]

Although most of us would no doubt like the clinical prediction to be the most accurate since it flatters our sense of personal acuity, in fact, the anamnestic are the most reliable predictions followed closely by the actuarial. History and circumstance, are better predictors than human assessment, whether expert or not: 'the overwhelming evidence is that actuarial devices outperform human decision-makers irrespective of setting.'[52] But, as was argued above, this outstanding performance of actuarial devices is based on the prediction of the behaviours of large numbers of individuals, not necessarily on a singular John Doe. Hence, in actual decision making by the state, in parole cases, for example, most predictions are still made intuitively with the advice of clinicians – to the continuing dismay of statisticians and proponents of actuarial systems.[53] Jackson found, for instance, in a detailed study of the judgments made by experts – in this case psychiatrists and judges – that they were heavily biased by factors such as socioeconomic class, likeability, value system, personal preferences, and attitude. Worse yet, she found that once an initial diagnosis is made there is a definite tendency to look for confirming data and to ignore disconfirming evidence.[54] The experts are, in other words, too much like the rest of us to be relied upon to make unbiased judgments on such complex issues.

To the extent that prison programs like cognitive skills rely upon a diagnosis process that seeks to identify prisoners who are dangerous, violent, likely to recidivate, or in other ways be singled out for treatment, they are subject to the weaknesses involved in the prediction of individual behaviour. The implications of this can become quite serious even in cases as seemingly benign as selection or non-selection for a prison program, since if once selected the prisoner either fails or refuses to cooperate – as often happens – then he or she may be labelled as one who 'refuses treatment' which in turn has a dramatic impact on release from prison (as we saw in Allen's story in Chapter 4). The problem here goes by the name of 'false positives' and it plagues all attempts to apply such systems to individuals. Prediction systems almost always overpredict and at best can achieve only about a 50 per cent accuracy rate. Two examples of these systems in operation make the problem quite clear: 'Assume that one person out of a hundred will kill: a low "base rate." Assume also that an exceptionally accurate test is created which differentiates with 95 per cent effectiveness those who will kill from those who will not. If 100,000 people were tested, out of the 100 who would kill, 95 would be isolated. Unfortunately, out of the 99,900 who would not kill, 4,995 people would also be isolated as potential killers. In these circumstances, it is clear that we could not justify incarcerating all 5,090 people.'[55] In fact, of course, the 'exceptionally accurate test' does not exist and instead of 95 per cent the real successful prediction rate would be lucky to reach 50 per cent. In another example 592 male violent sex offenders were assessed in detail by Kozol and his colleagues at the Massachusetts Center for the Diagnosis and Treatment of Dangerous Persons. They recommended that 386 men be released and unsuccessfully opposed the release of forty-nine others. Over a five-year period, 8 per cent of those considered non-dangerous committed a violent offence, indicating some predictive ability. In the group of the forty-nine men considered dangerous, only 35 per cent committed a violent offence. This leaves a 65 per cent false-positive rate, making them wrong two out of three times despite intensive testing.[56]

This is not an argument for abandoning attempts to predict dangerousness or to attempt a diagnosis of individual needs and predilections, but rather to sound a cautionary note concerning the problems associated with such predictions – problems that will not likely disappear or even lessen in seriousness with 'improved' instruments. There are several prediction systems currently in use that identify with acceptable degrees of accuracy groups of individuals who, by sharing certain biographical characteristics, are more likely than individuals in other groups to recidivate, or engage in violent acts, or commit a sexual offence, and so forth. Two of these are in wide use in the United States, the Base Expectancy Scale and the Salient Factor Score; one in Canada, the Statistical Index on Recidivism (SIR); and one in the United Kingdom, the Parole Prediction Scoring System. They are used as a means of identifying career criminals or repeat offenders as part of the 'selective incapacitation' policy in the United States – despite the average 50 per cent accuracy rate – and are used as well in parole or probation decision making, assisting in identifying candidates for release who are at a high risk to recidivate.

As discussed in Chapter 5, prediction devices like the SIR are also particularly useful in research assessing the effectiveness of prison programs, giving researchers a set of benchmarks of expected post-release behaviour for a group of program participants. The individual placements on these benchmarks – displayed on a spectrum ranging from 'highly likely to recidivate' to 'not likely to recidivate' – are all constructed from pre-incarceration variables such as age at first arrest, number of previous convictions, violence on record, and so forth, and therefore give the researcher a predicted release outcome based on the characteristics of the offender prior to his or her most recent incarceration. It should be possible, then, to assess the effectiveness of a given set of prison-based experiences that aspire to affect recidivism based on whether significant numbers of participants in that experience or program improve on their post-release prediction. Such improvements over SIR predictions are, in fact, precisely what the advocates of the cognitive skills program proposed to rest their case on: 'In order to show that the program has a lasting impact, we will need to demonstrate that program participants recidivate at a lower rate than might be expected merely on the basis of their pre-program risk levels (e.g. as measured by SIR).'[57] Coincidentally, as was outlined in Chapter 5, this same procedure was applied to the former prisoner-students in the post-secondary program in British Columbia: 'The core methodology for evaluating the University Program will involve comparing the actual reconviction rates of a range of cohorts and subgroups who had "graduated" from the program with the expected rates according to their SIR ranking.'[58] A potential 'high noon' thus emerges on the scene, two competitive but yet incestuous rivals for the honor of dethroning the ideology of nothing works face off with similar subjects in the same environment and with an identical measurement system. But before we examine in more detail how that turned out, there is one other aspect of the resurgence of a science-based treatment model that deserves at least a glance.

From Thinking and Crime to Brains and Crime

Approaches to crime that ground themselves in a developmental theory presume necessarily that the origins of adolescent or adult deviant behaviour has deep roots. Cognitive theories in particular have this quality because thought patterns, aptitudes, and habits are seen as being constructed from childhood, not simply acquired in response to adult frustrations – at least that is the theory. This allows for the idea of a propensity to commit crime, a propensity that 'is established early in life (e.g., in the pre-school years) and is persistent thereafter.'[59] This is very different, it is important to stress, from a view of crime that sees it as a 'not very surprising reaction of normal people to oppressive circumstances.'[60] While it seems reasonable to conclude that both nature and nurture play important roles in the production of deviant propensities and behaviours, in the world of professional understandings inhabited by experts the tendency is to favour one over the other. Once one moves towards the 'nature' as opposed to the 'nurture' explanation, a number of paths of inquiry open up, including a drift towards sociobiological, chemical, and genetic explanations, and in the past few years there has been a lot of traffic on those paths.

The old idea that criminals are born as much as they are made received a contemporary boost in 1986 with the publication of *Crime and Human Nature* by James Q. Wilson and Richard Herrnstein, a book that argued for looking at both nature and nurture but which quickly became a case for the former. Two of the most outspoken supporters of this view and proponents of a new 'science of criminology' are Stuart Yudofsky of the Baylor College of Medicine and C. Ray Jeffrey at Florida State University. Yudofsky, taking us right back to the postwar origins of the medical model, feels that 'we're going to be able to diagnose many people who are biologically brain-prone to violence' and as a result insists that we must move criminal justice towards a 'medical model based on prevention, diagnosis and treatment.' Jeffrey zeroes in on the repeat offenders and urges an effort to 'identify high-risk persons at an early age and place them in treatment programs *before* they have committed the 10 to 20 major felonies characteristic of the career criminal.'[61] These zealots of the new age of science are not troubled by Rousseau's insistence that recalcitrant or deviant individuals should be 'forced to be free' since they are convinced of the truth of both their science and their moral position. Indeed, Adrian Raine from the University of Southern California, an advocate for the genetic roots of deviance, argues in almost pure if 'vulgar' Rousseauean logic that if deviance is seen as a clinical disorder, then punishments would be less harsh and the whole criminal justice system would become more humane in the shift from a punishment to a medical regime.[62]

A more complex and balanced version of the argument that criminal predispositions may be at least in part biological in origin comes from the prominence of the new evolutionary psychology school of Darwinian thought and is very close to some of the key ideas of developmental theory. Robert Wright in his book *The Moral Animal* says Darwinian thought suggests that from a very early age many poor children have their very capacity for sympathy and guilt restricted or underdeveloped by the environment they live in and that this carries over into adult life: 'Many people in the inner city face limited opportunities for "legitimate" cooperation with the wider world. And the males, risk-prone by virtue of their gender to begin with, don't have the long life expectancies that so many people take for granted ... the "short time horizons" for which criminals are famous may be an adaptive response to predictive information about one's prospects for longevity and eventual success.'[63]

While the behaviours of these (mostly) males whose fortunes are threatened or truncated by circumstances thus make evolutionary sense, the actual mechanisms governing these behaviours are chemical rather than rational. In this case the neurotransmitter serotonin has been identified as the most likely agent of causation. Serotonin it is believed either has a role in the initiation of aggressive acts or functions as some kind of regulator within the brain. Whatever the actual mechanism, it is clear that low levels of serotonin are linked with aggressive behaviour. This is not, however, some form of biological determinism. Wright points out that serotonin levels are thought to be highly affected by social conditions, by diet, and even by one's sense of self-esteem. When someone feels depressed or oppressed, serotonin is low and in some circumstances may be the cause for a lashing out against the causes of that depression or oppression. In this case evolution may be providing, through lowering a chemical inhibitor like serotonin, a means or avenue for an individual to address an unsatisfactory social situation – for example, through aggression, an attempt to put the situation right. 'Violence is eminently functional – something that people are designed to do. Especially men.'[64] One study has concluded that the role of serotonin is a 'facilitator rather than an initiator of aggressive behaviour.'[65] Despite research being only in its early stages, Wright and others conclude that 'low serotonin encourages crime ... it seems to reflect a person's perception of foreclosed routes to material success; natural selection may "want" that person to take alternate routes. Serotonin and Darwinism together could thus bring sharp testament to otherwise vague complaints about how criminals are "victims of society." A young inner-city thug is pursuing status by the path of least resistance no less than you; and he is compelled by forces just as strong and subtle as the ones that have made you what you are.'[66] Most of our understanding of serotonin and its link with violence remains speculative. Certainly, we know that its role in the brain is too complex to allow us to reduce violence and aggression by simply administering serotonin boosters like Prozac to individuals deemed at risk. The Darwinian insight that aggression and violence are often rational and functional human responses, and the insights from neurophysiology that such responses may be governed by chemicals in the brain both, have important implications for understanding crime and our response to it. Certainly these developments call into question the cognitive model's presumption that criminal deviance springs from errors in thinking or deficits in some 'normal' process of cognition.

Indeed, evolutionary psychology moves us towards an understanding of crime as a 'reasonable' response of young males to circumstances they perceive to be limiting their 'life chances.' It is, one can just as reasonably argue, a 'wrong' response, and efforts should be undertaken in every way possible to dissuade them from that path and to turn them away from it once taken lest they make it their career and profession. This persuasion would seem to be most effectively undertaken using an educational approach (that is, the choice is wrong and there are options) instead of a therapeutic approach (that is, the choice comes from illness which can be cured), a cognitive approach (that is, the choice indicates deficits), or a punitive approach (that is, the choice reflects meanness which must be deterred). This brings us back, then, to the issue of cognitive skills versus education, a treatment approach to deviance versus an educational approach. What kind of evidence, if any, is there of the effectiveness of either approach?

The Empirical Issue

By the 1990s the work of assessing the effectiveness of prison programs had progressed considerably beyond the 'it works or it doesn't work' questions posed by Martinson in the 1970s. Gendreau and Ross had helped set the research agenda in their work in the 1980s, asking not 'whether' programs were effective but rather which programs 'work' and why.[67] That kind of research had already shown fairly clearly what kinds of programs did *not* work, the list including 'confrontation' programs such as Scared Straight that were designed to deter, 'diversion' programs, virtually all group counselling and therapy programs, as well as individual counselling and therapy.[68] But even among program types that appeared to be effective, it was clear that there would be no panaceas, no magic bullets. Part of the agenda was to discover not only which intervention works and why, but also to discover 'for whom' it was effective. This last point became especially important given the work done by Andrews and others on the need to focus prison interventions on high-risk offenders; to be deemed 'effective' in the 1990s one would have to show improvement here and avoid having success linked to low-risk cases.

Both of the evaluations being reviewed here took this approach. The evaluation of the cognitive skills program done in 1995 and the evaluation of the post-secondary program completed in 1996 both utilized a risk prediction system – in this case the SIR – in order to categorize their samples by recidivism risk and as well to find out whether various subgroups in the sample improved or not over their SIR-predicted rate of recidivism. There were important differences in the methodologies employed, the cognitive skills evaluation including a 'control group' of eligible inmates who did not participate in the program, while the post-secondary evaluation focused on comparing the actual post-release performance of selected subgroups with their SIR-predicted performance in an effort to identify for whom the program was most effective. Another important difference was the length of the follow-up period, the cognitive skills study following up its subjects for only one year after release, while the post-secondary study used a three-year follow-up period. Because of this one might expect higher recidivism rates for the latter study if only because of the difference in follow-up time. Finally, there was an important distinction in the definitions of recidivism used by the two studies, the cognitive skills evaluation including return to prison for technical parole violations and the post-secondary study restricting recidivism to reincarceration for a new indictable offence. This difference should result in a comparatively lower 'failure rate' for the university sample. Still, as evaluations go, these two efforts were remarkably similar even though done independently of each other.

What do these evaluations tell us? The cognitive skills evaluation carried out by the Correctional Service of Canada proclaims the program a success, but the actual data make the claim a difficult one to sustain. Researchers followed up a total of 2,125 men for one year after their release. Of these subjects, 1,444 had completed the cognitive skills program, 302 had dropped out of the program, and 379 were part of the control group of eligible subjects who had not been admitted to the program. Two key data points gave the researchers problems from the start given their expectations and the theory from which they started. First, there was only a small difference between the recidivism rates (defined as 'a readmission for technical violation of conditional release or a reconviction for a new offence within one year of release'[69]) of program completers and the control group, 44.5 per cent of the former returning to prison compared with 50 per cent of the control subjects. This is, as the report stresses, an 11.2 per cent decrease and therefore important to note, but obviously not the success that had been hoped for.

Second, and perhaps even more serious, the cognitive skills program was shown to have had no effect on improving the post-release performance of subjects deemed by the SIR to be at high risk to reoffend. Thus, 57.4 per cent of the high-risk subjects in the control group and 56.9 per cent of the participant subjects recidivated within that first year of release. On the other hand, lower risk participant subjects recidivated at a much lower rate than did control subjects.[70] As Robinson admits, this finding contradicts all the prognostications by Andrews and others that offenders in the high-risk categories would benefit more from appropriate interventions and should therefore be the primary recipients of those interventions. One might have concluded at this point that (a) the theory was wrong, (b) the cognitive skills program was in fact not an 'appropriate' intervention, or (c) cognitive skills was a failure. Robinson, however, found another way out of the dilemma, declaring that all the subjects were in fact 'high risk' independent of the SIR categories: 'our low risk offenders would likely fall toward the high-risk extreme on a risk continuum of all criminal offenders.'[71] This argument, weak on the surface, is made all the more implausible when one recalls that the SIR system used in dividing the cognitive skills subjects into high and low risk was developed by the Correctional Service of Canada using subjects from its own prisons, the same institutions from which the cognitive skills subjects were drawn.

As an adjunct to this reversal in the risk-level effectiveness result, the researchers also discovered that even with their own diagnostic systems assessing the relative 'need levels' for cognitive intervention, subjects with high need levels showed no improvement while those with lower need levels did show improvement. As in the case of risk level, the researchers' response to this result would appear problematic, since they posit that higher need subjects may just need 'a larger dosage of the program.'[72] The use of the metaphor 'dosage' does seem to indicate that although Robert Ross may have rejected any linkage between cognitive skills and the medical model, its corrections service advocates slide rather easily into a return to clinical language.

There were some promising results hidden amid the charts and tables of the research report on cognitive skills. Sex offenders, drug offenders, and violent offenders (all types generally ranked as a low risk to recidivate by SIR) did well after completing the cognitive skills program. On the other hand, the typical 'robbers and thieves' (always the highest risk to re-offend type) showed no change. There were indications in the data, however, that these high risk-career criminal types did do better when they completed their cognitive skills program in a community as opposed to prison setting, leading the researchers to suggest 'post-treatment booster sessions' – again falling into that consistent medicalized language in which offenders are literally 'inoculated' against crime.

One must conclude, however, that all things considered the research on the cognitive living skills program is 'not a pretty sight' and unlike earlier, more speculative predictions, these data have remained buried in a government of Canada report, and not touted in the learned journals of academia, let alone the popular media.

What of the post-secondary program? We have already established its record of overall effectiveness in the earlier discussion of the analysis of data from the total group. But the real ambition of the study was to identify particular subgroups of offenders for whom the program was effective, particularly those deemed by the SIR to be at a high risk to re-offend. The results from this research have appeared in a variety of publications, but in order to establish the significance of the results and, more importantly, to illustrate the complexity of the task facing those who wish to pursue the rehabilitation objective, a detailed look at a few examples is in order. Given the importance that prisons, politicians, and the public assign to high-risk offenders, it is especially appropriate to focus in on the specific fate of these highest risk prisoners after enrolling in university courses.

Looking in a Black Box – High Risk Offenders and Education

The relative success of the group of 654 former prisoner-students, while certainly encouraging, told us little about how these results could be linked to the education program itself. To explore that more 'micro'-issue we have to interrupt once again the narrative flow and re-enter the detail of the evaluation study, the world of numbers, subgroups, mechanisms, and variables that are the substance of evaluation research. The central vehicles for this exploration are the 'working groups,' subsets of subjects drawn from the total group and based on shared backgrounds (for example, juvenile delinquents from broken homes who dropped out of high school, our so-called hard cases) or on the basis of common patterns in the pursuit of education (for example, our 'Improvers' whose grade point average improved over their course of study).

The 'Hard Cases' Working Group

In creating the working group of hard cases it was hypothesized that selecting for delinquent school drop-outs from broken homes would constitute a group of prisoners more hardened in their commitment to a criminal lifestyle, more estranged from society and hence more likely to re-offend. With these three criteria a working group of 118 men was established, with SIR predicting that only 42 per cent of them would *not* re-offend (compared with the 58 per cent for the total group). The criminal profile of the group was as imagined, with 100 of the 118 having had three or more convictions in their criminal careers, 51 described as being opiate addicts, 81 having violence in their offence pattern, and well over half being held exclusively in maximum or high-medium security while in prison and denied any form of early release on parole.

What of the effect of educational experience on breaking this sorry cycle? Interestingly, discussions between researchers and the educational practitioners had not singled out a subgroup of this ilk for particular mention. 'Hard cases' were not seen, in the general course of program activities, as 'special cases.' This is borne out in the data. Like the total group which showed a 'relative improvement' over its SIR prediction of 30 per cent, the hard cases as a group showed a relative improvement of 31 per cent (55 per cent actual success rate compared with 42 per cent predicted success rate). Education seems to succeed for this group – but in much the same measure as the broad run of prisoners who enter the program. Trying to fathom how education might (or might not) penetrate these deeper-seated cycles of criminality required looking further inside the black box for any subgroups within the 'Hard Cases' whose relative improvement over SIR was significantly better than 31 per cent, or significantly worse.

Turning first to the variety of measures of levels or intensity of engagement or involvement with the university program, no differences were found in the post-release success of those students deemed to be actively engaged compared with those less engaged. Likewise, men who worked in the school library or were employed in jobs such as clerks or tutors or who were members of the student council (23 per cent of the total) – all indications of a more formal involvement in the education program – fared no better after release than their peers who merely took courses. Given the paucity of previous educational experiences, indeed the presumption that such experiences may have been decidedly unpleasant, it is perhaps not surprising that this group of men kept a relatively low and cautious profile within the university program.

More traditional academic variables revealed greater variation, but still very much as a mirror of the pattern of success and failure of the total group. As might be expected, those men who completed more courses did better than those who completed only a few. Thus, the thirty-one men in the group of 118 who completed more than thirty credits (one full year of university study) showed a relative improvement over their SIR prediction of 42 per cent, while the thirty-six men who completed less than ten credits showed a relative improvement of only 18 per cent , well below the average for the group as a whole. Actual academic performance within the program, however, revealed a more complex picture. The forty-three men who received the highest grades (in the A to B range) achieved only a 16 per cent relative improvement over SIR, while their peers whose grade point averages were in the C and D range bested SIR by 41 per cent, exactly the opposite of what might either have been expected or hoped for. Such a result might be explained as a strong echo of the 'high flyer' and 'improver' hypotheses generated early in the research process – the high grades coming too easily for some (the 'high flyers'), while for others even average grades are, in fact, a significant personal accomplishment. Looked at in terms of the movement of academic achievement over time, the case for the 'hard slog' is confirmed for 'hard cases,' with members of this working group whose grades improved beating SIR by 38 per cent (from 43 per cent predicted success to 59 per cent actual success), while those whose grades declined bested SIR by only 11 per cent.

Since the hard cases remained after this initial analysis a distinctly grey box, the next step was to look to processes outside of attainment and achievement per se to search for pockets of success within the working group. Several other features showed more promise than the traditional academic benchmarks in differentiating the hard cases and thereby offered some insight into programming policies that might be important in dealing with this type of offender. While there were indications of the importance of age in the analyses of the total group, and one of the hypotheses involved both younger and older students possibly doing better, the role of age emerged in full view with the hard cases. Table 7.1 reveals a remarkably clear inverted bell curve, with once again men in their twenties being strong losers in terms of post-

Table 7.1.   Percentage of hard cases by age at current conviction (*n* = 118)

Subgroups (*n*)	Predicted	Actual	Difference	Relative improvement
Age (years)				
16–21 (32)	43	69	26	59
22–25 (29)	43	41	−2	−5
26–30 (34)	40	41	2	4
31–5 (14)	40	57	18	44
≥36 (9)	47	89	42	90

release success. The 59 per cent improvement over the SIR prediction for the sixteen- to twenty-one-year-old subgroup provided a strong incentive to examine further the idea that younger offenders with a less firm commitment to a criminal career may use their prison education experience to start a new life – the second-chancer hypothesis. With this group education might be a means of avoiding the fate that seemed to await them as they moved into their twenties. Of course, the impressive if dismal accuracy of the SIR in relation to the twenty- to thirty-year-old subjects made a deeper look into that category a top priority as well.

Another variable that proved significant with this group of hard cases centred on the management of release and what happens after release. Since the education program had as one of its objectives encouraging the prisoner-students to reintegrate with society as citizens rather than remain on the edge as outlaws, staff in the program hypothesized that men released into the community as soon as possible after completing their courses would do better than men held in prison for extended periods after withdrawing from or completing the education program. To test this hypothesis, the total group of 654 men was analysed on the basis of the gap between last enrolment in courses and release date. As Table 7.2 indicates, the results somewhat opposed expectations, with men released within the same year of completing their course work doing the worst relative to their SIR prediction, and those held in prison for five or more years following course work doing marginally better than their peers released earlier. Although interesting, with the total group the differentiations among subgroups are seldom decisive. When the same analysis is done for the group of 118 hard cases, the results as seen in Table 7.3 are much more striking.

While a gap between program and release of two years and beyond

Table   7.2. Gap between prison eduation program and release – percentage of total group (n = 654)

Subgroups (n)	Predicted	Actual	Difference	Relative improvement
Years				
1 (169)	57	70	13	22
2 (199)	59	78	19	33
3–4 (165)	57	73	16	29
≥5 (121)	59	80	21	36

Table 7.3.   Gap between prison eduation program and release – percentage of hard cases (n = 118)

Subgroups (n)	Predicted	Actual	Difference	Relative improvement
Years				
1 (29)	41	34	−6	−15
2 (32)	41	56	15	36
3–4 (31)	41	61	20	50
≥5 (26)	46	69	23	50

seems to make little difference for the rehabilitation of Hard Cases, it apparently can be disastrous if men from this group are released immediately upon completing courses. What could account for this counter-intuitive pattern? Upon close examination we find that the group of twenty-nine men who were released within the same year of taking courses contains a much higher percentage of mandatory supervision and sentence expiry cases (72 per cent) than the total group of hard cases (56 per cent). It would appear that most of these high-risk (according to SIR) hard case prisoners tended to serve their full sentence within medium and maximum security institutions where the education program operated, rather than being 'cascaded' through minimum security work camps, halfway houses, and then full parole. In some cases they were simply held in the prison until their mandatory supervision date, but in most cases they were persistent failures on institutional passes and day paroles. The 'system,' via firsthand staff experience, had concurred with SIR in identifying this subgroup of twenty-nine individuals as particularly dangerous and likely to re-offend. The system was correct: 69 per cent of this group – twenty of

Table 7.4.   Percentage of hard cases and further education

Subgroups (n)	Predicted	Actual	Difference	Relative improvement
Further education (26)	43	69	27	62
No further education (83)	41	52	10	25
Withdrew from education (9)	46	44	−2	−3

the twenty-nine – did re-offend within three years of their release. The failure of the university program to counteract this particular set of massively loaded dice is, of course, instructive. Inmates spent only a fraction of their imprisonment on programs and an overall regime of sentence planning is thus vital to the success of any program.

The proof of this is again demonstrated by the data. Having identified a subgroup of hard case losers, it follows that the working group will also contain a phalanx of winners. Since the place of the program part within the rehabilitative whole seems vital, we might look again to the management of the post-release period for possible answers. As described earlier, following release a substantial proportion (33 per cent) of the total cohort of prisoner-students made the transition – albeit often for only a short time – to educational institutions in the community. The expectation was that such a transition would have a beneficial impact on post-release success. Indeed, this turned out to be the case, the 213 subjects who did manage to continue with some kind of education endeavour after release improved on the SIR predicted performance by 42 per cent – one of the most dramatic indicators to emerge from the overall research data (see Table 5.8). Table 7.4 shows the impact of further education for this group of hard cases.

The relative improvement of 62 per cent for those who continue with education after release highlights the importance of this mechanism with this most fragile group of subjects. As might be expected, fewer of our hard cases (22 per cent) managed to make the transition to post-release education, but those who did scored a triumphant improvement over what SIR predicted for them.

The 'Worst Cases' Working Group

To focus in further on the higher risk cases in the group of subjects, another working group was selected based on the two most obvious variables. First, because both the literature in criminology and the

Table 7.5.   Grade point average – percentage of worst cases (*n* = 119)

Subgroups (*n*)	Predicted	Actual	Difference	Relative improvement
A/B GPA (49)	36	53	17	47
C/D GPA (70)	35	40	5	13

work with the total group indicated that men in their twenties were highly likely to recidivate, subjects who were in their twenties when they first enrolled in the education program were selected. This resulted in a list of 327 subjects out of the 654. Selecting from that list those who fell within the SIR scales two highest risk categories, D and E, resulted in a final working group of 119 subjects, the 'worst cases.' They were a dismal lot: 78 per cent having grade 10 or less education, 62 per cent with a record of juvenile incarcerations, 98 per cent with three or more adult convictions, 77 per cent currently incarcerated for robbery, theft or breaking and entering, and 70 per cent with violence on their criminal records.[73]

As one would expect, the SIR was pessimistic about this group, predicting that only 36 per cent would manage to be successful after release. In fact, the group as a whole did only modestly better, managing a success rate of 45 per cent for a 27 per cent relative improvement over the prediction – encouraging, but slightly below the average for the total group and hardly numbers to trumpet too loudly.

In looking for subgroups that performed at a rate better than the 27 per cent for the working group as a whole, objective academic variables were considered to find out if doing well academically increased the odds of beating SIR. The initial results were not all that encouraging. The number of university credits earned did not prove useful since men who earned fewer than fifteen credits (about one full-time semester of work or five courses) did about the same in terms of SIR as did those who completed more than thirty credits. Likewise the number of semesters completed failed to yield any really interesting subgroups, although the forty subjects finishing three to four semesters (twelve to sixteen months) did improve over SIR by 36 per cent. Actual academic performance proved more interesting. As Table 7.5 illustrates, the men who received higher marks in their courses did substantially better than poorer students and much better than the working group's average. While a 53 per cent success rate on parole is by no means outstanding, given average success rates in North America of about 50 per cent for this group of high-risk, but high-achieving young men, the 47 per cent relative improvement over their dismal prediction rate is quite definitely outstanding. In this subgroup of forty-nine individuals, only eighteen were supposed to remain out of prison for three years after release. Instead, twenty-six of them remained free of prison after release.

As one might expect, men who performed better on the various academic variables ended up with the higher grade point averages. The forty-nine A and B students enrolled in more semesters, earned more credits, took part in more extracurricular activities, and they continued their education after release at a much higher rate (43 per cent compared with 16 per cent) than their peers who earned more average marks. In terms of prior education, the differences between the subgroups were minimal, with 76 per cent of the above average students entering the program with grade 10 or less education compared with 80 per cent for the other subgroup.

In another analysis of academic achievement it was found that men whose grade point average improved over their time in the program (n = 14 only) in turn improved over their SIR prediction by 36 per cent, while the twenty-nine men whose grades declined managed only an 18 per cent improvement on SIR, well below the average for the group. It would appear from these data that for this worst case group academic performance is an important component of post-release success. One could view this assumption in two ways. On the one hand, it might be argued that among high-risk subjects, high levels of academic achievement are a kind of self-selection indicator, identifying men who are in fact more likely to succeed than their preprison background might indicate. On the other hand, one could argue on the basis of these data that greater efforts should be made to promote high levels of academic achievement among high-risk groups in order to enhance their chances of success after release. The former approach presumes a fundamentally passive role for education, it being merely an indicator, while the latter presumes a more active role with education being more in the nature of a cause than a reflection. Deciding between these two approaches would mean entering a number of black boxes for which mere data do not have the key.

Shifting from the academic core to a more subjective set of variables associated with participation in various activities within and adjacent to the education program a measure of intensity of engagement was used, with twelve men judged to be 'very intensely engaged' with the

Table 7.6.   Further education after release – percentage of worst cases (n = 160)

Subgroups (n)	Predicted	Actual	Difference	Relative improvement
Further education (32)	36	66	30	84
No further education (86)	36	37	2	5

program having a relative improvement over SIR of 86 per cent, but the number of subjects seemed too small to be more than an indicator of the potential importance of this kind of engagement. Using another measure of engagement there was a substantial 42 per cent improvement over SIR for the subgroup of thirty men who participated in some formal way in program affairs, through such mechanisms as student councils, tutoring, or employment.

As with the hard cases, by far the most outstanding finding with this working group concerned the fate of those men who chose to continue with their education after release (Table 7.6). Once again, as might be expected, the men who went on to some kind of post-release education and improved so dramatically over their SIR prediction were better students in terms of the academic variables discussed earlier, were formally involved in the program at a higher rate, and contained a lower percentage of men convicted of robbery or theft. The success of this subgroup hints at the importance of putting emphasis on academic achievement within prison education programs and as well the need for such programs to be highly participative, even democratic, in structure in order to involve as many students as possible in the actual administration of the program. Were this particular program, for instance, still in operation the program administrators might reasonably aim for high-risk men in their twenties to (a) place a higher cultural value on academic achievement within the program, (b) expand opportunities for student involvement or participation in program affairs, and (c) make greater efforts to encourage continuing with education while on parole in order to move even a few individuals from the larger subgroup to the smaller.

The 'Young Robbers' Working Group

As if the hard and worst cases were not bad enough, in digging deeper into the total group in search of an even greater exemplar of the high-

Table 7.7.   Further education – percentage of young robbers (*n* = 160)

Subgroups (*n*)	Predicted	Actual	Difference	Relative improvement
No further education (95)	43	41	−2	−4
Withdrew (21)	45	33	−12	−27
Further education (43)	47	72	25	54

risk offender, a working group of 160 men under the age of thirty whose last conviction had been for robbery or breaking and entering was created. This turned out to be the most intractable group yet, with SIR predicting a success rate of only 44 per cent, and the group managing only a 10 per cent improvement on that with only 49 per cent of the young robbers remaining free of prison for three years. These twenty-something robbers and thieves seemed immune to virtually any academic mechanism, indeed often showing perverse results such as subgroups earning fewer credits and achieving lower grades having greater post-release success than their more academically successful peers. Fortunately, the responses to the academic variables were chaotic enough that it was not possible to conclude that the education program had actually done harm. There were, for instance, some encouraging results in that the thirty-three men whose academic performance improved during their time in the program bested their SIR prediction by 18 per cent and the seventy-two men deemed to be intensely involved with the program outperformed SIR by 13 per cent. Still, compared with other subgroups, these percentages were modest.

The young robbers proved perverse on other sets of measures as well. Contrary to most other groups, non-participants in the theatre programs did better than participants (12 per cent improvement over SIR compared with 4 per cent). Men from the group released on parole to halfway houses actually underperformed SIR by a −4 per cent compared with a 22 per cent relative improvement for men released directly into the community, and parolees in general did considerably worse than those released on mandatory supervision. The SIR beaters in the group only really emerge with the calculation for further education after release (Table 7.7). The forty-three men in this subgroup are interesting in particular because thirty-one of them are high school drop-outs, two-thirds of them completing only grade 10 or less. Of these drop-outs, twenty-one or two-thirds end up 'beating' SIR. Something within their experience of the education program had sufficient impact to persuade these exceedingly difficult-to-reach young men to alter, at least temporarily, a life plan that seemed firmly set on further criminal activity. Unfortunately, while the box may no longer be black it remains largely opaque, the individuality driving the choice of mechanisms and circumstances making it impossible to find a simple answer to 'what worked' and 'why.' As is the case with other promising subgroups, it is the self-selection by students from among a variety of mechanisms and circumstances that accounts for successful outcomes in education – not the isolation of a single factor.

The results as outlined here point to several specific mechanisms within the education program and within the procedures involved in the transition from prison to community that may serve to enhance the program's contribution to the individual high-risk offender's chances of beating the SIR prediction. The data indicate that to address the needs of this category of prisoner-students, prison education programs should aim to encourage a culture of academic achievement, focus in particular on those students who show signs of improvement, provide opportunities for participation in program administration and governance, offer extracurricular activities such as theatre, and both encourage and facilitate a continuing engagement with education after release. While some or all of these may be important for other groups of prisoner-students besides these high-risk younger men, this is not necessarily the case. The subgroup methodology undertaken here enables program administrators to discriminate among a prisoner-student population that has different needs and responds differently to the various mechanisms inherent in the education program.

Returning to the claim that education 'works' for high-risk offenders, we can argue that the evidence collected validates the claim – but it could be made to work even better if we mastered the match between mechanisms and students. In the next chapter we will take a more detailed look at some aspects of successful prison programs that this kind of research indicates should be central components to all efforts at rehabilitation of prison inmates.

CHAPTER EIGHT

From Object to Subject –
The Potential for a Room of One's Own
within the Prison

The purposes of the treatment of persons in custody shall be such as to sustain their health and self-respect and, so far as the length of sentence permits, to develop their sense of responsibility and encourage those attitudes and skills that will assist them to return to society with the best chance of leading law-abiding and self-supporting lives after their release.[1]

Council of Europe, *European Prison Rules*, 1987

In 1979 the organizers of a conference on prison education to be held at the University of Victoria in Canada invited a prominent radical criminologist to be the keynote speaker. In his rejection of the invitation, he complimented the organizers of the conference on the apparent success of their prison education efforts, but since he was convinced that on the whole nothing positive could emanate from such institutions he did not want to lend his name to an enterprise that might only serve to justify the idea of prison-based rehabilitation. Such was the impact of Foucault, Martinson, Morris, and all the other critical theorists and criminologists on the very idea of rehabilitation in the 1970's. The conference organizers – and I was among the group – were left with the dilemma of agreeing in large part with these critiques of the prison, while at the same time observing positive transformations among the prisoners they worked with.

For me this incident was the trigger, though I was hardly aware of it at the time, that set off the process of questioning that has finally manifested itself in this book. Are there subversive possibilities in the carceral archipelago? Can the corrections system 'correct' in spite of itself? Can a diamond emerge in the rough? Given that the Enlightenment model cannot 'work' because it leads only to fragmentation of selves and a crude sort of positivism, what accounts for observed successes in that most 'enlightened' of institutions, the prison? As we have seen, there is solid research that demonstrates that some programs in prison are remarkably effective in reducing rates of recidivism, changing the lives of prisoners, and perhaps even transforming the prison itself, if only temporarily. In this final chapter some common features of these programs are explored in the context of the 'counter-public sphere' notion that even within the bureaucratized and authoritarian institutions spawned by the Enlightenment tradition, there exist spaces, interstices, and experiments that can effect transformative changes in lives.

A clue as to how this might work was given at this same conference by Michael Ignatieff, who did accept the invitation to speak. He talked at length about the moral dimension implicit in providing education to prisoners and insisted that such programs would fail if they attempted to inculcate only normative values. Instead, Ignatieff argued for the inclusion of a critical perspective on social issues, including issues that prisoners might seek to use in constructing an excuse for their criminal actions. Such a critical perspective would demonstrate, if done skilfully, that one could take issue with the inevitable injustices, inequalities, and imperfections in society without needing to resort to criminal acts. A decade later, Ignatieff's radical perspective on this essential human right, even for the prisoner, of freedom to dissent and maintain a critical perspective on law and society would become codified in the Council of Europe's insistence that the prisoner need not 'capitulate psychologically to the prison system.'[2]

This seems an absolutely central point to any discussion of the rehabilitation or transformation of criminals into citizens. It is acknowledged at the outset that society as we find it is unjust, unequal, and often uncaring, but at the same time is a social structure within which one can live, be reconciled to, and even attempt to change. In the first instance, living with society as it is, some prisoners can be taught skills, motivated, or otherwise persuaded to take advantage of the opportunities that there are in society despite inequalities and injustices. Many education and training programs in prisons have this as their objective. Or, if this is not a likely or preferred possibility, one can be reconciled to the status quo by a contemplative inward turn or by the cultivation of alternative priorities, the option encouraged by many prison arts, counselling, and religious initiatives. Finally, the kind of critical approach discussed by Ignatieff, and pursued in its most extreme fashion in our earlier example of the SCWPP program at the California Institution for Women, could encourage a shifting of the energy and innovative thinking involved in a criminal career towards active engagement with issues of social change and development. This latter point contained within it the challenging and radical idea that in the criminal act there was a nascent critical insight that needed to be preserved rather than expunged. As we will explore in this chapter, particularly successful prison programs such as the post-secondary program in British Columbia managed to contain elements of each of these possibilities.

The Argument So Far

In tracing the history of modern prison programs designed to have an impact on crime and recidivism I have argued that the high point in effectiveness was reached in the 1975–1990 period commonly characterized as an era of 'humane containment' or, in Canada at least, by the idea of 'opportunities' being made available to prisoners. Compared with the periods just before (the medical model) and just after (the cognitive model), this was a time in which 'common sense' could be seen the dominant paradigm, a recognition if you will of the ancient truth about leading a horse to water but not being able to make him or her drink. To string out the metaphor, while the dominant models offered the prisoner a single pond from which to drink (or not!), the commonsensical approach offered a river or, at least a multiplicity of ponds.

A further extension of this argument has highlighted the distinctions between corrections professionals and the amateurs or 'outsiders' who find themselves in correctional institutions. Casting myself in the latter role, my own progress through the prison was a case study of the advantages the outsider can bring to the task at hand. If the task of the prison is merely containment then, of course, the outsider is both unnecessary and a hindrance. But since the prison has taken upon itself the task of 'correcting,' the issue is raised immediately whether the keeper can also correct. The lion tamer can, of course, both contain the lion and train it to perform tricks. and in response the lion – if one believes such things – learns to love both the trainer and the tricks. Closer to the mark, perhaps, is the accusation by Rene Char that 'those who watch the lion suffer in his cage rot in the memory of the lion.'[3]

If the keepers are kind to the kept, assure them that they have their best interests at heart, and go to great lengths to help them see the errors of their ways, can this fundamental inequality be overcome? Can the inmate forget, suspend belief, or willingly accept that the individual who is integral to the system that enforces his or her inability to move beyond a fence, wall, or regulation is someone they should credit as a source of reformation? In my 'prison years' this seemed an overwhelming burden for the correctional staff member to overcome, and I concurred with the words of one former prisoner that the 'prisoner's need to live and the system's need to live for him (and off him) can never be reconciled.'[4] This prisoner's voice is not alone in this conclusion. The evaluators of the NewGate programs stressed the central importance for rehabilitation efforts of a 'separate identity' from the prison, noting that prisoners have a 'basic mistrust' of correctional staff that leads inevitably to a cynicism about prison programs. They insisted that some kind of 'insulation' from the prison was essential to avoid an automatic 'contamination by association.'[5] In contrast to this, as we have seen, the cognitive skills program, which is so much in vogue in these times, prides itself on its ability to engage all prison staff in the 'treatment' of the inmate to the virtual exclusion of outsiders. Indeed, here the prisoner's 'needs' are seen to be so complex that they can be addressed only if the entire professional and empathetic resources of the prison are mobilized to that end! Thus, once again we are confronted with an either/or, yet another dualism.

Back to First Principles: Dualism

Western culture was born of a convenient dualism, the competing world-views of Plato and Aristotle. Whether seen as the sum total of human possibilities in their time or a creation by subsequent generations seeking neatness of analysis, the impact of a dualist framework has been decisive in Western culture from ancient to modern times. For the purposes of applying this dualism to this discussion of prisons, reformations, and transformations, we can simplify each side of the foundational dualist equation as follows: Plato believed that what we have come to call criminal behaviour or deviance (and he called evil) stem from either lack of knowledge or skewed knowledge and in correcting this was content to settle for visible signs of virtuous behaviour. Aristotle, on the other hand, saw deviance as stemming from embedded character flaws that led to poor decisions and was insistent that virtuous actions could only flow from virtuous intentions.

In the praxis of living and creating social systems, these two approaches to establishing and sustaining a moral order involve quite different prescriptions and often clash, although in reality we rarely see pure versions of either. Systems like fascism may be more Platonic in their authoritarian demands for outward conformity but they also contain an Aristotelean interest in the inner life of at least some of their members. Likewise, typically Aristotelean moral and social systems like much of the medieval era of European history do focus on the inner life of intention but often use this as an excuse for enforcing a Platonic conformity. But how does this relate to prisons? Clearly, the modern, progressive prison reform movements of the late eighteenth and early nineteenth centuries were Platonic in their concern with producing conformity in the outward life of the offender, with only the Quakers nodding as well to the importance of arriving at an inner transformation through solitary study of the Bible. Just as clearly, the contemporary medical or treatment approaches are Aristotelean in their concern with the inner self, the conscience, cognitive structures, and moral intention. In its most extreme version this Aristotelean impulse even proposes heading off future evil by detaining individuals whose 'character' can be diagnosed as flawed. In the modern parlance, if we find a sexual deviant in our midst who has refused treatment designed to cure him, how can we justify not locking him away in order to prevent inevitable or even possible future harm to others?

As so many critics of the dualist tradition in Western culture have attested, such an either/or approach to the lived realities of both selves and systems can only lead to misunderstandings, failures, and even disasters. This is not to say that Plato and Aristotle have no value, but rather that the real strength of their insights into the human condition only emerges when they are held in common rather than apart. It is in the realm of the critical tension between these two world-views, the synaptic space between the poles as it were, that we should strive to place ourselves. Some philosophers attempt to occupy this space and, logically enough in a dualist culture, are subsequently criticized for attempting to hold opposite views that can only result in a paradox. Rousseau was one of these who insisted on the value of the paradox, arguing that social conformity in the Platonic and if necessary authoritarian sense was an essential feature of any human social contract community, while at the same time insisting that in reaching moral conclusions about an individual's behaviour (such as his own!) only intentions mattered, not actions.[6]

It is, then, to this space between the dualisms of action and intention, body and soul, conformity and deviance, keepers and kept that we should find the most energetic, challenging, and therefore transformative attempts to address the problem of moving individuals from life as criminal to life as citizen. But we must be aware that this is a potentially messy space, difficult to tolerate, and often dangerous. While some criminals are truly transformed into citizens and others stubbornly remain openly criminal, the middle realm of paradox remains occupied by our untreated sex offender who lives a normal life but may harbour deviant intention, the heroin addict who has become an alcoholic, and the thief who learns to cheat within the law rather than steal outside it.

The Space Between

The era in corrections in which a 'hundred flowers were allowed to bloom' was characterized, I have argued throughout, by its tolerance for action in this neutral space between the dualisms. The prison systems examined here could not, of course, tolerate a complete breakdown or erosion of their mechanisms of control which might have followed on from a true 'opening up' of the prison to outside forces. There could be no copying of the penal situation in some developing countries with families living inside or adjacent to the prison, a money economy allowed to flourish, and inmate self-government rampant. But neither could these prison systems any longer mimic their more authoritarian counterparts in countries like China or the Soviet Union, where no doubts about proper treatment were ever entertained. The result was a kind of paralysis, temporary as we have seen, but sufficiently extended in time to allow for a significant history of successful innovation to occur.

This innovation manifested itself in many forms. There was a flowering of religious vitality within these prison systems. The Black Muslims, Evangelical Christians, and Native Brotherhoods, as well as proponents of more traditional religiosity grew dramatically in prisons during this period and remain powerful to this day. In each case the prisoners who identified in some way with these spiritual movements found ready advocates and sponsors in the community who in turn demanded access to the prison to work with their converts and, more controversially, demanded that the prison acknowledge this new-found religiosity as a valid factor in rehabilitation and release. Local community groups such as Chambers of Commerce and Lions Clubs also found within neighbouring prisons a worthy cause, and they made a strong case both for a presence within the prison of shadow groups and for the 'good works' performed by prisoners, while active in these groups, to be credited in terms of evidence of rehabilitation and in decisions about release. As both illiteracy and learning difficulties came to be seen as important inhibitors of social and economic well-being in the community as a whole, they were quickly seized upon as factors in crime causation as well, resulting in prisons being increasingly popular locations for volunteer tutoring by well meaning community people. Finally, as in the case of Barlinnie, the discovery of latent creative talents within the prison led to an intense interest in prisons on the part of the artistic community, an interest easily transformed into a demand that this new-found creativity also be credited as rehabilitative. As I have stressed throughout, education programs enjoyed a true renaissance during this era of opportunities, a renaissance the evidence for which provides the central empirical proofs offered in this book.

For the more successful of these incursions into the formerly closed world of the prison, I have identified three common factors, which taken together account for their success. They are:

1   Community, self, and authenticity: An ethical stance towards the prisoner based on interacting with him or her as a subject rather than an object. In its structural form this often centres on creating a democratic participatory environment within which the program operates.
2   Bonds with the conventional world: A politics of prison programming that stresses the connection between the specific initiative and an institutional or social affiliation external to and separate from the prison or the criminal justice system.
3   A structural approach that relies on diversity and complexity rather than singularity and simplicity, acknowledging that prisoner needs are many and unique and the intervenor's skills and abilities both various and limited.

Each of these factors contributes to the task central to any effort at encouraging individual change or development, namely, addressing the needs and aspirations of that individual in an intimate, equitable, and practical manner. 'Intimacy' may seem a strange requirement in such a process, but it goes to the heart of the task by acknowledging, even 'privileging' to use a more contemporary term, the singularity and complexity of the person. Try as we may to make them so, the imprisoned are not the 'dead souls' of Gogol's Russia, nor are they the numbered 'inmates' of the modern corrections institution. They can never be mere 'raw material' awaiting transformation, nor are they all benighted deviants awaiting or resisting correction.

If intimacy and even equity are dissonant-sounding words in the popular vernacular of that demonized deviance, there is more difficulty to come. The ethical, political, and structural prescription outlined above also requires that attention be paid to the preservation of individual 'dignity' and the development or enhancement of 'character.' Nelson Mandela in his autobiography, Long Walk to Freedom, singled out the importance of the former when he insisted that 'prison and the authorities conspire to rob each man of his dignity.'[7] Occupying as it does such prominent 'moral ground,' the state and its agent the corrections system can hardly do otherwise. The dignity of the criminal, assuming any is left after the degradation intrinsic to much of criminal and prison life, cannot be seen as an asset despite all the rehabilitative talk about the importance of self-esteem. The criminal must first be deconstructed via transformation into an object of study and control, and then filled with a unique sense of self- esteem and dignity formed by his new subjectivity as 'inmate.'[8]

The sense of character, dignity, and self-esteem that the prison regime attempts to impose on the prisoner is one that prepares the person for a life of submission to authority, rule-following, and self-discipline, all qualities of functional value within the prison and, as perceived by some, in society. In the dark vision of modern industrial society put forward by Christopher Lasch over the past thirty years this submissive, image-conscious, uncritical, and non-reflective persona is seen as the norm, a world in which 'the self becomes almost indistinguishable from its surface.'[9] It is not likely, however, that many prisoners are going to esteem or aspire to that kind of persona or character, their criminal careers in some ways being evidence of an early rejection of exactly that. True, there may be some, perhaps a significant number, of imprisoned criminals whose life chances were so poor or whose insights so limited that they were denied the opportunity of successfully becoming submissive, self-disciplined rule-followers, but they are not likely the more seriously dangerous residents in our prisons. Rather, they are the ones who upon questioning that path found the only option to be one of crime, violence, and self-destruction.

It is the success of traditional, conformity-encouraging prison programs with low-risk and older offenders and with their corresponding dismal failure with high-risk and 'mid-career' criminals that highlights for us the central dilemma. The current U.S. solution of merely holding these more dangerous offenders in prison until they are old and 'burnt-out' (that is, willing to conform at last) is likely too expensive, inhumane, and ineffective since it simply creates social space in the world of crime for other individuals. The success of programs like cognitive skills with low-risk offenders is interesting, but once again does nothing to address the social chaos being caused by multiple offenders – often aggressive, insightful, and intelligent – who perceive crime as their only reasonable career option.

What, then, is to be done? The title of this chapter borrows a phrase from one of Virginia Woolf's most influential books, A Room of One's Own, and her insistence in that book that 'a woman must have money and a room of her own if she is to write fiction' points the way towards a solution.[10] If 'writing fiction' is transposed to mean achieving an authentic sense of self in relation to the whole, and if 'money' can mean resources and the social connections they embody, and a 'room' can mean a space within which the private self can determine its interactions with the public sphere, then we are close to being able to move Woolf's prescription from the particulars of early twentieth-century women to late twentieth-century human beings, with prisoners being a particular subset. Indeed, we return via this reworked Woolf to our original three factors deemed essential to any successful transformation from criminal to citizen: a democratic ethics, a diverse set of political linkages, and an inevitably complex set of needs and relations.

Community, Self, and Authenticity

Throughout this book I have argued that criminals and prisoners are less unique or truly 'deviant' than simply extreme versions of individuals and groups present in society as a whole. I said at the outset that we would be more interested in the Adolf Eichmanns than the more sadistic fascists, more concerned with robbers and thieves than with Ted Bundy. Taking this approach enables us to leave more easily the specialist world of criminology and those concerned with exotic psychopathologies and look instead for a means to address crime and rehabilitation within the vast body of literature and thought applicable to individual development and social issues in general. I have often called upon literature, philosophy, and political theory in the search for insights into these issues. Given the pervasive concern with the fate of the self in mass society, the pressures on human and social authenticity caused by technology, and the threat to community posed by globalization, there is no shortage of links between prison and society on the issue of the self and the preservation of an authentic subjectivity, while at the same time ensuring a humane and supportive social community.

If the first step in constructing an approach to facilitating transformations in the lives of prisoners is to imagine a means of relating to the individual prisoner as a subject rather than an object, this task has immediate parallels in the society outside the prison. The philosopher Charles Taylor constructs his argument for an 'ethics of authenticity' on the idea that 'each of us has an original way of being human,' that we individually comprise a unique subjectivity that is ours and ours alone, and that this selfness includes or is embedded within a conscience, an 'intuitive feeling for what is right and wrong.'[11] This approach can easily lead to an unimpeded individualism, as Taylor acknowledges and de Tocqueville warned 150 years earlier. Clearly, if the 'innate sense of right and wrong' is present within us, it is too easily and readily masked by either the pressures towards conformity or the pressures towards narcissism and an excessive cult of individual 'self-fulfilment.'

The novels of Jane Austen survive so well in the late twentieth century because she wrote at a time when her idealized notions of community – grounded largely in the landed gentry families of eighteenth-century England – was coming under the corrosive pressure of early capitalist-driven individualism. In her most 'political' of novels, *Mansfield Park*, the two daughters of Sir Thomas Bertram, the typically Austenesque inept but well-meaning father, make poor choices in the mating game, and he muses at the end of the novel about what had gone wrong: 'Something must have been wanting *within*, or time would have worn away much of its [his severity as a father] ill effect. He feared that principle, active principle, had been wanting, that they had never been properly taught to govern their inclinations and tempers by that sense of duty which alone can suffice. They had been instructed theoretically in their religion, but never required to bring it into daily practice. To be distinguished for elegance and accomplishments – the authorized object of their youth – could have no useful influence that way, no moral effect on the mind. He had wanted them to be good, but his cares had been directed to the understanding and manners, not the disposition; and of the necessity of self-denial and humility, he feared they had never heard from any lips that could profit them.'[12]

This will warrant some dissection. At the start Austen has introduced the idea of an '*active* principle,' not merely a set of rules or commandments, but an internalized set of beliefs and principles that were grounded in social engagement rather than just learning – Aristotle's intentions again. It is a 'sense of duty which can alone suffice,' and duty here is understood to be a disposition formulated within a self in interaction with community. Presuming for a moment that our prisoners are like Sir Thomas Bertrams's daughters in that they have 'gone wrong,' then merely teaching or imposing a set of principles or rules will not suffice. Bertram rightly sees that his daughters have only 'theoretical' knowledge obtained independently of any requirement to put it into 'daily practice,' and here the 'daily' part seems particularly significant. The 'inclinations and tempers' of the two young girls were insufficiently touched by their abstracted lessons, just as the inclination of the criminal to steal or to shift quickly from frustration to violence will unlikely be altered by lessons in anger management, literacy, or positive reinforcement. Austen has Bertram see through the level of mere 'understanding' – what the correctional establishment often calls 'insight' – to the dispositional core. The task set for us, then, is to create a means of influencing the disposition of the prisoner in such a way as to allow him or her to bring into play what Taylor calls his or her innate sense of right and wrong and to do so in a manner that is at the same time both socially responsible and true to themselves.

As a born-again pedestrian who eschews the automobile whenever possible, I have ample time for reveries and speculations about the criminal habits of the drivers I observe on daily walks to buses and trains. What set of rules – internally or externally derived – governs or fails to govern the behaviour of the thousands of drivers that surround me? The ubiquitous yellow caution light that follows green and precedes red provides fuel for speculation. What cognitive and moral operations are at play when the driver sees the yellow appear and has to decide to stop and obey the law or speed up and evade the law? Fear of apprehension? Deterrence? Obligations to one's fellow humans? The decision in many cities to install cameras at intersections is an admission of moral defeat and a late twentieth-century lament akin to Austen's Sir Thomas Bertram – our drivers are 'wanting within.'

This raises a second major issue, namely, identifying what might be 'socially responsible' in an unequal and often unjust but still open society. In their opening line the authors of the very influential American exploration of this issue, the book *Habits of the Heart*, address this very point: 'How ought we to live? How do we think about how to live? Who are we ...? What is our character?'[13] Acknowledging the centrality in the American tradition of a kind of radical individualism – that unique way of being a self – the authors of this text nonetheless insist that it must be through community that this self can be realized. John McKnight, another important communitarian thinker, also affirms that it must be through a combination of 'person, place and peer' that the moral order so necessary for socially responsible action in the world can be discovered and nurtured.[14]

The direction of inquiry taken in *Habits of the Heart* and similar explorations directs our attention towards the 'space between' the individual and the social world of which he or she is a part, rather than to the intensely internal world of the psychology of deviance. The 'problem' we face with many criminals and prisoners is that they have abandoned by and large any notion of a middle ground between self and society. Ever since the research by Yochelson and Samenow, the work of Robert Ross, and the testing done by many psychologists and criminologists, it has become a commonplace to describe criminals as 'egocentric,' as seeing the social world revolving about them, an oddly pre-Galilean perspective. As reviewed earlier, we know from the research done by Piaget that such egocentrism is 'normal' for children and often extends well into adolescence; indeed, it is a central feature in the crucial developmental process of constructing a 'self.' We know as well, or at least can easily intuit, that such an egocentric self can become dangerous as an adult, its most extreme version being the psychopath who knows only the self.

It is in the realm of self and society that what we think of as the rehabilitation or, more properly, the transformation of prisoners must occur. Again, remembering Austen's point delivered through the musings of Thomas Bertram, it must be stressed that neither coercion, conditioning, or fear of punishment will work in the long run in moving these individuals closer to the centre-point in the self-society continuum. In one of my favourite renditions of this lesson, Jean-Jacques Rousseau has the heroine of his novel *Julie, Or the New Eloise* remind her lover that in choosing to marry someone else in order to please her family, she makes the hard but morally necessary choice: 'which is really more important to me, my happiness at the expense of the rest of mankind, or others' happiness at the expense of mine? If the fear of shame or punishment prevents me from doing wrong for my own advantage, I have only to do wrong secretly, there is nothing virtue can reproach me with. And if I am caught in the act, it is, as in Sparta, not the crime that will be punished, but the ineptness.'[5] This is Rousseau at his stoical best, counselling satisfaction with the inner well-being derived from obeying an ethics grounded in community. To have run away with the ill-born lover would have meant abandoning family, culture, and country for life with another single self – a twentieth-century fantasy of self-fulfilment grounded in the celebration of ego, passion, and rootlessness. Just as important in the passage is the fixation of the character on 'intention,' on the fallibility of a moral system based only on utility or self-interest – on not getting caught. Only a slight immersion in the conversational world of the prisoner – or random observations of the modern automobile driver – will make one aware of just how far that moral world is from the admittedly excessively self-sacrificing world of Julie.

That egocentric world of the prisoner is so powerful, and so powerfully reinforced every day by the struggle for psychological survival imposed on each prisoner by the prison, that one must enter the fray with modest expectations. 'Transformation' in this context may mean only slight movement towards the 'space between,' that certainly being the case for the more experienced and hardened members of the group. Still, given my argument as to the centrality of self-society issues in the dispositional qualities of the criminal, creating a stronger sense of 'self-in-community' must still be a core value in prison programming.

How are we to accomplish this, especially given how far removed the imprisoned are from any community one might want them to consider a stronger affiliation with? To suggest an answer we can turn to the general field of education and to the particular case of the post-secondary program in British Columbia. The work of Piaget remains at the core of our thinking about education, and Piaget starts from the premise that the essential educative task is to move individuals from the childish unilateral respect for authority to a position of mutual respect for autonomous wills. To do this he advocated a democratic approach to education, involving students from an early age in coop-

erative endeavours and in the self-discipline so central to true democratic life.[16] Instead, of course, we traditionally force young people to
wage constant war against authority in our institutional schools. We
have known since the teachings of Socrates that the way to create
responsible citizens who will exercise right reason in public affairs is
to draw them into public inquiry, to force the individual to become an
active associate in discussion. Our political theorists from Jefferson on
have taught us that to participate responsibly in democratic institutions we must practise doing so by taking responsibility and making
decisions. We know as well from educational theorists that independence of thought is increased by independence of action and that in
our maturation from childhood to adult these two processes should be
dynamically related – not treated in a linear or abstract fashion.[17]
More specifically, we know that actual learning is enhanced when students are actively engaged in the learning process. Thus, it has been
argued that

1   The amount of student learning and personal development associ-
    ated with any educational program is directly proportional to the
    quality and quantity of student involvement in the program.
2   The effectiveness of any educational policy or practice is directly
    related to the capacity of that policy or practice to increase student
    involvement in learning.[18]

Besides the evidence for this kind of engagement with the very process
of education being central to both learning and individual development, there is strong evidence in the research on the effectiveness of
higher education that substantive engagement with the social environment of the school is of at least equal importance. The so-called Ben-
nington effect indicated that the student's 'reference group' rather than
curriculum or teachers was the principal mechanism in whatever
changes took place during the period of schooling. Further research
done at Michigan State University singled out the first two years at
university as the period when friends, living situation and social life
were the most powerful influences on students, the period when 'campus climate plays the crucial role in changing the values and attitudes
of the students.'[19] These insights ring true, I am sure, for anyone who
has pursued higher education and as well for the earlier period of secondary school. Colleges and universities often go to great lengths to
ensure the 'right' kind of atmosphere within which students can

mature in relative safety and absorb those social and moral values deemed essential to life in a democratic society. Indeed, it was for this reason that the evaluators of the effectiveness of the prison post-secondary program in British Columbia put such great stress on the issue of student 'engagement' or 'involvement' with the education program as a possible causal agent in post-release success, more importance, in fact, than on the actual content of the educational material being learned.

Knowing what we do about the atmosphere or 'campus climate' of the modern prison, this research can only lead us to predict dismal results. Jack Arbuthnot, a writer on moral education from Ohio University, with extensive experience with prison programs, poses the central question: 'Can effective changes in moral reasoning be achieved in more narrowly focused programs with an unaltered correctional environment?' He says not, unless the following provisions are met:

1 Creation of an educational setting within the prison that maximizes not only growth in both logical and moral reasoning skills but also provides for practice in translating these skills into very real, everyday conflicts or dilemmas
2 Relative isolation from the remainder of the prison in as many aspects of daily life and governance as possible
3 Provision of a post-release program to provide support for the practical use of newly acquired reasoning and interpersonal skills[20]

Here Arbuthnot borrows liberally from the earlier (1976) final evaluation of the Project NewGate programs with their call for a separation of the program from the prison in whatever ways possible and the creation of a 'college-type atmosphere inside the prison [with] a wide variety of courses ... an extensive library with a wide assortment of books and periodicals, research and study facilities, major university involvement, informal and personal contact with college professors, extensive association with other students, lectures, debates, seminars, outside speakers.'[21] This all sounds very idealistic, perhaps even naïve, but in the late 1970s and the 1980s such steps were possible in a wide variety of penal institutions in Canada, the United States, and Western Europe. The post-secondary program in British Columbia included all of this and more in its four program sites, albeit in a somewhat truncated form in the maximum security setting. In visits to programs in

Wisconsin, Massachusetts, Washington, Oregon, Arizona, Ontario, and Great Britain, I observed very similar programs in operation during these years, all with variations of these structures and activities. If there was a weakness in virtually all of them it was in the area of post-release support facilities, and this no doubt did seriously inhibit their degree of effectiveness.

There was yet another dimension to these kinds of programs that, while not universally implemented, was present to some degree in most, namely, the idea of democratic decision-making structures within the program. If the objective outlined above is to create a situation in which prisoners are addressed 'naturally' and reciprocally as subjects rather than objects, that is, something other than what could happen in the traditional prison or even a therapeutic community which sometimes appears to foster reciprocity but is in fact highly manipulative, then more than mere 'atmosphere' or a 'campus climate' is necessary.[22] There must be in place as well a theoretical understanding of the importance of democracy in providing the basis for sustaining an authentic subjectivity, the will to implement that understanding, and the structures essential to its survival in the hostile environment of the prison. We need to examine each of these requirements in turn.

The theoretical importance of a democratic environment is centred on its role in providing a space for participative action, for the exercise of accommodation, compromise, and fairness along with guile, bluff, and force in social interactions. Within the prison the creation of such an environment makes it possible to recreate a version of the 'public sphere' that was taken away at the point of incarceration. As noted above, the skills and dispositions so essential to the operation of such a public sphere are not strictly speaking 'teachable,' but rather require a space for practice and experimentation. For most citizens, family life, schooling, and adolescent social relations provide at least a minimal mix of necessary learning and practice, but for the men and women we end up imprisoning, as their biographies demonstrate, these experiences are often truncated, skewed, or lead only to skills and dispositions that provoke a break with civic culture and authentic social relations. The case for the crucial role of democratic praxis in prison programs has a long tradition, but it was given a contemporary theoretical rationale through the work of Lawrence Kohlberg and his colleagues at Harvard. Focusing on the need for moral development, Kohlberg included a prison in the various moral development projects undertaken by his group. The program at the Niantic women's prison in Massachusetts was built around an 'intensive community life' employing what was seen as 'primary democracy' complete with group meetings, equal votes for staff and prisoners, and open discussion of all issues.[23] While it was similar in many ways to the smaller program described earlier at Barlinnie Prison in Scotland, that program had used democracy as a prison management tool, while Kohlberg had more grandiose objectives; and the realization of a 'just community' in the prison was the crucial *deus ex machina*:

> We can see that democracy is central to moral development if we see that the heart of morality is a sense of fairness and justice. Morality means a decision of what is right where there is a conflict between the interests and claims of two or more people. Justice means fairness in deciding the conflict, giving each person his due and being impartial to all. Democracy is a form of government designed so that the decision-making process will be considered fair by all. Only in a democratic setting can inmates have any sense of living in a community which is fair. While most inmates do not care about society's morality, they do care about justice and fairness. Because they are treated unjustly and live in an unjust world, they do not try to be fair to others. To be motivated to act fairly, inmates must feel they are part of a just community.[24]

This is an intensely pragmatic analysis, built not around trying to convince prisoners to love what they perceive to be an unjust world, but rather to convince them of a version of the Golden Rule, that the world will be less unjust if they move closer to an ethic of fairness and justice in their daily interactions. This message would appear patently absurd to a street-wise prisoner, violating all his or her instincts about survival. But if given an opportunity to experiment with fairness, accommodation, and compromise in a constructed just community, Kohlberg argued that the lessons learned and dispositions acquired could be transferred to the larger public sphere the prisoner enters upon release.

How can this actually be done in prison? At the Niantic moral development project the just community *was* the project, employing mass meetings of prisoners and staff from the 'cottage' or living unit to discuss everything from daily activities to food to serious disputes between prisoners and between prisoners and staff. Since everything was open to discussion (except release!) there were often tense moments, as in the case in which a planned escape by two prisoners threatened to jeopardize the whole project and group interest came into conflict with the inmate code. Like the SCWPP project in California but unlike Barlinnie, the Niantic experiment was closed down by the prison at the first convenient opportunity, in this case a serious disturbance in another part of the institution.

The approach taken by the post-secondary program in British Columbia was different in significant ways from Niantic, SCWPP, and Barlinnie. Staff in that program talked about creating an 'alternative community,' one with democratic structures and with the same ambitions as Kohlberg's just community but implemented in a more gradual and, in a sense, combative manner. Unlike the other examples, the post-secondary programs in the British Columbia prisons existed in areas or buildings separated off from the rest of the prison – not as permanently as was the case in Barlinnie, but one could approximate a feeling of 'leaving the prison' when entering the university area. This meant, of course, that the university staff could set about the creation of this alternative community relatively independently of correctional staff, who might be in the vicinity but were not participants.

Given that this program operated simultaneously in as many as four prisons, each with a unique security rating and 'atmosphere,' the actual manifestation of the university alternative community varied from site to site. The common premise was that democracy is less a right than a privilege and is something to be struggled for rather than granted. As well, it was presumed that without due care and attention, cultivation as it were, it could be seriously eroded and even lost. The evolution of these communities over the twenty-year life span of the program therefore seemed to move in cycles, roughly following the pattern of a staff-driven paternalism leading to consultation with a student elite and then to a kind of constitutional democracy through elected student councils – and then more often than not back to one of the earlier stages before moving forward again. These stages did tend to occur in sequence since each was dependent on there being prisoner-students in the program who had outgrown the forms and demands of the earlier stage. At times, of course, these stages had to coexist, since any given program had a constantly shifting population which made political consensus very difficult, much as it is in any political community in a state of flux. This was not, therefore, a closed experimental group but rather much more like any other community that must cope with 'outsiders,' immigrants, the loss of leaders, and the stress of demographic change.

In describing this alternative community in a 1983 article on the history of one of these programs, I referred to the program staff initiating the process through a kind of 'cultural offensive,' starting with changes in the organization of the physical space, the starting of a library, the introduction of a film series, and the decoration of walls and rooms with art prints.[25] These steps plus a visiting speaker series, visits by groups of students from the main campus, and the start of a theatre project were directed 'from above,' not in response to student demands or requests. They were designed to stress the uniqueness of the school area and to test the outer limits of institutional flexibility, not through confrontation but by argument and, occasionally, guile. While the changes were driven by a paternal sense of the need to create change, the staff were careful not to allow this to become transformed into authoritarianism. Interestingly, authoritarian solutions to the various problems and crises generated by these changes were generally preferred by both prisoner-students and correctional staff. When some men abused the new freedoms and opportunities available in the school area, as some inevitably would, other students would invariably put pressure on the program staff to 'solve the problem' by using their authority or calling in the prison authorities (for example, having the troublemaker transferred from the program) rather than dealing with the issue themselves.

Gradually, an elite group of prisoner-students began to emerge who were in fact more 'student' than 'prisoner' when they were in the school area (presumably when they returned to their cells in the prison a different persona was called upon). They managed to impose a more consultative set of procedures – not atypical for the prison environment – in effect negotiating with the program staff on a wide range of issues. For instance, the selection of upcoming courses, the dispersal of some budget resources, the selection of outside visitors, and the allocation of space in the school were all now decided upon in consultation with a student committee ostensibly if not actually elected by the student body. In return for this increased say in program affairs, the staff gave the students more responsibility, including recovering missing library books, building maintenance, and various administrative tasks. Gradually, the education progam was, in fact, becoming 'theirs.'

From this highly consultative but still very much 'top-down' structure the program began to move gradually towards a more truly democratic structure in response to increasing student pressure for 'actual' power instead of just a consultative voice. These became turbulent times, as the more 'engaged' students worked to balance their prisoner and student selves, tried to deal directly with the prison administration on behalf of the program, and at the same time struggled to bring along the majority of their fellow students. Rather than simply giving over power to the students the program staff saw these increased demands as an opportunity to enage in some actual politics, transforming the process into a struggle, complete with confrontations, complex negotiations, with victories and losses on both sides. To outsiders the actual issues would no doubt seem trivial or banal, but in the highly restricted atmosphere of the prison access to a coffee machine or the enforcement of quiet hours in a library can assume tremendous import. Obviously both students and staff were aware of the larger restrictions in the form of walls, fences, gun towers, and parole boards, but even in a make-believe democracy that operates in a small space within a large autocracy remarkable things can happen. Conflicts were always resolved 'in-house' since neither side wanted to 'call the police,' mutual respect was expected from all parties, and the art of compromise became a finely tuned skill.

In virtually all of the various subgroups or types of prisoner-students in the Canadian program examined in the follow-up research, those who were judged to be most 'involved in' or 'engaged with' the program did better after release than their counterparts whose participation was more diffident. This research tended to verify one of that program's central hypotheses, for while 'the university program was successful for many reasons, the most important was the creation of an effective learning culture in which adult education in prison could find an effective operational context – effective because it allowed prisoner-students to put into practice values and ideas percolating through the community, and because it converted the Prison Education Program part of the prison into an around-the-clock educational experience for some prisoners.'[26] Obviously in a multi-site, complex, and long-term prison program like the post-secondary program in British Columbia the impact will vary considerably over time, between institutional sites and among the hundreds of prisoners who experience different facets of the program in different ways. Some students may experience the contrast between prisoner-object and student-subject in an intensely personal way and be literally transformed as a result, never willing to return to the role of object. Others may have a much less intense notion of the difference, while still others may only observe the phenomenon from afar. This is, of course, no different from the experience of any random sample of university students in terms of their relationship with their temporary institutional affiliation. The central point, however, is the awareness that there are other roles one can adopt, even in the prison and even when released from prison back into communities in which their roles seemed defined by their histories.

Educational programs are by no means the only means through which these realizations can come about. For some prisoners vocational or religious experiences might serve the same end. I can recall one highly individualized case when I taught in a prison in which a prisoner assigned to assist the staff electrician in his daily rounds of replacing light bulbs and making general repairs was said to have been completely transformed by the daily conversations the two men had as they wandered about the prison, this being the prisoner's first intimate contact with a 'straight' person.

Perhaps the most dramatic forum in which this vibrant sense of community is made manifest and in which it leads to a more powerful sense of an 'authentic self' is in prison theatre. Because the post-secondary program in British Columbia spawned and then supported an active theatre program in several prisons, an examination of the impact of theatre became a central part of the research into that program's effectiveness. Time and again in examining the post-release lives of various subgroups of prisoner-students we found that among the most serious offenders, the most hardened criminals, and the men predicted to recidivate in great numbers, participation in theatre had the most dramatic impact. In a detailed examination of the impact of the theatre program on the participants, Knights and Jeffries argued that it operated at three distinct levels:

1   As a (counter) public sphere in which the voices of the incarcerated could be made public
2   As a civic sphere in which democratic decision making was the order of the day
3   As a private sphere, a place for intimate self-reflection[27]

One of the theatre directors hired to work with the men in staging a production of *Macbeth* speculated on the potential impact of this kind of experience: 'I have no idea if doing Shakespeare would make any of them give up stealing. But I wouldn't be surprised. The in-depth emotional and intellectual study required to play a role gives the prisoner a different perspective and conceivably could influence him to be more socially aware. The effect of most literature and drama has made peo-

Table 8.1.   Participation in theatre program – percentage of worst case group (n = 119)

Subgroups (n)	Predicted	Actual	Difference	Relative improvement
Theatre (29)	36	55	19	52
No theatre (90)	35	42	7	19

ple more aware of other people. That is one of the things "the arts" does. The effect of doing Macbeth could be that subliminally the prisoner realizes if a person tries to make everything for himself, totally imposes his will on others, regardless of the hurt to them, as Macbeth did, then, well, he's just asking for it.'[28]

In 1996, when the Knights and Jeffries paper was written, the results from the follow-up study of the university program students were not yet in. Wagner's insight or supposition, that acting Macbeth might bring about the transformation from criminal to citizen remained a hypothesis awaiting confirmation or refutation. The research team did subsequently, in fact, treat this as a working hypothesis, and two examples from that research are indicative of the validity of the original insight. The first comes from the 'worst case' group examined in Chapter 7. This group of 119 subjects was divided into two subgroups, one being the twenty-nine who participated in theatre projects and the other being the ninety who did not. While as we saw earlier the whole group behaved particularly badly after release compared with the rest of the 654 subjects, as Table 8.1 below shows, the theatre participants improved over their predicted rate of recidivism by an impressive 52 per cent.

These twenty-nine men outperform the other ninety members on virtually every academic variable selected, taking more courses, earning higher grades, and staying in the program for a longer time. Interestingly, for the total group of 654 men there is no difference in the post-release success of those who participated in theatre and those who did not. It would seem, therefore, that participation in theatre activities is especially effective with higher risk inmates and that there is a correlation between that participation and their success in other programs.

Knights and Jeffries in the conclusion to their essay offer their perspective about the reasons for this success, a perspective that meshes well with the overall argument in this book:

By dividing the theatre experience into public, civic and private spheres, the dimensions of an 'efficacious context' for prison education are highlighted. None of these spheres can be isolated from the other, if only because underlying them is a persistent theme: the ability to detach an educational program and its offshoots from the institutional imperative of prison and its strategies of rehabilitation and control is fundamental to the perceived success of programs. Adults enmeshed in institutions like prisons strain against the identities, roles, activities and attitudes prescribed for them. Perversely, the fact that prescribed behaviour is a consequence of previous actions means that the insistence on remorse and responsibility tends to create an opposite effect: to embrace identities, values and 'behaviours' that only guarantee the tightening of those same prescribed bonds. The desire for a socially desirable construct, the autonomous ego, is frustrated by imposed identities. Apparently, only an alternate learning culture that reconnects the prisoner (the exile) to society, that encourages a kind of spontaneous civility and citizenship, and that recasts his relationship to himself and others, can overcome the perverse outcomes of 'forcing men to be free.' It will also make sense of statements such as this: 'I don't think it (theatre) rehabilitates. I think it offers alternative and different points of view'; for some prisoners, anyway, there is a clear distinction between rehabilitation and the value of an alternative community.[29]

To summarize, before moving on to the argument for the importance of links to external institutions, the key words that seem to characterize successful prison programs, programs that do contribute to transformations from outlaw to citizen, are 'participatory,' 'democratic,' 'reciprocal,' 'community,' and 'authentic.' It has been argued that for new knowledge, perspective, and attitudes to be internalized in a fundamental manner, the subject must be an active participant in the learning process – a subject considering change rather than an object being changed. With adults in particular, this participation should as far as possible be structured around democratic norms and procedures, acknowledging, of course, that all manifestations of democracy operate within consensual and circumstantial limits. This not only provides a forum to practise democratic solutions, but allows the outlaw-exile-prisoner the option of adopting the role of citizen, even in its truncated carceral form. Because prisons are structurally authoritarian and dehumanizing it is especially important that staff working in such participatory and democratic programs accept the limitations on their authority that reciprocity implies. Since the environmental pressure will always be to encourage a subject-object relationship, staff must take extra care to establish as great a subject-subject relationship as possible. All of this can occur most easily in some kind of alternative, just, or democratic community that while it exists in the prison is yet in some way apart from it. Indeed it is argued by some that an alternative community can thrive in prison precisely because of the daily, even hourly contrast between it and the authoritarian nightmare of the prison community. Finally, the individual development that these steps allow to occur is in the end a private affair and as such can indeed lead to authentic and willed transformations rather than mere forced adaptations or the adoption of tactical masks.

Bonds with the Conventional World

The central purpose of all the efforts that go into the creation of democratic, participatory, and just communities within the prison is to create the possibility of a subject-to-subject discourse. We know from experience that adults resent and resist attempts at a top-down, subject-to-object form of discourse, that while they may be forced to conform to such a relationship for short periods of time, its impact will be limited and short-term at best. Once the potential for a reciprocal conversation between subjects is established, within the context of the prison the objective from the point of view of the teacher-counsellor is to engage the prisoner in a discussion of values and goals and the politics of living that is integral to both. The conversation centres on the 'quality' of the prisoner's subjectivity – and, indeed, in true reciprocal fashion on the quality of the subjectivity of the citizen as well. In a truly vibrant, dynamic setting the conversation becomes a debate, inevitably heated at times, concerning the relative merits of the subjective selves of criminal and citizen.

Attaining this position of mutual respect that is so crucial for any kind of transformative conversations, the 'outsider' must suspend any a priori moral judgments or social condemnations of the subject-as-criminal. In some ways, the teacher-counsellor becomes almost a part of the inmate subculture, refusing to accept a categorization of 'other' for the criminal-prisoner. This can be a difficult task given the nature of many of the acts committed by these individuals. If one is outside the correctional world – a contract employee or volunteer, for instance – one can attempt to simply 'not know' and maintain an easy illusion that prisoner X is simply another person, another student like any other. If, however, for whatever reason the act behind the person is known, then the illusion sometimes requires great effort to sustain. This process of suspending judgment is what makes any kind of reciprocal discourse difficult if not impossible for correctional staff. They are, in most cases by statute, required to know intimately the details of the prisoner's crime. Thus, in any interaction between correctional staff and prisoner the 'file' is a silent third party, almost inevitably transforming the prisoner into an object.

The central importance and complexity of this reciprocity is at the core of what is perhaps the most enlightened discussion of prison programming currently in circulation, the aforementioned Council of Europe's *Report on Education in Prisons*. There the need to respect the prisoner as adult person is front and centre: 'Clearly, crime cannot be condoned and the futility of a criminal life may well be raised as an issue in class, but there are aspects of the prisoner's culture which the adult educator must respect or at least accept.'[30] There can be no such reciprocity in a dualist world of victor and vanquished.

As has been stressed throughout this book, there are tremendous forces operating in the carceral world that seek to make these kinds of relationships impossible to maintain. On the one hand, the 'inmate culture' derives its strength and longevity from the alienation of the prisoner from his or her connections with the outside world, most prisoners agreeing that the best way to 'do time' was to forget about the outside. The alternative moral and social universe constructed within the prison by prisoners is designed to assist survival but, as is so often the case with such systems, it easily assumes a life and purpose of its own. Nurtured by long-term prisoners and those committed to a criminal lifestyle that must incorporate the virtual inevitability of intermittent time in prison, the inmate culture seeks converts wherever possible. At the same time, the correctional side of the prison, a kind of culture in its own right, sustains itself in large part through a clear understanding of what it is not. Hardly a high- prestige vocation, corrections professionals often feel underappreciated and under attack by the rest of society and are aware that most people would prefer that their work be hidden from public view. In the past few decades this condition has been exacerbated by the popular perception that prisons are a failure at all but containing. The prisoner becomes the essential other to whom correctional staff can be superior and whom they can blame for the poor reputation they are forced to endure – hardly the basis for a reciprocal conversation.

In the case of the post-secondary program in British Columbia,

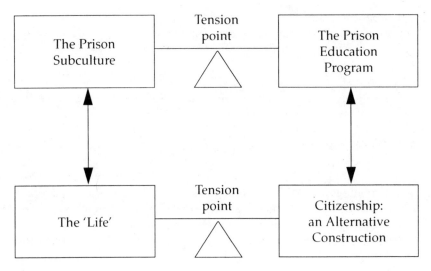

Figure 8.1.   Tension points in the corrections system.

which we examined in terms of the notion of an 'alternative community,' this environment was confronted by a deliberate attempt to create a sense of tension between the education program and the inmate
subculture of the prison. While existing in a state of conditional mutual
respect based on the acknowledgment by the program of the subject-
hood of both prisoner and teacher, the two realms or communities
were nonetheless in direct competition in terms of defining the quality
of both the institutional and the post-release lives of the prisoner-students. As Figure 8.1 illustrates, two key tension points are generated
by this competition, tension points that in effect existed within each
prisoner who crossed between these communities on a daily basis.

Since no one could actually ever 'leave' the prison subculture while
incarcerated, it had a definite advantage in this competition for affiliation, and men quite often withdrew from the education program
because they found the daily transition too stressful. On the other
hand, the education program had the advantage of a strong and very
public link with a high-prestige social institution, the university, which
exercised a powerful draw on many prisoners. In the judgment of the
education program staff, this tension was creative and worked to their
advantage since they were convinced that given the opportunity they
could make the more humane and 'enlightened' culture of the educa-

tion program a more powerful attraction than the vulgar Darwinian-
ism prevalent in the inmate culture. The real test, of course, came after
release when the tension point shifted to the alternative of citizen or
the criminal 'life.'

By contrast, the prison itself was seldom able to generate such 'tension points,' if indeed it ever wanted to. The prison operated from the
position of 'winner,' of the player holding all the cards and thereby
insisting on surrender rather than negotiation. By insisting that it could
and should 'change' or 'cure' people and that this cure worked by
turning subjects (outlaws) into objects (remorseful, pliant deviants)
before releasing them as (reformed) subjects. The transparency of this
agenda made it unnecessary in the case of the post-secondary program
to create or encourage a state of tension between it and the prison, the
latter being unable to generate any competing loyalty or affiliation.

Post-secondary programs had a tremendous advantage within the
prison because of their affiliation with a university. In virtually all
prison college or university programs great pains are taken to accentu-
ate this connection, with graduation ceremonies featuring fully robed
faculty and university administrators, visits by regular students to the
prison classes, and the replication within the prison program of as
many features of typical undergraduate education as can be managed.
In the British Columbia program there were student councils, prisoner-
students were allowed to vote on campus issues, the men had library
cards and could order books from the university collection, guest
speakers were a regular attraction, and a fine arts component was built
into each program site. Similar efforts were undertaken by universities
and colleges across North America. When possible, prison administrators were drawn into this somewhat make-believe world by consultative visits from university administrators, invitations to speak at
academic convocation ceremonies, and participation in university-
sponsored conferences and research activities.

All was never just smooth sailing, however, as the central missions
of these two institutions, prison and university, were quite distinct.
When conflicts did occur between the prison and the education program, however, the latter had the ability to bring into play its primary
link with the university and as a result often fend off undue interference. All independence within the authoritarian (or, to use Foucault's
language, disciplinary) world of the prison is, of course, relative to the
final and absolute authority of the prison as institution. While a contract employee working independently was at the almost complete

mercy of that power, and programs with weak institutional links very much at a disadvantage, even those programs with strong outside institutional support had to be very careful in any confrontation with the prison. Nonetheless, the NewGate evaluator John Irwin's point remains valid: 'An effective rehabilitation program must have continued and vigorous support from an outside powerful organization or organizations. Without this support [a] rehabilitative effort will more likely be converted into a conformity-producing mechanism or be removed entirely.'[31] Note the strong language: 'continued,' 'vigorous,' 'powerful.'

In North America the Correctional Education Association has often played this role for literacy, remedial, and secondary education, lobbying on behalf of individual programs and maintaining a high public profile for the profession of correctional education. In England professional associations like the National Institute for Adult and Continuing Education have played this role, and in Europe as a whole the Council of Europe has done the same. The council's report on education in prisons insisted: 'Adult educators in any situation must come to terms with the context in which they are working and pay attention to special needs therein, and this adaptation has particular significance in the prison setting ... However, professional integrity requires teachers and other educators working in prisons, like those in other professions, to take their primary aims, their underlying orientation, from within their own professional field.'[32] In other cases national and international literacy organizations have taken the lead in urging improved standards in prison literacy programs, and religious institutions have made representations on behalf of specific individuals and prison conditions in general.

Aside from these advocacy roles, there is another important function for the external institution. Once released from prison, where does the former inmate go? Most often family, friends, and community – the traditional sources of support in society – are the first points of contact after release. Having lost important 'time' while in prison, in need of money, and desiring a burst of self-esteem to counter the effects of correctional objectification, the former prisoner is in a hurry to make things happen. Employment opportunities are few and most often involve a long, slow process of advancement that runs counter to the need to make up for 'lost time.' In this situation, family, friends, and former community may all be, in fact, toxic. That is, they may all conspire, deliberately or not, to bring the former criminal back to old ways, comfortable ways. Add to this mix the vulnerability to drug and/or alcohol abuse and the situation is ripe for a return to crime.

There are many ways to intercede in this scenario. A good parole or probation officer will see trouble coming and try to head it off. Family, addiction, and career counselling services may be available. Religious or peer counsellors may be able to intercede and head off dangerous steps. In an ideal world all these would be present for the ex-offender, but we know that, in fact, compared with the resources allocated for incarceration, post-release care gets short shrift. As a result, recidivism rates are high across all criminal justice systems, with the bulk of the failures occurring in the first six months following release. As we have seen, the follow-up research on the former prisoner-students in British Columbia hints at one way this crucial transition period could be bridged, namely, post-release affiliation with another institution. It seems logical to presume that the shock of moving quickly from institutional supervision to freedom, even the relative freedom of parole or probation, is severe. Exhilarating to be sure, but also frightening, unnerving, and anxiety-producing. On the other hand, moving from the carceral institution to an educational institution, even if only for a few months, might make a crucial difference in those early returns to prison.

The data seem to support this idea. As noted earlier, the subgroup within the 119 'worst cases' group that managed to continue with some kind of educational activity after release improved over their SIR predicted outcome by an impressive 84 per cent. The results were similarly impressive with a group of 'second chancers,' 218 men who were under the age of thirty when sentenced to their latest prison term, were under age thirty when they entered the university program, and had a pre-incarceration education level up to grade 11. It was presumed that the education program might give this group of younger men a second chance at sorting out their lives and for those who carried on their education, the improvement over expectation was once again dramatic (Table 8.2). The same pattern held for the working group of 119 men whose grades had improved while they were in the prison education program (Table 8.3). For the entire group of 654 men there was some improvement for those who carried on with their education, but not nearly as dramatic as for these specific groups, indicating once again that this is no panacea, but rather is a particularly effective 'bridging' process for some ex-offenders.

It is important to note here that 'continuing with education' did not

Table 8.2.   Further education after release – percentage of second chance group
(n = 161)

Subgroups (n)	Predicted	Actual	Difference	Relative improvement
Further education (52)	52	82	30	57
Withdrew (19)	47	48	1	3
No further education (90)	49	54	5	10

Table 8.3.   Further education after release – percentage of improvers (n = 105)

Subgroups (n)	Predicted	Actual	Difference	Relative improvement
Further education (52)	56	90	34	61
No further education (53)	59	74	15	25

require enrolling at university after release, but could mean a trade school, college, or other educational institution. The important factor was less the content of the experience than the affiliation itself. Men often referred to this as providing a sense of 'belonging,' a place to meet new friends, put some distance between them and their old neighbourhoods, and generally to buy some time to think about what it was they really wanted to do. In most cases the actual time involved was quite short, the desire for money, a vocation, and more independence persuading them that the educational route was just too long and complex.

Respect for Diversity

The way to the head must be opened through the heart. The development of man's capacity for feeling is, therefore, the more urgent need of our age ... because it provides the impulse for bettering our insights.[33]

Friedrich Schiller, *Essays*, 1795

Friedrich Schiller's point may seem out of place in a discussion of crime, deviance, and transformation that has had so little to say about the affective, emotional side of the issue compared with the concentration on education, insight, and thinking. If we posit, however, that reason may be the closest we come to a universal quality in the human, a set of mental procedures that are discernible and subject to understanding by other reasoners and to modification, then feeling or emotion may come to epitomize the particular, that which makes each person unique, mysterious, and to the erstwhile change-agent, frustrating. Earlier, in reviewing the mental component of making decisions for deviance I referred to 'dispositions,' to some people being 'predisposed' to respond to situations in certain ways, sometimes criminal ways. This disposition is, I would argue, the final step before action, and it is the combination of whatever reasoning processes are in place with the emotional particularity of the person. To alter that person's potential actions, therefore, one must address more than just half the equation – more than just thinking.

This is an argument, then, for respecting diversity. Not just the popular, politically correct diversity of cultural backgrounds, but the daunting fact that each of us is unique, that the combination of mind, emotion, and biography means that people are complicated, and, despite the best efforts of carceral objectification, prisoners are still people. While medical science continues to move in the direction of acknowledging that, unlike experimental rats, people may respond to interventions in unique and mysterious ways, corrections 'science' still seems wedded to experimental models from an earlier era. Thus, we are plagued by studies of intervention effectiveness like the one recently completed in Texas that 'followed up' 14,411 inmates, some who were in education programs and others who were not. They found no significant differences between the two groups in their rates of recidivism.[34] One can easily imagine a similar study using 14,411 cows, one being given a vitamin supplement, the other not, in order to determine productivity outcome. Within that Texas study, of course, were many diverse groups of prisoners and ultimately 14,411 individuals. Both the groups and the individuals experienced their education or lack thereof in different ways, and the task in both program intervention and in effectiveness evaluation is to acknowledge that diversity and work with it rather than in spite of it.

As was reviewed in the earlier section on prediction theory, acknowledging the ultimate uniqueness of each individual does not mean one has to abandon any attempt to deal with groups or other collectivities of individuals. In a particular prison program dealing with a finite number of such individuals it makes sense to maximize the variety of potentially meaningful interactions by, for instance, recruiting staff with diverse interests and approaches, creating optional means by which the core of the intervention can be delivered (the university program's classroom courses, plus correspondence, plus theatre activities is a case in point), and keeping an open mind about admissions, scheduling, and evaluation. Since I remain convinced that our predictive instruments, tests, and other devices are far too clumsy to actually settle on the needs or appropriate learning styles of individuals, I encourage a more voluntarist model, one in which the individual chooses a preferred mode of interaction from among a series of options. For example, in the university program some prisoners preferred to study full-time and others part-time, some attended sequentially while others frequently took semesters off, and some wanted to concentrate while others preferred browsing. Yet each prisoner-student had to complete an English literature and a history course, each had to maintain a satisfactory grade point average, and each was responsible for completing the courses registered for. One can imagine comparable scenarios in vocational programs, industrial shops, and fine arts activities.

When moving beyond such a collection of individuals to examining larger collectivities, such as was the case in the follow-up study of the post-secondary program in British Columbia, the group rather than the individual becomes the carrier of diversity. Thus as mentioned earlier, that study looked at worst cases, improvers, and second chancers, among others, groups that coalesced around a hypothesis that had been generated by consulting the 'folk wisdom' of people familiar with the program and the individuals. But these groups only emerged after the case; there was never an attempt to identify individuals as 'second chancers' while they were in the program and treat them in some way differently from another individual deemed a 'worst case.' The crucial argument being made is that individual humans remain unpredictable and at the level of specific intervention programs in prisons or the community we must confront the 'clients' as individuals rather than as types, categories, or cohorts. All of the education programs referred to in this study operated on a loose, open admissions policy, accepting that adults are too complex to stream as a result of test results or pre-set categories.

Reflections

Democratic communities, strong institutional affiliations, and respect for diversity and individuality are anethema to the traditional prison.

Jacobo Timmerman, who endured imprisonment in an Argentinian brutal parody of the modern prison, reflected on the experience in terms of the authoritarianism – whether well-meaning or evil – that lies at the root of modern carceral systems: 'The chief obsession of the totalitarian mind lies in its need for the world to be clear-cut and orderly. Any subtlety, contradiction, or complexity upsets and confuses this notion and becomes intolerable.'[35] The authoritarian institution, shaping the reality of both keepers and kept, uses its monopoly of power to implement its 'compelling need to simplify reality.'

Following the crisis of confidence experienced by those in corrections in the 1970s and 1980s, limited versions of democratic communities did flourish, outside institutions did become interested in prison reform and programs, and there was an acknowledgment that prisoners were individuals with specific needs and desires. The resulting sets of policies, what I have grouped under the label 'opportunities model,' allowed for an opening up of prison systems to outsiders. The results were often messy, untidy, chaotic, but seldom if ever disastrous. Programs like the SCWPP at the California Institution for Women were perhaps too avant-garde for even a more open prison system, but new programs took their place, including a wide range of education programs. Project NewGate was too ambitious and high profile, but it opened the way for a renaissance of college and university engagements with prisons across North America. Popular interest in literacy and a new thrust of religiosity in the culture resulted in thousands of lay volunteers entering prisons to work one-to-one with prisoners.

These interventions did not 'cure crime'. There were other demographic, cultural, and economic engines in charge of that phenomenon – but as the research results from the university program in British Columbia show, significant numbers of men who were predicted to continue with criminal careers after release, chose other options, and one can make a strong case that it was their experiences while in prison that in large part accounted for the choice. This research also shows beyond any doubt that there is no simple correlation between taking education courses and doing well after release, but rather that the mechanisms that contribute to such outcomes are multiple and varied. For some individuals the mere completion of high school, learning to read, or completing college courses might be a sufficiently influential mechanism that would cause a rethinking of career options, attitude, and social life. For others it might be the friendships and collegiality formed in a theatre workshop or life skills class, or the insights gained by assuming a leadership role in a student council or participatory community. These are the engines that drive change in the 'real' world and there is no reason that they should not be just as powerful in the prison if that institution allows them to flourish.

Conclusion

The materialist doctrine that men are products of circumstances and upbringing and that, therefore, changed men are products of other circumstances and changed upbringing, forgets that it is men that change circumstances and that the educator himself needs educating.[1]

Karl Marx, Theses on Feuerbach, 1845

Men make their own history, but they do not make it just as they please; they do not make it under circumstances chosen by themselves, but under circumstances directly found, given and transmitted from the past.[2]

Karl Marx, 18th Brumaire of Louis Bonaparte, 1852

In the space between these two quotations from Karl Marx lies the ground we have been working. In the first, written in 1845, Marx was addressing the great themes of materialism and determinism, asserting the power of the self in the production of historical and individual change. Here the actors – in our case the prisoner and the keeper – are empowered and are charged in a truly Jeffersonian sense to educate themselves in order to transform both self and circumstance – a position firmly grounded in the optimism of the Enlightenment. In the second quotation, written in 1852, Marx's impulse to empower is tempered, and he speaks as a realist who has experienced firsthand the difficulties of individual transformation within the modern bureaucratic apparatus. He has, after all, witnessed the failures of revolution in 1848.

I repeated Marx's experience in my own much more confined journey through reality in my prison career in the 1970s. Initially I saw only possibilities for personal transformations that could flow from immersion in a critical process of self-education for both my students and myself. Then, as transformed prisoners too often returned to prison having failed either to attempt or succeed at the citizen's role, I became acutely aware of the weight of circumstances they carried with them into the community. But, to repeat a theme stressed throughout this discussion, understanding lies at neither pole of the dualism, not with the educated and empowered actor, not with the weighed down victim of context. It is in the tension-ridden space between the poles that the 'action' takes place. We know, thanks to the kinds of data reported on at length in this book, that within this space even the most circumstance-ridden individuals, the worst cases, hard cases, addicted, and deprived can, in fact, 'make their own history,' can educate themselves, and, as Jefferson put it, 'inform their discretion.'

What does it really mean to 'inform one's discretion'? The word itself provides some important clues:

Dis-cre-tion: 1. The quality of being discreet; prudence, circumspection, tact, wariness, restraint, moderation, delicacy; 2. [archaic] The act or quality of discerning, discriminating or judging. 3. A power of decision – individual judgment – power of free decision or choice within certain legal bounds.[3]

It is really the blending of the archaic content-laden usage – no doubt Jefferson's – with the modern more action-oriented meanings that gives the word 'discretion' a special relevance to prisons and issues of rehabilitation and individual change. Dr Johnson, in his dictionary (1755), which was no doubt Jefferson's guide to proper usage, equated discretion directly with 'prudence, knowledge to govern or direct one's self.' As we have seen, great efforts are made by the prison to deny the individual as prisoner the freedom and authority to make decisions and choices, thereby severely handicapping efforts to carry out Jefferson's suggestion. Nonetheless, even within that authoritarian frame we have seen that subversion of at least this element of the prison agenda is possible. Structures can be created in which prisoners may exercise choice and situations nurtured within those structures that encourage prudence and sensitivity to others in the exercise of choice. Finally, through education and other means the substance of those decisions and choices can be affected, influenced, and changed. But to what end?

Again, as implied throughout this book, the end must be a renewed commitment to citizenship on the part of the released prisoner and, in the inevitable dialectic, a renewed commitment by society to assist those individuals in sustaining their efforts. There are rules attached to citizenship, some derived from long-standing ethical standards and others from generation-based social consensus. Living compatibly with these rules requires a sense of discretion, prudence, and judgment. The importance of creating, nurturing, and sustaining this ability to *be* a citizen, when one has as often as not rejected the role, was a context oddly parallel to that being examined here when Vaclav Havel told the Czech people in 1990 that their real enemy was their 'indifference to public affairs, conceit, ambition, selfishness, the pursuit of personal advancement, and rivalry.'[4]

One could easily argue that Havel was simply describing here the average citizen in a competitive, materialist, advanced capitalist or socialist society. If so, what right do we have to expect the former convict to aspire to higher ideals than seem to prevail in the mass culture? Here the moral imperative becomes quite complex. The former convict or prisoner must aspire to attain a finer discretion, one might argue, because the implications of his or her not doing so are too serious for both the individual and the society. Others within society may be inordinately selfish, indifferent to social obligations, or crassly ambitious, but they normally have too many links with the conventional world to allow those traits to carry them too far beyond the pale. The former criminal is vested with too many illegal skills, too little fear of apprehension, and too many chemical and psychological weaknesses to risk treading on that ground. While no doubt unfair, the fact that we must ask so much of the former prisoner in terms of efforts at becoming a full citizen in turn provides the rationale for expending extra resources in helping him or her to accomplish this. Thus, if a liberal education in prison proves efficacious in helping prisoners become citizens, it is in our interest to provide that education in spite of the fact that we feel their earlier actions make them among the least deserving of such a gift.

This is a bitter pill to swallow, a kind of utilitarian ethic that calls upon society to look to its interests rather than its passions. The Western nations took this step in international politics following the Second World War and rewarded their former enemies with aid in order to thwart a new enemy and at the same time ensure their own prosperity. Why not the same step for our 'former' enemies from within?

In chapter 1 I argued that there were essentially three paradigms or models for guiding how societies that grew out of the European Enlightenment could respond to crime, deviance, and prisons, models built around idea systems associated with Voltaire, Rousseau, and de Sade. Each of the modern justice and prison systems discussed in this study – the United States, Canada, and the United Kingdom and European Community – contains elements of Voltairean pragmatism, Rousseauean idealism, and Sadean fatalism, with policy trends shifting among these paradigms throughout the postwar era. Mindful of the danger of allowing theory or modelling to overwhelm reality, it does nonetheless seem fair to say that each of these systems has, in fact, come to focus on one of these paradigms as the century of modernity comes to a close.

The descent of the criminal justice system in the United States into a Sadean nightmare world of massive prison construction, lengthened sentencing, rampant executions, and an ever-expanding definition of deviance appears as a direct response to the shift from wars on communism and poverty to a massive war on crime. The ground for the shift was well prepared, however, with the socio-biologist and criminologist James Q. Wilson declaring as early as 1975 while the treatment model was still largely intact that 'wicked people exist. Nothing avails except to set them apart from innocent people.'[5] The fatalism in this call for incapacitation could be borne, perhaps, if the definition of 'wicked' remained constrained by an enlightened social conscience, but in the post-1980 United States the borders of that definition blew apart and that nation began 'celebrating' in a perverse way the 'difference' (there's that postmodern notion again!) of the criminal by creating an archipelago, a vast prison system designed not to transform but rather to contain the individual until that difference is driven out of the individual or he or she is dead.

One senses in casting an eye and ear towards public discourse concerning crime, criminals, and prisons in the United States that this acceptance of 'difference' is not merely labelling or scapegoating, but rather contains a strong element of accepting what is perceived as the criminal's desire to be singled out, to be confirmed as it were with the identity of the 'other.' In this public discourse (which is quite distinct from the professional discourse of criminologists and other experts) the lesson learned from 'nothing works' was that the criminal did not *want* treatment to work, that the criminal had entered the Sadean and anti-Socratic utopia in which pleasure alone guided action, and individuals could willingly and with knowledge choose to do evil. It is an upside-down world in which the man who is robbed rather than the thief is at fault 'because he was not vigilant enough to prevent the theft.'[6] A world in which the criminal believes along with the great and ruthless Jacobin St. Just that 'nothing resembles virtue so much as a great crime.'[7] Believing that the criminal commits crime because it gives him or her pleasure and identity, the public in turn is thereby freed to derive equal pleasure in punishing the criminal. The Sadean circle is complete and potentially perpetual.

Operating within this paradigm there is room for compassion and 'treatment' only for the few who (a) have not participated in the two areas of crime singled for special reprobation – sexual assault and drug dealing – and who (b) are young enough to warrant consideration for a 'second start' at a law-abiding life. The remainder – mostly young males 'of colour' – make up a new underclass in the United States for which little or no sympathy is generated. By accepting that this group has willed itself into crime and prison, the majority in this otherwise compassionate and freedom-valuing political culture can more easily turn a blind eye to what for most outsiders seems a horrendous penal system driven only by punishment, retribution, and incapacitation.

Our second national system, the Canadian, seems still wedded to a Rousseauean set of policies that maintain a faith in rehabilitation, even if by coercion when necessary. The rehabilitation ideal suffered a setback in the 1980s but has re-emerged full force with the commitment to the cognitive model. Canadian prisoners are in their own way conceived of as ill, as suffering deficits in key areas of either personality or mental structures, or as victimized by thinking or reasoning errors stemming from deprived circumstances. In either case there remains the firm conviction within the Canadian system that these needs can be addressed. There is, of course, an ever-increasing level of public fear and loathing about crime and criminals, much of it spilling over from the United States. But with the exception of a few high-profile cases and, of course, virtually all cases involving sexual offences, there remains a public and professional expectation or hope that the prison system ought to be able to reform and rehabilitate.

While encouraging in a humanitarian sense, and certainly responsible for the Canadian systems, both federal and provincial, being able to avoid the worst excesses of the American prison and incarceration pattern, the Rousseauean position has generated its own set of problems. The treatment approach typified by the cognitive skills programs creates optimism about 'corrections' by a process of mystification. Using complex diagnostic language and specialized programs designed to 'penetrate' the personality of the offender, crime and deviance are once again transformed into a benign-appearing medical-psychiatric realm that must be kept under the control of experts. The result is a more humane but still closed penal system increasingly filled with desperate experts seeking to find just the right prescription that will enable them to meet the promises they have made to government and the public. While many of the interventions – from penile-metres to Prozac to literacy – have great value for individuals, none of them can deliver the promised rehabilitative cure. Thus, this approach invites another Martinson, another cynic intent on puncturing the naïve idealism of the experts. As we have seen in some of the cases discussed earlier, the belief in the cure leads directly to other elements of Rousseauean abuse, including extended sentences, coerced treatment, and unnecessary and damaging labelling.

The third set of prison systems discussed in earlier chapters is broadly speaking the European example. Despite Kevin Warner's view that the United Kingdom has moved much closer to the American than to the other European systems, the official iterations of the Anglo-European approach share the pragmatism and concern for the integrity of the individual prisoner that is at the heart of a Voltairean approach to criminal justice. Here the ambitions are much more modest, and there is a determination to try and avoid the fixation on 'otherness' so typical of the American approach. The word 'corrections' is avoided in favour of the more straightforward 'prison' and 'prisoner' is more common than 'offender.' Having been steeped in the Foucaultean critique, the punishment component of the system is determinedly held to be the prison sentence itself and coercive manipulations within the sentence are regarded with skepticism (though they still exist).

Above all, within the European approach there is very little anticipation that the prison itself can do very much for the prisoner. As we saw in the case of education, prisoners are held to be adults like anyone else and should have the same rights to educational opportunity as adults in the community. Likewise, educators should demand no more in terms of change or transformation from their prisoner-students than they would from adult students at the local college or community centre. While admirable in a kind of anti-Foucaultean sense, and realistic in terms of both the inevitability of scarce resources and the intractability of many prisoners, this approach like the other two has its share of problems. The determination to avoid at all costs the task of 'correct-ing' can lead to the often unrealistic assumption that the prisoner is capable of undertaking his or her own reformation once a minimal provision of tools is provided.

As stressed before, none of the actual prison systems being dis-cussed here fits neatly into these models or paradigms. There are reha-bilitative prisons in the United States, brutal and retributive penal practices in Canada, and therapeutic institutions in Europe. But, broadly conceived, these models do capture the dominant trends in penal practice. But do they work? Are they effective? Do they achieve their objectives? Perhaps they do if their objectives are defined in terms of incapacitation or peaceful prisons, but they fail utterly as I have argued throughout in both lowering the rate of return to crime and prison and in helping transform criminals into citizens.

So, in concluding this discussion, let us return to the these two closely related objectives that common sense might lead us to expect from our prison systems: lowering recidivism and creating productive fellow citizens. The prison programs we have examined in some detail in this book – the NewGate programs, the British Columbia university program, the Santa Cruz women's prison program, and the Barlinnie experiment – all carried these objectives and while degrees of success varied, the results from the most highly evolved of the species, the B.C. program, certainly point towards the possibility of significant levels of success. While no single program, educational or otherwise, can be held responsible for providing the full range of resources necessary for members of a highly disparate population to make a successful transi-tion from criminal to citizen, it can within the confines of the prison be the essential catalyst for such transitions.

What do prisoners need to make this transition? What are the ele-ments of citizenship that are required? There are at least five compo-nents or elements that come to mind that are universally valid but that would be especially important in the context of the prison, and each has a potential programmatic counterpart:

1   *Economic well-being*: the job skills necessary to find a niche within the local economy and the social skills essential to succeed at work, whether self-employed or salaried. Vocational training programs and accompanying social and life skills programs oriented towards employment issues should be available to all prisoners. As well, programs designed to introduce prisoners to the idea of a rapidly

changing economy and the necessity of ongoing retraining should be part of any pre-release program, thereby encouraging individual prisoners to consider new employment possibilities rather than returning to previous occupations which in many cases were linked to their criminal history, often seasonal, or no longer as prevalent.

2 *Critical thinking*: the skills, abilities, and perspectives necessary to judge properly the actions of others, potential actions of the self, and the relations of self to others – including the state and other corporate bodies – and the ability to communicate verbally and in writing. Educational programs focusing on the liberal arts, discussion groups, and courses in critical thinking are all avenues towards enhancing one's thinking and communicating abilities, and they can be made accessible to individuals at virtually all educational and literacy levels. For prisoners in particular, whose 'troubles' have to some degree at least had their origin in dysfunctional, inappropriate, or impractical relations with others, it is crucial that they be encouraged to think through in as sophisticated a manner as possible the history of these relations and consider at least alternative possibilities.

3 *Ethical self-reflection*: closely linked with critical thinking, prisoners should be encouraged to reflect upon the ethical norms, of society, their own ethical norms and the personal and social implications of violating either. Religious programs, counselling services, and some educational programs can provide opportunities for such reflection, providing they are cast in an exploratory, non-judgmental context. The objective should remain one of 'integration' of the prisoner as moral being with the society rather than the forced inculcation of a set of moral rules or norms. Central to engaging the prisoner in this process of ethical self-reflection is the creation of an atmosphere of mutual respect.

4 *Social participation*: in analysing that most overtly democratic of modern societies, the United States, Alexis de Tocqueville singled out the participatory spirit, indeed habit, among its citizens as the true source of its strength and vitality. For individuals to participate fully as socially conscious, engaged citizens, however, they must (a) know how to initiate that participation, (b) believe that it welcome and possible, and (c) imagine some benefit to be derived, both for self and society. Specifically denied all three of these possibilities by the very nature of their imprisonment, the prison must foster, as best it an, a 'false democracy' within its walls, a human laboratory

in which prisoners can experiment with various forms of democratic participation, decision making, and conflict resolution. Individual prison programs should likewise include participatory management as part of their mandate to prepare prisoners for release.

5   *Bodily health*: Last but far from least is the centrality of the body to citizenship. At far higher percentages than is found in the general population, prisoners suffer from addictions to drugs and alcohol that plague their bodies, undermine their spirits, and often make it impossible to bring to bear any of the occupational, cognitive, ethical, or social skills, abilities, or predispositions otherwise acquired. Indeed, it is no understatement to insist that each of these is, in fact, dependent on bodily health and on physical addictions or dependencies that are either eliminated or at least properly managed. Prisons must make available a full range of drug and alcohol counselling programs and make every effort to persuade the individual prisoner of the interdependency of body, mind, spirit, and social realms of community and employment.

What is required to carry this off is, in fact, a delicate combination of all three of the paradigms referred to above. From de Sade the modern prison needs to acquire a sense of the pride, self-respect, and powerful identity that the prisoner as criminal carries with him into the encounter with the prison and the suggestion that personal change ought to be considered; from Rousseau a sensitivity about the special backgrounds from which prisoners as a rule emanate and the special needs that may therefore be manifest; and from Voltaire a realistic assessment of just what can be accomplished and a determination to address the prisoner as an autonomous person rather than an offender or degenerate. From my own experience in prison, I always considered that the education program I participated in, when it was operating well, fulfilled this integration reasonably well and was indeed a reasonable model for others to emulate.

Above all, the persistent focus on citizenship as the primary objective in all prison programming makes it possible for one to approach the 'normal' within the prison, to approximate the conventional within the bizarre. It was with this end in mind that the university program in the prison struggled to establish what was called an 'alternative community,' which was in turn a version of Lawrence Kohlberg's idea of a 'just community.' Ideally, a prison dedicated to facilitating the five components of citizenship reviewed above would itself comprise an alternative community, but that possibility seems a long way off. Instead, as our review of selected prison programs during the 'era of opportunities' has shown, the 'normal' environments within the prison have typically been islands, in some cases such as Barlinnie literally walled off from the 'real' prison.

Within these prison communities that strive to establish civil and ethical relations between teachers, counsellors, and volunteers on the one hand and prisoners on the other, it is the starting point of mutual respect that kick-starts the process of individual development that can lead to the kind of transformations revealed in the follow-up research. As one prisoner-student said in an eloquent graduation address, 'Here we are granted our humanity; it is in fact demanded of us. Here we function as responsible human beings.' In a less polished way, a beginning student in the university program in British Columbia spoke just as eloquently about his reaction to being a member of the university community in the prison: 'It's more relaxed, you're treated more humanely, I think. And one doesn't have to put up a front, you just act yourself. You know that you're accepted by these people, these teachers accept you like they would anybody on the street. *This is all new to me.*'

Notes

Chapter 1 Introduction

1 Michel Foucault, *Discipline and Punish: The Birth of the Prison* (New York: Vintage, 1979), p. 17.
2 Hannah Arendt, *Eichmann in Jerusalem* (Hammondsworth: Penguin, 1963), p. 230.
3 In this I follow the lead of Foucault for whom prison is the place 'where modern techniques of control are revealed in their full unbridled operation. Consequently a close analysis of the machinery of imprisonment, and of the knowledge on which it is based, can form the basis for a general anatomy of modern forms of power and control.' Cited in David Garland, *Punishment and Society* (Chicago: University of Chicago Press, 1990), p. 134; my emphasis.
4 Robert Merton, 'Insiders and Outsiders: A Chapter in the Sociology of Knowledge,' *American Journal of Sociology* 78:1 (1972), p. 33.
5 James Hamilton, *Rousseau's Theory of Literature* (York, SC: French Literature Publications, 1979), p. 16. In its prescription for a reformed life, the state also reveals the persistence of severe gradations in lived modernity – qualitative gradations in the expectations allowed in the 'corrected life.'

Chapter 2 The Origins of Curing Crime and Similar Popular Delusions

1 James McConnell, professor of psychiatry at the University of Michigan. Cited in Sharland Trotter and Jim Warren, 'The Carrot, the Stick, and the Prisoner,' *Science News* 105 (1974), p. 180. McConnell spent years training flatworms to run through mazes by administering a series of electric shocks.

2 P.E. Meehl, 'Psychology and the Criminal Law,' *University of Richmond Law Review* 5 (1970), p. 14.
3 Romans 7: 18–19.
4 Augustine, *Confessions* (Hammondsworth: Penguin, 1961), p. 47.
5 Thomas Hobbes, *Leviathan*, in Edwin Burt, ed., *The English Philosophers from Bacon to Mill* (New York: Modern Library, 1967), p. 161.
6 Sigmund Freud, *Civilization and Its Discontents* (New York: W.W. Norton, 1961), pp. 65–6.
7 Aristotle, *Ethics* (Hammondsworth: Penguin, 1976), p. 123.
8 Plato, *Timaeus and Critias* (Hammondsworth: Penguin, 1977), p. 117.
9 'I am pretty sure that none of the wise men thinks that any human being willingly makes a mistake or willingly does anything wrong or bad. They know very well that anyone who does anything wrong or bad does so involuntarily.' Plato, *Protagoras*, translated by Stanley Lombardo and Karen Bell (Indianapolis: Hackett Publishing 1992) p. 42.
10 Being typically idiosyncratic, Rousseau parted company with the others on the innate sociability of humans, arguing that in the 'state of nature' they were isolates.
11 Adam Smith, *The Theory of Moral Sentiments* (Oxford: Oxford University Press, 1976), p. 86.
12 Cited in Michael Ignatieff, 'State, Civil Society and Total Institutions: A Critique of Recent Social Histories of Punishment,' in Norval Morris and Michael Tonry, eds., *Crime and Justice: An Annual Review of Research*, vol. 3 (Chicago: University of Chicago Press, 1981), p. 183.
13 Jean-Jacques Rousseau, *Discourse on the Origins of Inequality* (Hammondsworth: Penguin, 1984), p. 100.
14 'Enlighten the people generally, and tyranny and oppressions of body and mind will vanish like evil spirits at the dawn of day. Altho' I do not, with some enthusiasts, believe that the human condition will ever advance to such a state of perfection as there shall no longer be pain or vice in the world, yet I believe it susceptible of much improvement, and, most of all, in matters of government and religion; and that the diffusion of knowledge among the people is to be the instrument by which it is to be effected.' Letter to Dupont, 1816, in Adrienne Koch, *The Philosophy of Thomas Jefferson* (Gloucester, Mass.: Peter Smith, 1957), p. 118.
15 Jean-Jacques Rousseau, *The Social Contract* (Hammondsworth: Penguin, 1968), p. 71.
16 Clarence Darrow, *Crime and Criminals* (Chicago: Charles Kerr, 1902), reprinted in John Burr, ed., *Philosophy and Contemporary Issues* (New York: Macmillan, 1984), p. 66.

17 Erich Lowey, *Suffering and the Beneficent Community* (Albany: State University of New York Press, 1991), p. 30.

18 Robert Wright, *The Moral Animal* (New York: Vintage, 1994), p. 13.

19 In Thomas Lickona, ed. *Moral Development and Behavior* (New York: Holt, Rinehart and Winston, 1976), p. 108.

20 'At Home with Charlie Manson,' Vancouver *Sun*, 28 July 6, p. 4 1979.

21 Mary Warnock, 'An Inside Job,' *Times Higher Education Supplement*, 10 Feb. 1995, p. 18.

22 David Garland, *Punishment and Society* (Chicago: University of Chicago Press, 1990), p. 270.

23 Ian Taylor, Paul Walton, and Jock Young, *The New Criminology* (New York: Harper, 1973), p. 33.

24 B. Seashore, S. Haberfeld, J. Irwin and K. Baker *Prisoner Education: Project NewGate and Other College Programs* (New York: Praeger, 1976), p. 158.

25 Stuart Yudofsky of the Baylor College of Medicine asserts that with the expected advances, 'we're going to be able to diagnose many people who are biologically brain-prone to violence.' He argues that we must trade our traditional concept of justice based on guilt and punishment for a 'medical model based on prevention, diagnosis, and treatment.' Cited in W.W. Gibbs, 'Seeking the Criminal Element,' *Scientific American*, March (1995), p. 102.

26 A. Nassi and S. Abramowitz, 'From Phrenology to Psychosurgery and Back Again: Biological Studies of Criminology,' *American Journal of Orthopsychiatry* 46:4 (1976), p. 605.

27 Note that this was discovered by Dutch researchers in one family.

28 Note that this is the same researcher referred to in the 1984 report.

29 S.A. Mednick and Jan Volavka, 'Biology and Crime,' in Norval Morris and Michael Tonry, eds., *Crime and Justice: An Annual Review of Research*, vol. 2 (Chicago: University of Chicago Press, 1980), p. 87.

30 Dorothy Nelkin and M. Susan Lindee, 'Genes Made Me Do It: The Appeal of Biological Explanations,' *Politics and the Life Sciences* 15:1 (1996), p. 96.

31 Robert Worth, 'A Model Prison,' *Atlantic Monthly*, Nov. (1995), p. 44.

32 Thomas Jefferson to Edmund Pendleton, 26 August 1776, in Julian Boyd, ed., *Papers of Thomas Jefferson* (Princeton: Princeton University Press, 1950), p. 505.

33 John McKnight, *The Careless Society: Community and Its Counterfeits* (New York: Basic Books, 1996), p. 138.

34 Friedrich Nietzsche, *Birth of Tragedy* (Hammondsworth: Penguin, 1993), p. 65.

35 Ibid., p. 73.

36 B. Karpman, 'Criminality, Insanity and the Law,' *Journal of Criminal Law and Criminology* 39 (1949), cited in Donald Cressey, 'Limitations on Organization of Treatment in the Modern Prison,' in Richard Cloward and Donald Cressey, eds., *Theoretical Studies in the Social Organization of the Prison* (New York: Social Science Research Council, 1960), p. 88.

37 David Garland, 'Sociological Perspectives on Punishment,' in Michael Tonry and Norval Morris, eds., *Crime and Justice: An Annual Review of Research*, vol. 4 (Chicago: University of Chicago Press, 1991), p. 135.

38 David Cohen, 'Preface,' Special Issue: Challenging the Therapeutic State,' *Journal of Mind and Behaviour*, 11: 3–4 (1990), p. 246.

39 Norman Fenton, 'The Prison as a Therapeutic Community,' *Federal Probation* 20, June (1956), p. 28.

40 Jean-Jacques Rousseau, *Confessions* (Hammondsworth: Penguin, 1953), p. 46.

41 Jean Starobinski, *Jean-Jacques Rousseau: Transparency and Obstruction* (Chicago: University of Chicago Press, 1988), p. 246.

42 Irvine Welsh, *Trainspotting* (New York: W.W. Norton, 1996), p. 14.

43 Michel Foucault, *Discipline and Punish: The Birth of the Prison* (New York: Vintage, 1979), p. 151.

Chapter 3   Insight Wars: The Struggle for the Prisoner's Mind and Soul

1 Lionel Trilling, cited in Francis Cullen and Karen Gilbert, eds., *Reaffirming Rehabilitation* (Cinncinati: Anderson, 1982) p. 15.

2 Michel Foucault, *Discipline and Punish: The Birth of the Prison* (New York: Vintage, 1979), p. 239.

3 Ibid., p. 101.

4 Ibid., p. 246.

5 *Oxford Endlish Dictionary,* 2nd ed., (Oxford: Clarendon Press, 1989), vol. 7, p. 1027.

6 Ronald Zuskin, 'Developing Insight in Incestuous Fathers,' *Journal of Offender Rehabilitation* 18:3–4 (1992), p. 207–8.

7 Christopher Webster, Grant Harris, Marnie Rice, Catherine Comier, and Vernon Quinsey, *The Violence Prediction Scheme: Assessing Dangerousness in High Risk Men* (Toronto: University of Toronto, Centre of Criminology, 1994), p. 50.

8 Fred Greenstein, 'Personality and Political Socialization: The Theories of Authoritarian and Democratic Citizenship,' *Annals of the American Academy of Political and Social Science* 361, Sept. (1965), pp. 86–7.

9 D. Claster, 'Perception of Certainty: Delinquents and Non-Delinquents,' in

Richard Henshel and Robert Silverman, eds., *Perception in Criminology* (New York: Columbia University Press, 1975), p. 93.

10 Robert Ross, *Time to Think: A Cognitive Model of Delinquency Prevention and Offender Rehabilitation* (Johnson City, Tenn.: Institute for Social Sciences and Arts, 1985), p. 162.

11 George Spivak, Jerome Platt, and Myrna Shure, *The Problem-Solving Approach to Adjustment* (San Francisco: Jossey-Bass, 1976).

12 Paul Wagner, 'Punishment and Reason in Rehabilitating the Offender,' *Prison Journal* 58, Spring (1978), p. 37.

13 Hannah Arendt, *On Revolution* (Hammondsworth: Penguin 1963), p. 93.

14 Michel Foucault, ed., *I, Pierre Riviere, Having Slaughtered My Mother, My Sister, My Brother* ... (Lincoln: University of Nebraska Press, 1975).

15 Foucault, *Discipline and Punish*, p. 172.

16 Ibid. pp. 202–4.

17 Ibid. p. 184.

18 Thus, Foucault asks us to 'imagine the power of the *education* which, not only in a day, but in the succession of days and even years, may regulate for man the time of waking and sleeping, of activity and rest, the number and duration of meals, the quality and ration of food, the nature and product of labour, the time of prayer, the use of speech and even, so to speak, that of thought ... this education which, in short, takes possession of man as a whole, of all the physical and moral faculties that are in him and of the time in which he is himself.' Ibid., p. 236.

19 Ibid. p. 189.

20 Michael Ignatieff, 'State, Civil Society and Total Institutions: A Critique of Recent Social Histories of Punishment,' Crime and Justice: An Annual Review of Research, vol. 3 (Chicago: University of Chicago, Press, 1980), p. 164.

21 Evelyn Baring and Lord Cromer, Modern Egypt, vol. 2 (London: Macmillan, 1908), p. 124.

22 Perversely, given the ambitions and intentions of the 'system,' these inadequacies only become evident long after the prisoner is released or deceased, and the various files, papers, medical reports, psychiatric reports, and other ephemera are collected by a government archival process and finally stored together in a warehouse, accessed only by the odd researcher.

23 Robert Garber and Christina Maslach, 'The Parole Hearing: Decision or Justification?' Criminology Review Yearbook, vol. 1, Sheldon Messinger and Egon Bittner, eds., (Beverly Hills: Sage, 1979), p. 447.

24 Irvine Welsh, *Trainspotting* (New York: W.W. Norton, 1996), p. 187.

25 Charles Taylor, *The Malaise of Modernity* (Concord, Ont.: Anansi Press, 1991), p. 61.

26 Mary Bellhouse, 'Rousseau under Surveillance,' *Interpretation* 1:2 (1994), p. 176.
27 Kevin Kennedy, 'Man at 50,' *California Magazine*, May (1985), p. 81.
28 Donald Gutierrez, *The Dark and Light Gods: Essays on the Self in Modern Literature* (New York: Whiston, 1987), p. 181.
29 Andre Furtado and Don Johnson, 'Education and Rehabilitation in a Prison Setting,' *Journal of Offender Counseling, Services, Rehabilitation* 4:3 (1980), p. 252.
30 Robert Martinson, 'What Works? Questions and Answers about Prison Reform,' *Public Interest*, Spring (1974) p. 49.
31 Ibid., p. 50.

Chapter 4   Let a Hundred Flowers Bloom, a Hundred Schools of Thought Contend

1 Mao Tse-tung, *Selected Readings* (Peking: Foreign Languages Press, 1971), p. 462.
2 Alexis de Tocqueville, cited in Joel Stewards, 'The Penitentiary and Perfectibility in Tocqueville,' *Western Political Quarterly* 38:1 (1985), p. 18.
3 Robert Martinson, 'California Research at the Crossroads,' *Crime and Delinquency* 22:2 (1976), p. 190.
4 Cited in Constance Holden, 'Prisons: Faith in Rehabilitation Is Suffering a Collapse,' *Science* 188:4190 (1975), p. 816.
5 Alfred Blumstein and Jacqueline Cohen, *An Evaluation of a College-Level Program in a Maximum Security Prison* (Pittsburgh: Carnegie-Mellon University, School of Urban and Public Affairs, 1974), p. 1; Robert Ross and Bryan MacKay, 'Behavioural Approaches to Treatment in Corrections: Requiem for a Panacea,' *Canadian Journal of Criminology* 20:2 (1978), p. 287; Louis Genevie, Eva Margolies, and Gregory Muhlin, 'How Effective Is Correctional Intervention?' *Social Policy* 16:3 (1986), p. 54.
6 Morgan Lewis, *Prison Education and Rehabilitation: Illusion or Reality? A Case Study of an Experimental Program* (University Park, Pennsylvania: Institute of Research on Human Resources, 1973), p. 2.
7 Daniel LeClair, 'Community-Based Reintegration: Some Theoretical Implications of Positive Research Findings' (Boston: Massachusetts Department of Correction, Publication 11625, Nov., 1979), p. 1.
8 Francis Fox, 'Prison Should Be Rehabilitation Last Resort,' Vancouver *Sun*, 30 Oct., 1976.
9 Correctional Service of Canada, *Orientation Manual for Contract Staff* (1987), p. 18.

10 Anon., 'The Career Criminal,' *The Angolite* (1973), p. 37.
11 David Rothman, 'The Crime of Punishment,' *New York Review of Books*, 17 Feb. (1994), p. 35.
12 Joy Mott, 'Adult Prisons and Prisoners in England and Wales, 1970–1982: A Review of Findings of Research' (London: Home Office Research Study 84. London: Her Majesty's Stationery Office, 1985), p. 2.
13 Denis Trevelyan (Director General, Prison Service), 'Education as Part of the Concept of Positive Custody,' *Coombe Lodge Reports* 14:2 (1981), p. 82.
14 Ibid., p. 81.
15 *The Role of Federal Corrections in Canada: The Report of the Task Force on the Creation of an Integrated Canadian Corrections Service* (Ottawa: Ministry of the Solicitor General, 1977), p. 32.
16 Wayne Knights, 'Culture in the Bureaucracy: The University in Prison,' *Yearbook of Correctional Education* (Vancouver: Institute for the Humanities, 1989). p. 70.
17 Robert Homant, 'Employment of Ex-Offenders: The role of prisonization and Self-Esteem,' *Journal of Offender Counseling Services and Rehabilitation* 8:3 (1984), pp. 5–23; Dennis Anderson, 'The Relations between Correctional Education and Parole Success,' *Journal of Offender Counseling*, 5:3–4 (1981).
18 Ibid. p. 13.
19 Jean Harris, *Stranger in Two Worlds* (New York: Macmillan, 1986), p. 221.
20 David Garland, *Punishment and Society* (Chicago: University of Chicago Press, 1990), p. 261.
21 John Irwin, 'The Trouble with Rehabilitation,' *Criminal Justice and Behaviour* 1:2 (1974), p. 141.
22 Victor Serge, *Men in Prison* (London: Writers and Readers, 1977), p. 21.
23 Jean Genet, *The Miracle of the Rose* (New York: Grove Press, 1966), p. 105.
24 Michael Enright, 'The Halls of Anger – Study in Failure, *MacLean's*, 21 March 1977, p. 32.
25 Victor Serge, *Memoirs of a Revolutionary: 1901–1941* (Oxford: Oxford University Press, 1963), p. 45.
26 Peter Scharf, 'Empty Bars: Violence and the Crisis of Meaning in the Prison,' *Prison Journal* 63:1 (1983), p. 117.
27 Lewis, *Prison Education and Rehabilitation*, p. 31.
28 Andre Furtado and Don Johnson, 'Education and Rehabilitation in a Prison Setting,' *Journal of Offender Counseling, Services, and Rehabilitation* 4:3 (1980), p. 250.
29 John Wideman, *Brothers and Keepers* (Hammondsworth: Penguin, 1984), p. 183.
30 Donald Cressey, 'Limitations on Organization of Treatment in the Modern

Prison,' in Richard Cloward and Donald Cressey, eds., *Theoretical Studies in the Social Organization of the Prison* (New York: Social Science Research Council, 1960), p. 100.

31 Genet, *Miracle of the Rose*, p. 193.

32 Martha Duncan, 'Cradled on the Sea: Positive Images of Prison and Theories of Punishment,' *California Law Review* 76:6 (1988), p. 1207.

33 Wideman, *Brothers and Keepers*, p. 201.

34 *Business Council for Effective Literacy Newsletter* 1:9 (1986), p. 4.

35 *Los Angeles Times*, 2 Nov. 1990.

36 Patricia Van Voorhis, 'A Cross Classification of Five Offender Typologies: Issues of Construct and Predictive Validity,' *Criminal Justice and Behaviour* 15:1 (1988), pp. 109–24.

37 S. Duguid, 'History and Moral Education in Correctional Education,' *Canadian Journal of Education* 4:4 (1979), p. 821.

38 Cited in Richard Matthews, *The Radical Politics of Thomas Jefferson* (Lawrence: University Press of Kansas, 1984), p. vii.

39 S. Duguid, 'Selective Ethics and Integrity: Moral Development and Prison Education,' *Journal of Correctional Education* 37:2 (1986), p. 61.

40 G. Sykes and S. Messinger, 'The Inmate Social System,' in Richard Cloward and Donald Cressey, eds., *Theoretical Studies in the Social Organization of the Prison* (New York: Social Science Research Council Pamphlet, 1960) pp. 5–19.

41 Ibid., p. 16.

42 G. Kassebaum, *Prison Treatment and Parole Survival* (New York: Wiley, 1971), p. 143.

43 Ibid., p. 154.

44 Garland, *Punishment and Society*, p. 173.

45 John Irwin and Donald Cressey, 'Thieves, Convicts and the Inmate Culture,' *Social Problems* 10:2 (1962), p. 155.

46 S. Cohen and L. Taylor, *Psychological Survival* (Hammondsworth: Penguin, 1972), p. 149.

Chapter 5   Reeling About: The Era of Opportunities

1 Barry MacDonald, *The Experience of Innovation*, Centre for Applied Research in Education Occasional Publication 6 (Norwich: University of East Anglia, 1978), p. 118.

2 *Times Higher Education Supplement*, 22 Sept. 1978.

3 Charles Dickens, *Hard Times* (London: Gresham, 1902), p. 1.

4 Harvey Graff, *The Literacy Myth* (New York: Academic Press, 1979), p. 242.

5 Thomas Mott Osborne, *Prisons and Common Sense* (Philadelphia: Lippincott, 1924), pp. 35–6; cited in Duncan D. Campbell, 'Developing Continuing Education in the Correctional Institution: Some Principles and Practices,' *Canadian Journal of Criminology and Corrections* 16:2 (1974), p. 118.
6 Henry Ehrmann, 'An Experiment in Political Education: The Prisoner of War Schools in the U.S.,' *Social Research* 14 (1947), p. 313.
7 'The prison offers – or seems to – the lure of the underground, the student as outsider, the rebel who in a literal sense has resisted "the system" to the extent of breaking its laws. Consequently the prison tends to attract those faculty not wholly comfortable themselves with that system.' Raymond Hedin, 'Teaching Literature in Prison,' *College English* 41:3 (1979), p. 280.
8 Raymond Bell, *Chronicle of Higher Education*, 18 Nov. 1981.
9 *NewGate Highlights* 1:1 (1972). See also Ray Allen, 'Inmates Go to College,' *Personnel and Guidance Journal* 53:2 (1974), p. 147.
10 *NewGate: New Hope through Education* (Paramus, NJ: National Council on Crime and Delinquency, n.d.), p. 4.
11 Richard Clendenen, John Ellington, and Ronald Severson, 'Project New-Gate: The First Five Years,' *Crime and Delinquency* 25:1 (1979), p. 58.
12 Marjorie Seashore, Steven Haberfeld, John Irwin, and Keith Baker, *Prisoner Education: Project NewGate and Other College Programs* (New York: Praeger, 1976), p. 185.
13 John Irwin, 'The Trouble with Rehabilitation,' *Criminal Justice and Behaviour* 1:2 (1974), p. 146.
14 Ibid., p. 147.
15 Jim Thomas, 'Teaching Sociology in Unconventional Settings: The Irony of Maximum Security Prisons,' *Teaching Sociology* 10 (1983), p. 232.
16 Morgan Lewis, *Prison Education and Rehabilitation: Illusion or Reality?* (University Park, Pennsylvania State University, Institute for Research on Human Resources, 1973), p. 2.
17 Frank Cioffi, 'Teaching College Humanities Courses in Prison,' *Alternative Higher Education* 6 (1981), p. 50.
18 K. Owen McCullogh, 'Our East Campus Is a Correctional Institution,' *Georgia Journal of Corrections* 3:1 (1974), p. 60.
19 Seashore et al., *Prisoner Education*, p. 172.
20 The sources for this section are from documents pertaining to the Santa Cruz project given me by its chief organizer, Karlene Faith.
21 The Santa Cruz campus of the University of California opened in 1965 and utilized a 'collegiate model' in an effort to encourage innovation, achieve a more 'personal' student experience, and in general present an alternative approach to higher education. The 'history of consciousness' graduate pro-

gram had few of the traditional graduate school requirements and prided itself on its interdisciplinarity and unconventional approach.

22 Santa Cruz Women's Prison Project, *Women in Prison*, n.d.

23 SCWPP, Progress Report, Nov. 1974.

24 SCWPP, Progress Report, 1973.

25 Response to project questionnaire.

26 SCWPP, Progress Report, Nov. 1974.

27 Roy Light, 'The Special Unit-Barlinnie Prison,' *Prison Service Journal* 60 (1985), pp. 14–17.

28 D. Barry, HM Inspectorate of Prisons for Scotland, *Report on HM Special Unit Barlinnie* (1982).

29 Christopher Carrell and Joyce Laing, eds., *The Special Unit Barlinnie Prison: Its Evolution through Its Art* (Glasgow: Third Eye Centre, 1982), p. 26.

30 Barry, *Barlinnie*.

31 Ibid., p. 4.

32 B. Conlin and D. Boag, Letter to *Prison Service Journal* 62 (1986), p. 22.

33 Ludovic Kennedy, 'Foreword,' in Carrell and Laing, eds., *Special Unit Barlinnie Prison*, p. 5.

34 Jimmy Boyle, *A Sense of Freedom* (Edinburgh: Canongate, 1977).

35 Walter Davidson, Chief Officer, Special Unit 1973–80, in Carrell and Laing, eds., *Special Unit Barlinnie Prison*, p. 32.

36 Carrell and Laing, eds., *Special Unit Barlinnie Prison*, p. 7.

37 Robert Deboe, 'Andragogy Locked-Up: The Enigma of Adult Education in Corrections' (Washingtonm, DC: U.S. Department of Education, National Institute of Education, ERIC ED237667, (1982) p. 2.

38 Will Hannam, 'A Foot behind the Door: An Historical Analysis of Adult Education in Prisons,' *International Journal of Lifelong Education* 1:4 (1982), p. 371.

39 Norman Jepson, 'Education in Penal Systems: The Perspective of a University Adult Educator and Criminologist,' *Coombe Lodge Reports* 14:11 (1982) pp. 570–7.

40 Ibid., p. 572.

41 Norman Jepson, *Stone Walls Do Not a Prison Make: Institutional Challenge to Education and Social Work* (Leeds: University of Leeds, Department of Adult and Continuing Education, 1986), pp. 27–52; also published in the *Yearbook of Correctional Education* (Vancouver: Correctional Education Association, 1989).

42 Council of Europe, Legal Affairs, *Report on Education in Prison* (Strasbourg, 1990), p. 17.

43 Kevin Warner, 'Prisoners Are People? Do We Perceive "Objects" of Treat-

ment or "Responsible Subjects"?' (paper delivered at the 53rd Correctional Education Association Conference, Salt Lake City, Utah, July 1998).

44 Council of Europe, *Report on Education in Prison*, p. 19

45 T.A.A. Parlett, 'The Criminal as Moral Philosopher,' *Journal of Correctional Education* 26:4 (1974), p. 19.

46 D. Ayers, R. Linden, and T.A.A. Parlett, 'An Evaluation of a Prison Education Program,' *Canadian Journal of Criminology* 26:1 (1984), pp. 65–73.

47 D. Ayers, S. Duguid, C. Montague, and S. Wolowydnik, *Effects of University of Victoria Program: A Post-Release Study* (Ottawa: Ministry of the Solicitor General, 1980).

48 S. Duguid, *Final Report: British Columbia Prison Education Research Project* (Burnaby, BC: Simon Fraser University Press, 1998).

49 D. Griffin, 'Report to the OISE Review' (Toronto: Ontario Institute for Studies in Education, 1978), p. 62, and Correctional Service of Canada, Education and Training, *Calendar of Studies* (1982–83), p. B–2.

40 This approach would agree with Diana Scully, who in her book *Understanding Sexual Violence: A Study of Convicted Rapists* (Boston: Unwin Hyman, 1990), demands a shift from a method or mode of 'understanding' that has led to attempts to excuse or even justify rape to one that focuses on male responsibility. While historically rape has been seen to spring from psychopathology, sexual frustration, overwhelming impulse, an unsatisfactory relationship with the mother, or childhood abuse, Scully is determined to show that men who rape are usually all too normal and in charge of their faculties, that *rape is a choice they make* in societies whose patriarchal system effectively gives them permission to do so.

51 Jepson, *Stone Walls Do Not a Prison Make*, p. 27.

52 A.R. Luria, *Cognitive Development: Its Cultural and Social Foundations* (Cambridge: Harvard University Press, 1976), p. 163.

53 See Elizabeth Fabiano and Robert Ross, *The Cognitive Model of Crime and Delinquency: Prevention and Rehabilitation* (Toronto: Planning and Research Branch of the Ontario Ministry of Correctional Services, 1983), vol. 1, p. 9. Ross recognized the power of this approach when he focused on the importance of the teaching method in the university program: 'Courses are taught primarily in intensive small group discussions in which the student's view on many controversial, historical and current social issues is continually challenged by his peers and the faculty. Through such exchanges the students learn to sharpen their thinking and communication skills, acquire the realization that there are alternative ways of viewing social and interpersonal problems and issues, and come to recognize that their egocentric view is not necessarily the only, or the best one.' Robert

Ross, *Time To Think: A Cognitive Model of Delinquency Prevention and Offender Rehabilitation* (Johnson City, Tenn.: Institute for Social Sciences and Arts, 1985), p. 90.

54 June Tapp and Lawrence Kohlberg, 'Developing a Sense of Law and Legal Justice,' *Journal of Social Issues* 27:2 (1971), p. 86. See also Jack Arbuthnot, 'Moral Reasoning Development Programmes in Prison: Cognitive-Developmental and Critical Reasoning Approaches,' *Journal of Moral Education* 13:2 (1984), pp. 112–23; Lawrence Kohlberg, 'The Just Community Approach to Corrections,' *Journal of Correctional Education* 37:2 (1986, pp. 54–8); Peter Scharf, 'The Prison and the Inmate's Conception of Legal Justice: An Experiment in Democratic Education,' *Criminal Justice and Behaviour* 3:2 (1976) pp. 107–22; and Norma Gluckstern, 'The Model Program at Berkshire,' *Personnel and Guidance Journal* 53:2 (1974), pp. 153–62.

55 William Perry, *Forms of Intellectual and Ethical Development in the College Years* (New York: Holt, 1970), cited in R. Morrill, *Teaching Values in College* (San Francisco: Jossey-Bass, 1980), p. 37.

56 Edward Eddy, *The College Influence on Student Character* (Washington, DC: American Council on Education, 1959), cited in Paul Dressel and Irvin Lehman, 'The Impact of Higher Education on Student Attitudes, Values, and Critical Thinking Abilities,' *Educational Record* 46:3 (1965), p. 249.

57 D. Heath, *Growing Up in College: Liberal Education and Maturity* (San Francisco: Jossey-Bass, 1968), p. 197.

58 N. Gluckstern and K. Wenner, 'The Model Program at Berkshire,' *Personnel Guidance Journal* 53:2 (1974), p. 153.

59 J.D. Ayers, Stephen Duguid, Catherine Montague, and Sonia Wolowydnik, *Effects of University of Victoria Program.*

60 Robert Marshall, in WHOS Program, *Mad Dog Blues* (1989), a play by Sam Shepard.

61 University of Victoria Staff Document, 'The Scholarly Community within the Federal Prisons in the Pacific Region' (1982).

62 Paul Gendreau and Robert Ross, 'Revivification of Rehabilitation: Evidence from the 1980's,' *Justice Quarterly* 4:3 (1987), p. 365.

63 Ralph Barton Perry, 'A Definition of the Humanities,' in T. Greene, *The Meaning of the Humanities* (New York: Kennikat Press, 1969 [1939]), p. 4.

64 D. Winter, D. McClelland, and A. Stewart, *A New Case for the Liberal Arts* (San Francisco: Jossey-Bass, 1981), p. 28.

65 W. Forster, *The Higher Education of Prisoners* Leicester: Vaughan Paper Number 21, Department of Adult Education, University of Leicester, 1977), p. 23.

66 Heath, *Growing Up in College*, p. 203.

67 George Steiner, 'Humane Literacy,' in *Language and Silence* (New York: Atheneum, 1977), p. 11.

68 U.S. Bureau of Justice Statistics, 'Recidivism of Prisoners Released in 1983,' April (1989).

69 Peter Hoffman and Barbara Stone-Meierhoefer, 'Post-Release Arrest Experiences of Federal Prisoners: A Six-Year Follow-Up,' *Journal of Criminal Justice* 7:3 (1979), p. 202.

70 Linda Smith and Ronald Akers, 'A Comparison of Recidivism of Florida's Community Control and Prison: A Five-Year Survival Analysis,' *Journal of Research in Crime and Delinquency* 30:3 (1993), p. 281.

71 A. Beck and B. Shipley, *Recidivism of Young Parolees* (Washington, DC: Department of Justice, 1987).

72 Stephen Duguid, Colleen Hawkey, and Ray Pawson, 'Using Recidivism to Evaluate Effectiveness in Prison Education Programs,' *Journal of Correctional Education* 47:2 (1996), pp. 74–85.

73 Ray Pawson and Nick Tilley, *Realistic Evaluation* (London: Sage, 1997).

74 Robert Haan and William Harman, *Release Risk Prediction: A Test of the Nuffield Scoring System* (Ottawa: Ministry of the Solicitor General, 1988), p. 9.

75 Correctional Service of Canada, *The Statistical Information on Recidivism Scale*, Research Brief B–01 Ottawa: Correctional Service of Canada Research and Statistics Branch, 1989), p. 7.

76 R. Cormier, 'Yes, Sir! A Stable Risk Prediction Tool,' *Forum on Correctional Research* 9:1 (1997), p. 6.

77 Alfred Blumstein and Jacqueline Cohen, 'Control of Selection Effects in the Evaluation of Social Problems,' *Evaluation Quarterly* 3:4 (1979), p. 584.

78 *Chronicle of Higher Education*, 18 Nov. 1981.

Chapter 6   The Return of the Criminal as 'The Enemy Within'

1 Jery Zaslove, 'Ten Fables for the Heroic Future,' *Vanguard*, Sept.–Oct. (1988), p. 19.

2 U.S. Department. of Justice, Office of Justice Programs, *Bulletin*; U.S. Bureau of Justice Statistics, 'Prisoners in 1994,' August 1995.

3 *Newsweek*, 23 March 1981.

4 Elliott Currie, 'Shifting the Balance: On Social Action and the Future of Criminological Research,' *Journal of Research on Crime and Delinquency* 30:4 (1993), p. 479.

5 Richard Posner, 'The Most Punitive Nation,' *Times Literary Supplement*, 1 Sept. (1995) p. 3.

6   Holly Johnson and Roger Boe, 'Violent Crime Trends in Canada since 1983,' *Forum on Corrections Research* 9:2 (1997), pp. 3–4.
7   Robert Reiner, 'The Perfidy of the Paramour: How Police Fell Out of Favour with the Conservatives,' *Times Literary Supplement*, 1 Sept. (1995), p. 9.
8   Thom Gehring, 'Correctional Education and the Cold War,' (keynote address, Correctional Education Association Conference, Whistler, BC, Oct. 1993).
9   David Garland, *Punishment and Society* (Chicago: University of Chicago Press, 1990), p. 239.
10 Karl Marx, *Communist Manifesto* (London: Oxford University Press, 1992), p. 6.
11 Max Horkheimer and Theodor Adorno, *Dialectic of Enlightenment* (London: Allen Lane, 1973), cited in Wayne Knights, 'Culture in the Bureaucracy: The University in Prison,' *Yearbook of Correctional Education* (Vancouver: Institute for the Humanities, 1989), p. 66.
12 George Steiner cited in the *New Yorker*, 15 Aug. 1977, p. 30.
13 Charles Dickens, *David Copperfield*, (New York: Collier, 1917), p. 192.
14 Jean Harris, *Stranger in Two Worlds* (New York: Macmillan, 1986), p. 237.
15 Jack Katz, *The Seduction of Crime* (New York: Basic Books, 1988), p. 217.
16 Peter Marshall, *William Godwin* (New Haven: Yale University Press, 1984), p. 395.
17 Madelyn Gutwirth, *The Twilight of the Goddesses: Women and Representation in the French Revolution* (New Brunswick, NJ: Rutgers University Press, 1992), p. 246.
18 Larry Motiuk and Ray Belcourt, 'Profiling the Canadian Federal Sex Offender Population,' *Forum on Corrections Research* 8:2 (1996), pp. 3–7.
19 Donald West, 'Sex Offences and Offending,' in Michael Tonry and Norval Morris, eds., *Crime and Justice: An Annual Review of Research*, vol. 5 (Chicago: University of Chicago Press, 1983), p. 196.
20 David Richards, 'Rights, Utility and Crime,' in Michael Tonry and Norval Morris, eds., *Crime and Justice: An Annual Review of Research*, vol. 3 (Chicago: University of Chicago Press, 1981), p. 250.
21 Garland, *Punishment and Society*, p. 192.
22 Michel Foucault, *Discipline and Punish: The Birth of the Prison* (New York: Vintage, 1979), p. 17.
23 Louis Genevie, Eva Margolies, and Gregory Muhlin, 'How Effective Is Correctional Intervention?' *Social Policy* 16:3 (1986), pp. 52–7.
24 *Corrections Digest*, 11 April (1980), p. 9.
25 Don Gibbons, 'Some Critical Observations on Criminal Types and Criminal Careers,' *Criminal Justice and Behaviour* 15:1 (1988), p. 19.

26 S. Ekland-Olson and W. Kelly, *Justice under Pressure* (New York: Springer-Verlag, 1993), p. 118.

27 Nick Gillespie, 'Less Crime, More Punishment,' *Reason*, May (1996), p. 17.

28 Alfred Blumstein, 'Prison Populations: A System out of Control?,' in Michael Tonry and Norval Morris, eds., *Crime and Justice: An Annual Review of Research*, vol. 10 (Chicago: University of Chicago Press, 1988), p. 237.

29 Samuel Pillsbury, 'Why Are We Ignored? The Peculiar Place of Experts in the Current Debate about Crime and Justice,' *Criminal Law Bulletin* 31:4 (1995), p. 312.

Chapter 7   A Cold Wind from the North – The Medical Model Redux

1 Michael Ignatieff, *Needs of Strangers* (Hammondsworth: Penguin, 1984), p. 11.

2 Ian Dunbar, *A Sense of Direction* (London: Home Office, Prison Department, Oct. 1985).

3 Ibid., p. 28.

4 T.J. Sawatsky, *Review of Offender Support Programs* (Ottawa: Correctional Service of Canada, 1985), p. 23.

5 Ibid. p. 25.

6 Ibid., p. 14.

7 A.J. Cropley, *Lifelong Education: A Psychological Analysis* (New York: Pergamon Press, 1977), p. 84.

8 Ibid., pp. 87–8; Long, Huey, Kay McCrary, and Spencer Ackerman, 'Adult Cognition: Piagetian Based Research Findings,' *Adult Education* 30:1 (1979), p. 4.

9 Jean-Claude Bringuier, 'Conversations with Jean Piaget,' *Society*, March (1980) p. 57.

10 Spivak, Platt, and Shure, pp. 5–7; Robert Ross, *Time to Think: A Cognitive Model of Delinquency Prevention and Offender Rehabilitation* (Johnson City, Tenn.: Institute for Social Sciences and Arts, 1985), p. 12

11 Michael Chandler, 'Adolescence, Egocentrism and Epistemological Loneliness,' in B. Presseisen, ed., *Topics in Cognitive Development*, vol. 2 (New York: Plenum Press, 1978), p. 144.

12 Thomas Lickona, ed., *Moral Development and Behavior* (New York: Holt, Rinehart and Winston, 1976), p. 33.

13 Reuven Feuerstein, *Instrumental Enrichment: Studies in Cognitive Modifiability* (Jerusalem: Hassadah-WIZO-Canada Research Institute, Report 3, 1977).

14 Samuel Yochelson and Stanton Samenow, *The Criminal Personality* (New York: James Aronson, 1976). Yochelson died soon after the book was pub-

lished, but Samenow has continued to pursue actively his aggressive understandings of the criminal mind, most recently in *Straight Talk about Criminals* (Northvale, NJ: Jason Aronson Inc, 1998).

15 Lawrence Kohlberg, K. Kauffman, Peter Scharf, and Joseph Hickey, 'The Just Community Approach to Corrections,' *Journal of Moral Education* 4:3 (1975) pp. 243–60.

16 J.D. Ayers, 'Education in Prisons: A Developmental and Cultural Perspective,' in Lucien Morin, ed., *On Prison Education* (Ottawa: Supply and Services, 1981), p. 75.

17 Yochelson and Samenow, *The Criminal Personality*, p. 23.

18 Daniel Claster, 'Perception of Certainty: A Comparison of Delinquents and Non-Delinquents,' in Richard Henshel and Robert Silverman, *Perception in Criminology* (New York: Columbia University Press, 1975), p. 93.

19 Chandler, 'Adolescence, Egocentrism and Epistemological Loneliness,' p. 331.

20 Ross, *Time to Think*, p. 10.

21 Lawrence Kohlberg, 'Adolescent as A Philosopher: The Discovery of the Self in a Post-Conventional World,' *Daedalus* 100 (1971), p. 1065.

22 Long et al., 'Adult Cognition,' p. 12.

23 Carolyn Eggleston and Thom Gehring, 'Correctional Education Paradigms in the United States and Canada,' *Journal of Correctional Education*, June (1986) pp. 86–92.

24 Paul Gendreau and Robert Ross, 'Effective Correctional Treatment: Bibliotherapy for Cynics,' *Crime and Delinquency* 25:4 (1979), pp. 463–89; Paul Gendreau and Robert Ross, 'Revivication of Rehabilitation: Evidence from the 80's,' *Justice Quarterly* (1987), pp. 349–407.

25 Robert Ross, Elizabeth Fabiano, and Roslynn Ross, '(Re)Habilitation through Education: A Cognitive Model for Corrections,' *Journal of Correctional Education* 39:2 (1988), p. 45.

26 James Houston, 'Shifting the Paradigm: Classification and Programs in Prison,' *Criminal Justice Review* 20:1 (1995), p. 66.

27 Donald Andrews, Ivan Zinger, Robert Hoge, James Bonta, Paul Gendreau, and Francis Culler. 'Does Correctional Treatment Work? A Clinically Relevant and Psychologically Informed Meta-Analysis,' *Criminology* 28:3 (1990), p. 374.

28 Johnson City, Tenn.: Institute of Social Sciences and the Arts, 1985.

29 T.J. Sawatsky, *Review of Offender Support Programs* (Ottawa: Correctional Service of Canada, 1985), p. 34.

30 'Something Works!' *Liaison*, April (1989), p. 6.

31 Andrews, et al., 'Does Correctional Treatment Work?' p. 374.

32 Donald Andrews, Jerry Kiessling, David Robinson, and Susan Mickus, 'The Risk Principle of Case Classification: An Outcome Evaluation with Young Adult Probationers,' *Canadian Journal of Criminology* 28:4 (1986), p. 377.

33 Correctional Service of Canada, Core Strategy Document, 20 Sept. 1991.

34 Elizabeth Fabiano, David Robinson, and Frank Porporino, *A Preliminary Assessment of the Cognitive Skills Training Pilot Project* (Ottawa: Correctional Service of Canada, May, 1990), p. 9.

35 Ian Benson, 'Report on Cog Skills Visit,' correspondence 17 Nov. 1993.

36 Elizabeth Fabiano. 'How Education Can Be Correctional and how Corrections Can Be Educational,' *Journal of Correctional Education* 42:2 (1991), p. 105.

37 Roger Cormier, 'Reducing Re-offending: The Steps Canada Is Taking,' *Prison Service Journal* 93 (1994), pp. 47–50.

38 Lynn Stewart and William Millson, 'Offender Motivation for Treatment as a Responsivity Factor,' *Forum for Corrections Research* 7:3 (1995), p. 5.

39 Robert Worth, 'A Model Prison,' *Atlantic Monthly*, Nov. (1995), pp. 38–42.

40 Doris Mackenzie, Robert Brame, David McDowell, and Clare Souryal, 'Boot Camp Prisons and Recidivism in Eight States,' *Criminology* 33:3 (1995), p. 352.

41 Michigan Department of Corrections, Internet 21 May 1996.

42 It may be the case that the other 'side' of the penal spectrum, the police, the criminals, and the judiciary may be at one with this popular perception that nothing works – hence, the frequent friction between police and prison staff and especially parole services and the distinctive attitudes of the criminal as prisoner and the criminal as citizen.

43 Hannah Arendt warns us that 'to be sure, every deed has its motives as it has its goal and its principle; but the act itself, though it proclaims its goal and makes manifest its principle, does not reveal the innermost motivation of the agent. His motives remain dark, they do not shine but are hidden not only from others but, most of the time, from himself, from his self-inspection as well.' *On Revolution* (Hammondsworth: Penguin, 1987), p. 93.

44 Adam Smith, *The Theory of Moral Sentiments* (Oxford: Oxford University Press, 1976), p. 9.

45 Morris Berman, *The Re-Enchantment of the World* (New York: Bantam, 1981), pp. 137–8.

46 Richard Rorty, 'Untruth and Consequences,' *New Republic*, 31 July 1995, pp. 32–6.

47 John Danford, *David Hume and the Problem of Reason* (New Haven: Yale University Press, 1990), pp. 19–20.

48 Norval Morris and Marc Miller, 'Predictions of Dangerousness,' in Michael

Tonry and Norval Morris, eds., *Crime and Justice: An Annual Review of Research*, vol. 6 (1985), p. 16.

49 See Katherine Hayles, *Chaos and Order* (Chicago: University of Chicago Press, 1991), p. 8. Stephen Kellert, *In the Wake of Chaos:Unpredictable Order in Dynamical Systems* (Chicago: University of Chicago Press, 1993).

50 Michael Ignatieff, 'Moral Education as a Reform Movement: A Historian's Perspective,' in *Proceedings* (National Conference on Prison Education, Victoria, BC, 1981), p. 12.

51 Morris and Miller, 'Predictions of Dangerousness,' p. 14.

52 Stephen Gottfredson and Don Gottfredson, 'The Long-Term Predictive Utility of the Base Expectancy Score,' *Howard Journal* 32:4 (1993), p. 278.

53 Christopher Webster, Grant Harris, Marnie Rice, Catherine Cormier, and Vernon Quinsey, *The Violence Prediction Scheme: Assessing Dangerousness in High Risk Men* (Toronto: University of Toronto Centre of Criminology, 1994), p. 20.

54 Margaret Jackson, 'Psychiatric Decision-Making for the Courts: Determining the Nature of Mental Health Expertise,' (PhD Dissertation, University of Toronto, 1985).

55 Joan Nuffield, *Parole Decision-Making in Canada: Research towards Decision Guidelines* (Ottawa: Solicitor General of Canada, 1982), p. 16.

56 Harry Kozol, Richard Boucher, and Ralph Garofolo, 'The Diagnosis and Treatment of Dangerousness,' *Crime and Delinquency* 18 (1972), pp. 371–92.

57 Elizabeth Fabiano, David Robinson, and Frank Porporino, *A Preliminary Assessment of the Cognitive Skills Training Program Pilot Project* (Ottawa; Correctional Service of Canada, 1990), p. 43.

58 Stephen Duguid, John Eksted, Margaret Jackson, Brian Burtch, and Jery Zaslove, Social Sciences and Humanities Research Council of Canada research funding application, 1993.

59 Daniel Nagin and David Farrington, 'The Stability of Criminal Potential from Childhood to Adulthood,' *Criminology* 30:2 (1992), p. 236.

60 Robert Wright, 'The Biology of Violence,' *New Yorker*, 13 March (1995), p. 71 – characterizing the view of Peter Breggin.

61 Quoted in W.W. Gibbs, 'Seeking the Criminal Element,' *Scientific American*, March (1995), p. 107.

62 *Times Higher Education Supplement*, 10 Feb. 1995.

63 Robert Wright, *The Moral Animal* (New York: Vintage, 1994), p. 222.

64 Ibid., p. 72.

65 Serena Lynn-Brown, Alexander Botsis, and Herman van Praag, 'Serotonin and Aggression,' *Journal of Offender Rehabilitation* 21: 3–4 (1994), p. 28.

66 Wright, *The Moral Animal*, p. 351.

67 Paul Gendreau and Robert Ross, 'Correctional Treatment: Some Recommendations for Effective Intervention,' *Juvenile and Family Court Journal* 34:4 (1984), p. 32.
68 James Houston, 'Shifting the Paradigm: Classification and Programs in Prison,' *Criminal Justice Review* 20:1 (1995), p. 71.
69 David Robinson, *The Impact of Cognitive Skills Training on Post-Release Recidivism among Canadian Federal Offenders* (Ottawa: Correctional Service of Canada Research Division, 1995), p. viii.
70 Ibid., p. 28.
71 Ibid., p. ix.
72 Ibid., p. 52.
73 Much of the discussion of this group of high-risk subjects is taken from S. Duguid, 'Confronting Worst Case Scenarios: Education and High Risk Offenders,' Journal of Correctional Education 48:4 (1997), pp. 153–9.

Chapter 8   From Object to Subject – The Potential for a Room of One's Own within the Prison

1 Council of Europe, European Prison Rules (Strasbourg: Council of Europe, 1987). Cited in Kevin Warner, 'Prisoners Are People?' (paper given at the 53rd Correctional Education Association conference, Salt Lake City, Utah, July 1998.
2 Council of Europe, *Report on Education in Prisons* (Strasbourg: Council of Europe, 1990), p. 19.
3 Cited in Elizabeth de Fontenay, Diderot: Reason and Resonance (New York: George Braziller, 1982), p. 100.
4 W. Kuenning, 'Letter to a Penologist,' in H. Cantine and D. Rainer, eds., *Prison Etiquette* (Bearsville, NY: Retort Press, 1959) cited in Donald Cressey, 'Limitations on Organization of Treatment in the Modern Prison,' in Richard Cloward and Donald Cressey, eds., *Theoretical Studies in the Social Organization of the Prison* (New York: Social Science Research Council, 1960), p. 100.
5 Marjorie Seashore, Steven Haberfeld, John Irwin, and Keith Baker, *Prisoner Education: Project NewGate and Other College Programs* (New York: Praeger, 1916), p. 172.
6 Voltaire's attitude was predictably quite different: 'What is virtue, my friend? It is to do good; let us do it, and that's enough. But we won't look into your motives.' Carol Blum, The Republic of Virtue (Ithaca: Cornell University Press, 1986), p. 58.
7 *Times Literary Supplement*, 30 Dec. 1994.

8 David Garland, *Punishment and Society* (Chicago: University of Chicago Press, 1990), p. 183.

9 Christopher Lasch, Minimal Self: Psychic Survival in Troubled Times (New York: W.W. Norton, 1984), p. 30.

10 Virginia Woolf, A Room of One's Own (New York: Harvest, 1957), p. 4.

11 Charles Taylor, *The Malaise of Modernity* (Concord, Ont.: Anansi Press, 1991), p. 26.

12 Jane Austen, Mansfield Park (Hammondsworth: Penguin, 1966), p. 422.

13 Robert N. Bellah, Richard Madsen, William Sullivan, Ann Swidler, and Stephen Tipton, *Habits of the Heart: Individualism and Commitment in American Life* (New York: Harper and Row, 1985), p. vi.

14 John McKnight, *The Careless Society: Community and Its Counterfeits* (New York: Basic Books, 1996), p. 139.

15 Jean-Jacques Rousseau, *Julie, Or the New Heloise* (Hanover, NH: University Press of New England, 1997), p. 295.

16 Thomas Lickona, 'Moral Development and Moral Education: Piaget, Kohlberg and Beyond,' in J. Gallagher and J. Easley, eds., *Knowledge and Development*, vol. 2 (New York: Plenum Press, 1978), p. 36.

17 See D. Winter, D. McClelland, and A. Stewart, *A New Case for the Liberal Arts* (San Francisco: Jossey-Bass, 1981), p. 142.

18 'Involvement in Learning,' *Chronicle of Higher Education*, 24 Oct. (1984), p. 39.

19 Paul Dressel and Irvin Lehman, 'The Impact of Higher Education on Student Attitudes, Values and Critical Thinking Abilities,' Educational Record 46:3 (1965), p. 255.

20 Jack Arbuthnot, 'Moral Reasoning Development Programs in Prison: Cognitive-Developmental and Critical Reasoning Approaches,' *Journal of Moral Education* 13:2 (1984), p. 121.

21 Seashore et al., p. 149.

22 Roburn reminds us that a therapeutic community relies on 'scientific control of the environment ... in which concerted efforts are directed towards making each aspect of the patient's daily experience contribute towards the ultimate goal of social and vocational rehabilitation.' Michael Roburn, 'The Therapeutic Community,' Canadian Journal of Corrections 9:4 (1967), p. 313.

23 Peter Scharf and Joseph Hickey, 'The Prison and the Inmate's Conception of Legal Justice: An Experiment in Democratic Education,' Criminal Justice and Behaviour 3:2 (1976), p. 112.

24 Lawrence Kohlberg, 'The Just Community Approach to Corrections,' Journal of Moral Education 4:3 (1975), p. 10.

25 Stephen Duguid, 'Origins and Development of University Education in Matsqui Institution,' *Canadian Journal of Criminology*, July (1983), pp. 295–308.

26 Wayne Knights and Bill Jeffries, 'Staging a Learning Community: Theatre in Prison,' (unpublished manuscript, Simon Fraser University Prison Education Research Project, 1996), p. 1.

27 Ibid.

28 Ibid.

29 Knights and Jeffries, 'Staging a Learning Community,' p. 2.

30 Council of Europe, Report on Education in Prisons, p. 19.

31 John Irwin, 'The Trouble with Rehabilitation,' *Criminal Justice and Behaviour* 1:2 (1974), p. 148.

32 Council of Europe, Report on Education in Prisons, p. 13.

33 Friedrich Schiller, Essays (New York: Continuum, 1993) p. 107.

34 Kenneth Adams, Katherine Bennett, Timothy Flanagan, James Marquart, Steven Covelier, Eric Fritsch, Jurg Gerber, Dennis Longmire, and Volmer Burton. 'A Large-Scale Multidimensional Test of the Effect of Prison Education Programs on Offender Behaviour,' *Prison Journal* 74:4 (1994).

35 Jacobo Timmerman, *Prisoner without a Name, Cell without a Number* (New York: Vintage, 1982), p. 95.

Conclusion

1 Karl Marx, *Theses on Feuerbach*, in Robert Tucker, ed., *The Marx-Engels Reader* (New York: W.W. Norton, 1978), p. 144.

2 Karl Marx, *18th Brumaire of Louis Bonaparte*, in Robert Tucker, (ed., *The Marx-Engels Reader* (New York: Norton, 1978), p. 595.

3 *Webster's Third New International Dictionary* (Springfield, Mass.: Merriam, 1993).

4 Michael Ignatieff, 'Tough Lessons for True Democrats,' *Observer*, 11 March 1990, p. 19.

5 James Q. Wilson, *Thinking about Crime* (New York: Random House, 1975). Cited in John Irwin, James Austin, and Chris Baird, 'Fanning the Flames of Fear,' *Crime and Delinquency* 44:1 (1998), p. 35.

6 Frank Manuel and Fritzie Manuel, Utopian Thought in the Western World (Cambridge, Mass. Harvard University Press, 1979), p. 546.

7 Hannah Arendt, *On Revolution* (Hammondsworth: Penguin), p. 87.

Index